Air Warfare

Air Warfare

History, Theory and Practice

PETER GRAY

Bloomsbury Academic
An imprint of Bloomsbury Publishing Plc

B L O O M S B U R Y
LONDON · OXFORD · NEW YORK · NEW DELHI · SYDNEY

Bloomsbury Academic
An imprint of Bloomsbury Publishing Plc

50 Bedford Square
London
WC1B 3DP
UK

1385 Broadway
New York
NY 10018
USA

www.bloomsbury.com

BLOOMSBURY and the Diana logo are trademarks of Bloomsbury Publishing Plc

First published 2016

British Library Cataloguing-in-Publication Data
A catalogue record for this book is available from the British Library.

ISBN: HB: 978-1-7809-3619-2
PB: 978-1-7809-3662-8
ePDF: 978-1-7809-3814-1
ePub: 978-1-7809-3310-8

Library of Congress Cataloging-in-Publication Data
A catalog record for this book is available from the Library of Congress.

Typeset by Deanta Global Publishing Services, Chennai, India
Printed and bound in Great Britain

CONTENTS

ACKNOWLEDGEMENTS

This book came about following numerous requests, from students at all levels, for a supporting textbook to go with their courses and research interests. The text is based, at least in part, on the structure and content of the MA in Air Power History Theory and Practice at the University of Birmingham. I am grateful to successive cohorts for their individual and collective enthusiasm for the subject, for their feedback, comments and questions and for their suggestions towards the book. I am also grateful to the anonymous reviewers of the book proposal and of the final text. I have been lucky in meeting many colleagues around the world who have contributed to my wider thinking on air warfare and to a smaller number who have helped directly. These include Annette Amerman for suggestions on American sources; Major Bill March and Dr Richard Goette for their help on Canadian materials; colleagues in the Royal Australian Air Power Development Centre; and successive Directors of Defence Studies for the Royal Air Force (RAF). I am grateful to Seb Cox, Head of the Air Historical Branch (AHB), for his help and support over the years and for his formal permission to quote from the Portal Papers held at Christ Church, Oxford. Finally, I am deeply indebted to my colleague Dr James Pugh for his detailed and incisive comments on draft chapters. Thanks also go to Daniel Pilfold for our discussions on Churchill. All errors remain entirely my own.

CHAPTER ONE

Introduction

Air power is the most difficult of military force to measure or even express in precise terms. The problem is compounded by the fact that aviation tends to attract adventurous souls, physically adept, mentally alert and pragmatically rather than philosophically inclined.

WINSTON CHURCHILL[1]

In this, much used, quotation, Churchill identified a number of paradoxes about the use of air power and the romance of air warfare. As a new form of warfare in the twentieth century, it consistently offered great promise. Arguably, it still does. Mastery of the third dimension, through the atmosphere and into space, facilitates attack at long range, information gathering, information transmission and an almost instant advantage over foes constrained to a two-dimensional battlefield. This mastery would obviously have to be fought for, and then maintained, as had also been stated by Churchill elsewhere. But the battles in the sky, from the earliest days of air combat, brought with them a degree of romance, chivalry and excitement in marked contrast to the popular portrayals of the gloom of the trenches. The new breed of aerial warriors had to be adventurous given the nature of the early machines; the descriptors physically adept, pragmatic and mentally alert also were very apt. Churchill, of course, understood this from his early attempts to learn to fly himself.[2] Although Churchill was not successful in his quest, those that did conquer the air were happy to assume the heroic mantle.[3] Churchill was again instrumental in maintaining this image with his famous speech on 'the Few'.[4]

It is, however, interesting to question Churchill's assertion that airmen were more 'pragmatically rather than philosophically inclined'. It could well be a reflection that airmen were happy to promise many things for the future of air warfare that, had they thought more deeply, they would have seen the myriad practical difficulties. The early days of the Second World War in France and then in the bomber offensive over Germany were to show this; Churchill's frustration over this is reflected in his wartime correspondence. But, is it that difficult to measure, or define in precise terms?

The Air Publication from which the Churchill quotation was taken defined air power as:

> The ability to project military force in air or space by or from a platform or missile operating above the surface of the earth. Air platforms are defined as any aircraft, helicopter or unmanned vehicle.[5]

It should be noted that this definition is service neutral; the platforms could be army, navy or air force. It encompasses naval aviation, tactical reconnaissance, air transport, rotary wing operations, deployment of airborne forces along with strike, interdiction and control of the air. A subsequent revision of British doctrine published as a joint document, defined air power as 'using air capabilities to influence the behaviour of actors and the course of events'.[6] One could take the definitions from the doctrinal publications of many air forces. But though the words may change slightly, the essence of any final definition would contain most of the sentiments expressed in the two definitions above. It is also, at this stage, worth noting the comment by David MacIsaac in his chapter 'Voices from the Central Blue: The Air Power Theorists' in which he acknowledged that the term 'air power' is variously used.[7] He also suggested that the term 'should be reserved for discussions of the full potential of a nation's air capability in peace as well as war, in civilian as well as military pursuits'; but he admits that this interpretation is rare.[8] The term 'air warfare' is equally liable to be defined in a number of ways. But the reality is that most students of the discipline are either practitioners, as aircrew, ground crew or are employed in other similar roles in the military, or they are attracted to the subject because it is about fighting and warfare. That was one of the prime reasons for its inclusion in the title.

Air power has traditionally been described as having four key roles. The first of these is control of the air and this applies whether it is referring to sovereign airspace or above a battlefield. Doctrine manuals wax lyrical about the subject and deservedly so. Control of the air is essential for naval or land forces to stand any chance of being able to carry out their core functions without interference from enemy air forces. By the same token, if friendly air is to assist sister forces (or components), they need to be free from aerial harassment. Control of the air can be limited in time and space, or in more ideal circumstances, amount to air superiority or supremacy. Airspace may be generally protected over a wide area such as the UK air defence region, or concentrated zones such as over the Olympic Games in London in 2012. All forms of delivering bombs, missiles and other ordnance against surface targets can be loosely termed as attack or strike. Movement of forces can equally be grouped under the heading of mobility; this includes air-to-air refuelling. Seeking and gathering intelligence and information forms the fourth role. None of these are specifically platform dependent and many aircrafts are capable of operating across a range of roles.

This book is unashamedly written and produced as a textbook. It does not pretend to have all of the answers on air power, or air warfare, within its covers; but the extensive referencing used throughout will give the student of air warfare adequate clues as to where wider research may be fruitful. Wherever possible, references have included online material and open-access sources. Producing a textbook is fraught with problems and challenges. The first of these is that experts in any particular field will be quickly frustrated that the text may not go far enough or particular favourite references have been omitted. Wherever possible, important sources have been chosen because they are in print and easily available. Inevitably, some are harder to find.

This book followed several years of designing and teaching an air power course at Master's degree level at the University of Birmingham and it is, to a certain extent, based upon that course. It is not, however, the product of a military academy where the interpretation of the core material has to suit the demands of the organization. As a textbook it is suitable for students at all levels who have an interest in the subject. It will certainly be of interest to military practitioners either at colleges, staff or war colleges, or more generally. The book will also be valuable for those seeking an academic rigour to their studies. This immediately begs a series of related questions including 'why study military history?'; 'why study air warfare?'; or more fundamentally, 'why study?' and 'why air warfare?' Some study for the qualification, either to progress to a higher degree and then into academe or for some professional advancement. Others study because they are passionately interested in the subject and want to put some structure into their reading and interest. Biddle and Citino have made the point that it is essential that, in a liberal education system, students are taught to 'think critically and wisely about issues of peace and war'.[9] For others, it is the culmination of a lifetime of interest in the subject from the days when their fascination was caught with childhood comics and plastic model aeroplane kits. I can probably plead guilty to all of these, as can many of my students.

There are some other guilty pleas that have to be acknowledged. This book is rather UK biased and concentrates on English, Commonwealth and American sources. There is some excuse for that in terms of availability and of language proficiency. Part of the rationale is based on my own familiarity with the materials and sources, especially archival. Where possible a wide range of authors and sources have been cited, but in parallel with the use of air power, Anglo-American works predominate.

Following this introduction the first substantive chapter will explore in more depth the fundamental question as to why we should want to study air warfare. Logically, its successor covers the basics of the historiography and the sources and therefore where some of the answers can be found. In this, every effort has been made to widen the scope and the author is very grateful to air power colleagues (in the Acknowledgements) who have assisted in the list of materials presented. The following chapter discusses air power theory without, hopefully, getting too bogged down in the literature. Again, there is plenty of scope for wider reading. The following chapter makes the transition from theory to practice and outlines the key roles of air power. It does not seek to replace texts or doctrine manuals, but does highlight some of the debates and controversies surrounding the practical employment of air power. The next chapter is on leadership and command in air warfare followed by a discussion on the thorny subjects of law and ethics. The final substantive chapter is on air warfare and the levels of warfare; this includes a discussion on intelligence and targeting. Each of the main chapters from the historiography onwards finishes with a case study. These have almost invariably been based on research carried out and they have been used extensively in a teaching environment to a wide variety of audiences. There may be small areas of overlap with the broader text and this has been maintained for reasons of continuity and flow.

War studies as an academic subject can be broadly taken either as a subset of political sciences (including international relations) or as a historical discipline. The author has done both and this comes through in some of the treatment of the materials. This also reflects the reality of the theory, practice and, indeed, history. From the historical point of view, it has to be acknowledged that authors change their minds over time, views mature or alter, or the person just dies. It is therefore good practice to use the past tense through the discussion and this has been attempted in the text. The Italian air power theorist Giulio Douhet is an excellent example of this especially on the bombing of cities and civilians. His early writings were strongly opposed, but swung around completely as a result of his observations on the First World War.

CHAPTER TWO

Air warfare, war studies and military history in the twenty-first century

Military history is one of those terms which inevitably means different things to different people. A very brief trawl through the curriculum vitae of a wide variety of people will show an interest in the subject and it often appears at the very end of the CV under 'other interests'. This is inevitably true of members of the armed forces, whether retired or not, as well as the wider public. But a brief visit to any bookstore in the United Kingdom, United States, Canada, New Zealand or Australia or indeed to one's favourite book search engine will reveal a vast range of topics and a huge diversity in target audiences. Significantly, bookstores in France and Germany tend not have military history sections and display far fewer books on the subject. The study of air warfare is no exception to this and the fascination with aircraft and their associated technologies arguably increases the appeal. This works at the basic level with (a largely male) addiction to gadgets; beyond this, Morillo has argued that technology has a specific role in the shaping of patterns of warfare.[1] At the academic end of the spectrum, military history has often been popular with students, but its intellectual standing has been questioned on many continents over the last century.[2] Sir Michael Howard has pointed out that professional historians have 'found it hard to think of the term in anything but a rather pejorative sense'.[3] Ironically, Howard's chapter in Murray and Sinnreich's study *The Past as Prologue: The Importance of History to the Military Profession* highlights one of the reasons for the disdain of other historians in that they perceive military history as having been written and studied precisely for the purpose of educating soldiers.[4] Although this is a perfectly reasonable use of military history it is by no means the only one and certainly does not prevent it, and the wider study of warfare, from being a genuine academic subject.

At this stage, it is worth pausing to question whether 'military history' is the most appropriate term to deploy. It is in widespread use and influential critiques such as Jeremy Black's *Rethinking Military History* take this broad view, at least in its title.[5] But it could be argued that 'military' only encompasses the land environment (i.e. armies) excluding maritime and air power. The natural extension to this in the quest for accurate terminology is to consider the history or war (or warfare) and the associated academic subject of 'war studies'. Howard has recounted the discussions within King's College, London in the early 1950s over the title of the chair which he was later to occupy with such distinction.[6] Sir Charles Webster is described as having thumped the table 'and demanded: "It's about war isn't it? So what's wrong with War Studies?"'[7] The title has stuck in London, at the University of Birmingham and in various publishers' series. It also resonates with the various War Colleges around the world, often differentiating these higher-level and more strategically focused institutions from the staff colleges.[8] Broadening the title, and subject area, to encompass warfare also invites consideration of the other strategic levers of power such as political, economic, diplomatic and so on. It also allows the academic discipline to overlap with ethics, law, international law, literature, political theory, economics and political science. It also encompasses cultural aspects along with relationships with wider society. The study of the history, theory and practice of warfare goes back therefore to the earliest writings of Herodotus and covers every geographical area.[9] The utility of war studies, or even occasionally the obverse of the coin, peace studies, would seem obvious, begging the question as to why a body of literature is needed to defend the subject.

The first issue is the misperception that military history is little more than a stand full of glossy publications detailing the exact colour schemes of particular weapons systems, the regalia and uniforms of various 'crack' or elite units and painfully detailed accounts of a tiny fragment of a greater campaign. The reality is that the public audiences are genuinely interested in these areas, and the books sell; after all, they support perfectly reasonable hobbies. This in turn builds a need among some readers to delve more deeply into battles, campaigns and the utility of different weapons systems. This then fuels the middle ground of bookstore material on warfare which again sells well, especially if published in parallel with a television series. Where the problems arguably begin is that the lucrative middle ground is also the province of journalists or TV historians some of whose rigour (or that of their research teams) is not always to the highest academic standards; it often relies on a single source chosen for convenience rather than scholarship. Many established military historians also either specialize in this field or have contributed to it. Again these books are generally marketed and sold well. But this arguably makes matters worse; for a minority of professional historians, it seems that popularity and accessibility are directly counter to intellectual rigour. But this is only a very small part of the issue. In practice, the academic publishing systems, in most countries, have a pecking order in terms of prestige. This is partly based on reputation, and also on the levels of academic scrutiny that the work submitted for publication has to undergo. The same is true with academic journals. One must, here, also take account of the business models utilized by book publishers who, naturally enough, have to turn a profit. The genuine academic works are often only produced in expensive hardback format intended either for academics who cannot afford 'not to have' a particular title or for the libraries of their institutions. Paperback editions are rare in this model, although e-versions are becoming increasingly available. Publishers also jump on anniversary bandwagons such as the Battle of Britain, the Somme and individual raids such as the Dambusters. Major events such as the centenary of the First World War become a feeding frenzy for publishers and authors alike; this may seem like a specious comment, but this process takes up a surprising amount of production capacity, arguably at the expense of more scholarly work. None of this endears war studies and military historians to their colleagues!

The second problem is the notion that the subject area is merely lists of battles and the lives of dead generals; the apparent coincidence that many of these have been written by nearly-dead generals only compounds the issue.[10] Those historians who challenge military history on this latter ground usually fail to acknowledge that for a significant part of the last two centuries the 'great deeds of great men' approach to history also encompassed politicians, diplomats and even academic historians.[11] The disdain is then exacerbated by a lack of understanding of the military instrument and its practitioners. Although many in the international politics field of study fully understand the wider issues around humanitarian intervention, nation-building and the wider sweep of security roles, these are easily swept aside by the cynic.[12] Some military historians have formally categorized the move away from the caricature version of military history as being about battles and generals, calling the emergent discipline 'new military history'. But Biddle and Citino, along with Joanna Bourke, have pointed out that it is no longer 'new'.[13]

Finally, distaste for the politics of a particular conflict, whether it be Vietnam, Srebrenica, Afghanistan (Russian intervention as well as American) and the Gulf wars apparently renders the academic study of these conflicts both inappropriate and pointless. This list of concerns and prejudices is not exhaustive, but gives a flavour of some of the challenges. There are, however, more serious issues to be tackled.

One of the more serious accusations against studying the history of warfare is that it may actually be of some use, rather than just being an abstract discipline.[14] The first of these is the use of history to educate servicemen and women of all ranks, along with politicians, officials and the general public.[15] This is especially relevant on the more senior military courses where aspects of higher command are studied.[16] Inevitably, this process of education is fraught with difficulty in that one has to be selective as to the sources chosen, including official histories of conflict which should not be taken as the last word.[17] Coupled with this is the normal historical caution on the need to examine who the author was, his or her standpoint, why it was written and what was left out and why.[18] The second issue surrounds the very natural desire to learn lessons. But as Howard has cautioned:

> The lessons of history are never clear. Clio is like the Delphic oracle: it is only in retrospect, and usually too late, that we understand what she was trying to say.[19]

It is important here that the embryonic military commander understands the importance of thinking through the real precedents in a clinical manner, avoiding the temptation to cherry-pick or attempting to force the evidence to fit the situation, but succeeding in doing so only on occasion. It is even more important for the war studies or air power student to do the same.

Extending the discussion beyond the quest for lessons, gleaning the best from history is a fundamental part of the process of formulating the doctrine whether it be for air power, for the joint arena or for the other environments. The 'lessons' theme is evident in the title of a journal article by the distinguished historian Richard Overy, where he commented that 'military doctrine is by definition historical'.[20] If one takes doctrine as being the 'fundamental principles by which military forces guide their actions' this becomes both logical and necessary.[21] One can extend that thinking further by following the approach taken by naval strategist Julian Corbett who suggested that doctrinal thinking would allow politicians and military planners to be able to utilize 'mental power and verbal apparatus' on a level playing field.[22] By further extension, a common understanding of the history upon which the thinking is based would prevent individual interpretations being used as ammunition in planning or budgetary skirmishes, or just plain misunderstandings.

Beyond the temptation to plumb the depths of military history for 'lessons' and contributions to doctrine is the more refined quest for *The Art of War*, or for either universal military principles or, often, a defined national way of conducting warfare.[23] An oft-quoted approach to the 'British Way of Warfare' is traditionally accredited to Basil Liddell Hart who argued that Britain was more successful in warfare when she adopted a flexible maritime strategy and largely avoided continental commitments.[24] For students of air warfare, Liddell Hart's work is worthy of study for his views on air power, before and after the Second World War.[25] Similarly, the thinking of Major General J. F. C. Fuller is worth examining in this field; both strategists will be looked at in greater detail in Chapter 4.[26] Ways in warfare also extend into counter-insurgency and the Cold War.[27] This broad section of the historiography obviously has its own merit and is certainly useful for studying the origins of specific schools of thought beyond the normally cited ideas of Trenchard, Mitchell and Douhet. But care has to be taken in all fields of military history, and for air warfare in particular, not to seek examples showing that there are sets of universal military principles based on universal military thought.[28] For this universality to be valid, it depends on assumptions of 'rationality' and a study of air power history would likely suggest the opposite.

Seeking a purely military set of rational or universal principles is also dangerous as it would tend towards omitting cultural and social aspects, not only of the immediate context, but also in the wider backdrop covering the full spectrum from scientific advances, through technology, to embracing the workforce (female and male) all on a world stage. While it is something of a truism to stress this aspect of military historiography, it is actually important to note the prevalence of parochialism.[29] This is evident, to a greater or lesser extent, in all air warfare history, with the enemy often being the target (on the ground or in the air) rather than being a full partner in the conflict. Recent research is, however, moving towards examination of the life on the receiving end of aerial bombardment.[30] It may seem a sweeping statement to point out that this parochialism is even worse among the allied or partner nations, with American literature seemingly 'unaware that the United States had any allies in the Second World War at all, in either Europe or the Pacific'.[31] There are obvious exceptions to this, including Richard Hallion, Carlo d'Este and Tami Davis Biddle.[32] Care also has to be taken to note that there are many examples of research which has been specifically targeted, and the title chosen, to address a given national contribution or air force.[33] Parochialism is evident in military history generally, and also in air warfare, in a number of forms. The first of these is the evident tribalism between services. Accounts of the use of the heavy bombers in the Normandy campaign in 1944 will very quickly demonstrate this; likewise with close air support in the same campaign. Arguably, the inter-service rivalry is at its most virulent in the debates over budgets in times of austerity such as the interwar years.[34] For any war studies historian, it is instructive therefore to look at discussions on a different topic from several perspectives. The three main secondary sources for interwar policy by Bond, Montgomery Hyde and Roskill will inevitably shed differing light on a given issue. This, of course, is mirrored in the primary files where the Cabinet or Committee on Imperial Defence minutes are common, but the papers prepared by each of the service ministries would have been written from his or her own perspective.

A different form of parochialism is reflected in the tendency for military history to focus only on the national myths, tales of bravery and of victory against the odds.[35] That said, the victory may be omitted if the defeat and suffering are part of the national myth such as the defeat of the Serbs on the Field of Blackbirds in Kosovo Polje in 1389.[36] Regrettably, the history of air warfare is not exempt from this malaise. One of the main disadvantages of this has been brought about by what Howard has called the 'peculiar introversion of the British Army itself'.[37] Part of this stemmed from the nature of soldiering in the United Kingdom, or as Howard points out, often a long way from home in the days of the empire. Military activity was on a small scale and centred on a particular community, be it a regiment or a garrison, each with its own problems specific to the region or district concerned.[38] As issues were solved, deeds were recounted and the histories and myths grew. This was so true for squadrons and air bases in far-flung places and is still probably the case. Occasionally the Squadron or Unit Operational Records (RAF Form 540) would record the details, but often they were made dry and 'safe' – sanitized before submission to higher authorities. The more substantial tales were left to oral history and occasional memoirs. Whether the sources were formal records, informal squadron diaries or personal notes, much clearly depended on the skills of the authors, their standpoints and who they expected to be their target readers. So at one end of the spectrum, military history is about the 'big stories' such as the Battle of Britain or the Dams raid and with 'individual's war stories' at the opposite. Many of the latter sources have serious problems in their utilization. The problems come from the reality that chroniclers since Thucydides are an inherent part of the history; none are independent witnesses to the events that they describe.[39] At a more mundane level, diaries and letters may have been written to reassure family members, to deprecate the author's own part (or the reverse), always assuming that they have not been censored. The problem with the spectrum thus described is that the efforts of the serious student of warfare or military historian is almost an outlier to the range and has to set his or her own research question and agenda; in many cases this will not necessarily have a body of reputable literature to support it.

Both Howard and Black have tended to mirror the theme of parochialism in their works on the nature of military history which comes starkly to the fore when they turn aside from land-based warfare to admit the growing strength in the United Kingdom of naval history.[40] Part of this has been due to the lack of a critical mass of naval historians in academe with the exceptions of Kings College, London and Exeter University. Expertise, globally, exists in the staff and war colleges, but most of their programmes are inward looking and not normally for wider exploitation. Neither of the distinguished authors mention air power history not least because, again, there are only isolated pockets of expertise outside the direct military sphere, or the institutions which directly support various military academies or colleges.[41] In maritime history and the study of air warfare, this lack of critical mass means that few programmes are available (almost anywhere) at undergraduate and masters' levels. This is then reflected in the low numbers of potential doctoral supervisors and the whole spiral of intellectual poverty tightens.

Having outlined why there is a body of literature on the purpose, role and nature of military history as a subject, it is worth looking at some of the issues that have been raised by key authors and examining how these apply to the world of air warfare. The detail of the historiography will be covered in the next chapter while the remainder of this chapter will concentrate in particular on some of Howard's and Black's warnings. The first issue worth considering is that of parochialism and the extent to which this applies to the history of air warfare. The simple answer is that it inevitably does for a number of reasons. The world's air forces came from parent services and brought with them elements of their culture, ethos, structure and staff systems. Values and attitudes also came and approaches to thinking about the history, traditions and practice were bound to be tainted. That said, the advent of military aviation immediately before the First World War brought with it a heady mixture of factors that allowed it to set real distance between the fledgling services and the parents. Part of this mix was the exciting and stimulating combination of science, technology, engineering and new military thinking. From what was supposed to be an era of decline, amateurism and the decay of empire, the spirit of dynamism and innovation was hugely impressive.[42] The wave of progress was avidly followed by the public and press. The wild excitement over aviation was matched with the real fear of the potential devastation that could be wrought from the air in future conflicts.[43] By 1918 therefore, air warfare had largely set itself free from the parochialism of its past and had to build its own history.

The problem from the interwar years onwards was that the history of air warfare followed, partly, the path of the developments in air power itself. Parochialism per se was replaced by an enduring fascination with the men and the machines and subsequently their weapons on a scale that far surpassed the interest in the other fields. This period, for virtually all air arms and forces, was one of survival, of fights for budgets and in trying to establish a degree of independence from the other services which would allow air warfare to be developed freely. This again resulted in an enduring (to this day) genre which sought to explain the virtues of air power and to counter its critics. This version of parochialism has manifested itself in a tendency for the researchers on air warfare to consider air battles either in isolation or, only grudgingly, in the wider context of war; the wider appreciation of the role of air power has often been left to general historians rather than air power advocates. There are inevitable exceptions to these statements and these are augmented by the reality that many of the scholarly air power works have been vital subjects in their own right. Equally parochialism to the point of deep partisan feelings is also evident in military and naval history.

One of the major challenges to all military, naval and air historians, and for that matter, their planners and practitioners in real life, is the need to explore warfare in its wider context. It is not enough to trot out the comfortable aphorisms from standard texts such as Clausewitz about war being an extension of politics, it is actually necessary to set the application of air power into the wider conflict taking due account of the political, economic, legal, industrial, social and other factors.[44] From the earliest days of flight, the media has taken an intense interest including Lord Northcliffe's

Daily Mail in and during the First World War with much coverage and even prizes for specific record-setting flights.[45] The same remains true today whether the conflict is in the Falklands, Libya or Afghanistan, and it could be argued that air power can be utilized by politicians for its impact in the press.[46] The need to take these factors into account seems self-evident, but often history at the operational level fails to do so. All that said, the wider context, and the position of military history within a broader church of 'war and society' should not detract too much from the core essential of '*fighting*'.[47]

Immediately as one steps back from the fascination with the real fighting, a whole stream of ancillary questions need to be answered. The first of these is the natural need to fathom the purpose of the conflict – what are we fighting for, how and with what? Again, it is not enough just to cite Clausewitz; the practitioner and the historian have to understand the real and implied objectives of the recourse to armed conflict. For example, it is not enough to start studying the role of air power in the Battle of Britain and in the fall of France in 1940 without a clear understanding of the political, economic, diplomatic, intelligence, industrial and social factors affecting not only the major contestant powers, but also their neighbours. Much of this work has been done, occasionally in stand-alone works and memoirs, but more usually within a wider bibliography. The Fighter Command order of battle in May 1940 is virtually meaningless without a comparative understanding of the British, German and French attitudes first to disarmament in the Geneva Conferences from 1932 to 1934 and then the helter-skelter rearmament phase with its all-consuming quest for 'parity' in aircraft strengths.[48] Equally one needs to take account of the inter-party politics in each of the nations' capitals, the internecine relationships between government ministries and the personalities involved.[49] Running parallel with these themes is the close examination that has to be made to the bureaucratic issues involving the Air Ministry's efforts to ensure that the organizational structure of the RAF was fit for purpose as it expanded rapidly and new Commands had to be formed.[50] Industry had to ensure that production targets were met, that skilled workforces were recruited or trained and that aircraft repair organizations were established.[51] Similarly, each nation had to balance, or choose to ignore, the ethics, legalities and legitimacy of its likely means of conducting operations.[52] The military historian also needs to look beyond the tactical aspects of the Battle of Britain to examine the effects on the respective populations and to examine what steps the governments were taking to safeguard their people.[53]

A similar analysis could be conducted over the formation of the RAF on 1 April 1918 which would take the military historian far beyond the single-dimensional discussion of the handling of the Smuts report.[54] Given that RAF, like most air forces, was formed from existing services – in this case, the army and the Royal Navy (RN) – there are interesting social and cultural history dimensions that must be added to the mix of politics, economics and logistics.[55] Part of the real issue here is that armies, navies and air forces do not exist in isolation: they reflect, to varying extents, the societies from which they are drawn and their histories facilitate an invaluable insight into the wider national and international tapestry.

After the war or conflict has ended, the military historian, or student of air warfare could be expected to analyse the impact of the fighting in each of the areas described with the addition of the process of reaching peace and the terms, if any, imposed on the losing side. With Versailles as an example, this field alone has huge ramifications for historical study and wider understanding. The social and cultural aspects of military history have generally not been extensively covered for air warfare so there is a rich field for study.[56] The same is largely true for the field of remembrance of air forces and their people.[57] A unique and vital niche in the study of air warfare is the research that has been carried out on the failure to withstand the stress of flying. This has been described in various ways, but the expression used during the Second World War was 'Lacking in Moral Fibre (LMF)'. Serious study in this area has to be multidisciplinary taking in work from past and present psychiatry and arguably more controversially, from discussions on class, ethnic grouping and background.[58]

A significant problem area with the historiography of air warfare is that not only is it Western-centric, but is also frequently written in English.[59] To some extent, the last point is inevitable in that English is the international and universal language of the air with all aircrew and air traffic controllers using it (other than in operational situations). Moyar has pointed out that in general military history, the involvement of Western nations in conflicts has been out of proportion to that of other groups of nations and that this is mirrored in the concentration of archives.[60] The concentration of air assets in air warfare in particular accentuates this. There are obviously exceptions to this in Russia and China and the inability of Western scholars to deal with the language barriers lends support to the Black criticism. That said, there are exceptions to this including Group Captain A. K. Agarwal's *The Third Dimension: Air Power in Combating the Maoist Insurgency* published in association with the United Service Institute of India and deals with the Indian Government's efforts to quell the insurgency.[61] Beyond such notable exceptions, many works dealing with air operations (not just warfare) in continents such as Africa tend to concentrate on Western operations.[62] Operations in Afghanistan and Iraq have generated a sizeable literature, including works incorporating air operations, but again these inevitably centre on Western operations.[63]

This brief review suggests that military history, certainly in the English-speaking world, is alive and well.[64] That is certainly true of the history of air warfare and its wider contribution to military operations (war fighting or otherwise). This chapter has not sought to provide an absolute, or even comprehensive, review of air power bibliography. What it has done has been to give an overview of serious air warfare literature to support the contention that many of the criticisms of military history are neither valid generally nor specific case of air warfare. Although the history of air warfare is by no means complete, or even uniformly covered, the works cited in the references to this chapter more than adequately illustrate the breadth, depth and overall scope of the research carried out. Whether the literature is composed of books comprising interviews and reminiscences, traditional biographies or classic memoirs, they are a real contribution to fabric of national experience.[65] The literature on air warfare is by no means devoid of context, nor does it focus exclusively on technical detail or tactical minutiae. There are obviously many works that fall into this category; these sell well and provide considerable pleasure to sizeable audiences – some of whom become encouraged to take on wider or more detailed academic study. The universal health warning that goes with all of the literature to be studied, and the various sources will be covered in the next chapter, is to analyse why it has been written, to what agenda and for whom.

Deconstructing the narrative

In normal usage, the word 'narrative' is relatively simple and uncontentious. It is simply a story, or 'a spoken or written account of connected events in order of happening'.[66] Yet Hayden White has suggested that the topic has been 'the subject of intense debate' within contemporary historical theory.[67] This is partly because the dictionary definition of 'narrative' is what old-fashioned history either was, or perceived to be: just storytelling with close attention to dates, times and places used as signposts along the way. Modern historians tend to look down on this as the lowest form of historical endeavour, with military history being one of the worst offenders in terms of the craft being seen as merely describing the tactical detail of battles in considerable detail and without context.[68] To some extent this is surprising given that narrative is an essential element of human discourse and forms the foundations of wider understanding. You have to know the story in the first place before attempting to work out what it all means; this is what E. H. Carr has described as the 'ultimate wisdom of the empirical, commonsense school of history'.[69] But he immediately went on to discount this as not being good enough. Rather, accuracy in this field was a necessary condition, but not the essential function.[70] In other words, in assessing a narrative, the analytical historian needs to know which facts are disputed and which are accepted. From there he or she is able to analyse critically what has been described and decide its importance and meaning.

The narrative, and it is worthy of note here that the word is used both as a noun and as an adjective, has a slightly darker side to it. In modern usage, it has been hijacked as shorthand for a process of telling the story to maximize political or other advantage. This has been true in the reports compiled following many major campaigns where the debrief is written in such a way as to tell the story, but with emphasis on more than just dates and places. There is often an underlying agenda, possibly to show a particular platform in the best light or to justify future expenditure on other equipment. It could be argued that this has been the case from the times of Herodotus and Thucydides.[71] This has been done internally within a service, for instance, when the RAF decided to write the 'narrative' of the air campaign over Libya, and also externally either through think tanks, memoirs or edited volumes.

So if Carr was correct in stating more was needed than just the story and there is suspicion that the narrative in question has been deliberately constructed, how does the analyst, or historian, decide on what it all means? The first point to make here is that understanding narrative, history and memory is not just the preserve of academic historians. It extends to encompass language, law, psychology, poetry and elements of the sciences, all with an extensive accompanying literature.[72]

Whatever the discipline, for those who are part of the organization, guild or craft, the overarching narrative is an essential part of understanding, and then assimilating, the culture of the 'unit'. As such it enables a sharing of the history, traditions and stories from the past without which the present makes little sense. As members of the 'unit' (of whatever sort) grow in seniority and confidence, they either actively, or subconsciously, contribute to the developing narrative. The formulation of the narrative is also an essential element of memory and of the formal process of remembrance and the various practices of commemoration. This can be on a large scale covering several countries with something like the First World War.[73] Or it can be narrower and focused such as the memorialization of the German Africa Korps in which the narrative was constructed to differentiate these soldiers from their counterparts in Eastern Europe. The fallen soldiers and their surviving colleagues sought to remove the stigma of National Socialism and depict the conflict in the desert as a chivalric war, or a war without hatred.[74]

In analysing a narrative, the historian will have a set of facts before her or him which are incontrovertible and provide the backbone for the piece. But as Marwick has pointed out, 'a mechanistic conception of "the facts" is not helpful'.[75] The sequence of events has to be set in a wider context and the interconnections between the facts analysed. Causal links have to be sought, and established with care taken not to assume cause and effect when there is no evidence to substantiate it. This can be implied within a narrative for a wide range of reasons ranging from laziness on behalf of the original author through to a deliberate ordering of events to invite the assumption in order to serve the narrative. The historian also has to take account of the attitudes prevailing at the time of compilation as they cannot be assumed to have remained the same; values and attitudes change. Similarly, institutions evolve and their working practices change over time; for example, the so-called 'smoke-filled rooms' of ministries in capitals are long gone. At a higher level, conditions in wider society change over time and these are reflected, often as unstated assumptions, in the ensuing narrative.

Beyond these considerations, the narrative has to be examined to establish the nature of the language that has been employed and the register in which it is written. Is it a polemic, a radical political statement, a simple rant or a measured piece of prose? Is it written with an underlying Marxist base structure, in the liberal tradition, or is it a postmodernist work? Superimposed on these questions, the historian has to consider whether the narrative is internally consistent and whether it fits externally with the wider historiography. It will not necessarily conform in all details, but major areas of divergence need to be identified and explained. Overall it is not just a question of telling a simple story. If the student of air warfare is to get beyond the superficial picture, this critical analysis is essential.

CHAPTER THREE

Air warfare historiography and sources

For any student of air warfare, whether a practitioner, someone on a degree-awarding course, a virtual student on something like a Mass Open Online Course (MOOC), or a person researching for one's own interest and education, one of the first issues this student faces is based around where he or she should get information from. This begs the question as to how accessible and how reliable it is, why it was written, by whom and for what purpose. In the vast majority of cases the answers to these questions are rarely simple; apparently authoritative sources often serve to raise yet more questions and offer further scope for interpretation. Events in history such as the Battle of Britain, the attack on Pearl Harbor and the Vietnam War provide instant examples of the lack of a definitive interpretation. The amount of critical analysis expended on securing answers will depend on the curiosity of the researcher and on his or her intended output of the research. This chapter will examine a range of potential sources, including official documentation, secondary sources and, of course primary and archival materials. The bulk of the examples will be UK-based, but mention will be made of other sources. Wherever one's sources, and in whatever language, the fundamentals tend to be the same.

Doctrine

Military doctrine, at its simplest, is that which is taught. The material is on the syllabi of military training courses, in staff colleges and is used more generally to explain widely held beliefs to a variety of audiences. But this definition has the potential to infuriate some scholars, partly because it is just too glib. A preferred definition which has been used by the North Atlantic Treaty Organization (NATO) and in both UK Air and Space doctrine is

> fundamental principles by which military forces guide their actions in support of objectives. Doctrine is authoritative, but requires judgement in application, it is dynamic and must be reviewed for relevance.[1]

In an air warfare context, this definition is not always as comprehensive as it may sound; with strategic bombing, for example, this contemporary definition is not helpful in that the doctrine was based upon both theory and practice.[2] For significant periods of the twentieth century these fundamental principles were no more than articles of faith and certainly unproven in practice. As discussed in the last chapter, an alternative approach to doctrine, and the use of theory, has been offered by maritime strategist Julian Corbett who suggested that doctrinal thinking could allow politicians and military planners to be able to utilize 'mental power and verbal apparatus' on a level playing field.[3]

It could be argued that the production of doctrine has become something of a cottage industry in the UK with the Ministry of Defence (MoD) Development, Concepts and Doctrine Centre supplementing the NATO doctrine with its own hierarchy of Joint Doctrine Publications and Notes. Longer-term conceptual work is managed through their *Global Strategic Trends* (GST) programme.[4] Other future work is covered in Joint Concept Notes such as the *Future Air and Space Concept* (FASOC).[5] This plethora of publications has been further supplemented with its own range of document launches, journal articles and conferences.[6] But the UK is not unique in this regard with the Royal Australian Air Force (RAAF) having a comprehensive range of publications including *The Air Power Manual*.[7] Similarly, the United States Air Force (USAF) has its own hierarchy of doctrinal publications including Joint Doctrine and the *Air Force Basic Doctrine, Organization and Command*.[8] United States Marine Corps doctrine is essentially marine-air and is in their *Marine Corps Operations* manual.[9] The Canadian Armed Forces also have their own suite of doctrine manuals including the *Canadian Forces Aerospace Manual*.[10] Students, and practitioners, interested in the development of USAF doctrine over the years should consult Meilinger (ed. for the School of Advanced Air Power Studies), *The Paths of Heaven: The Evolution of Air Power Theory* and Futtrell (ed.), *Ideas, Concepts, Doctrine: Basic Thinking in the United States Air Force*, with Volume I covering the period 1907–1960 and Volume II covering 1961–1984.[11]

There are several themes that emerge from this very brief summary. The first is how similar the air forces are with air power doctrine forming part of a hierarchy of thinking, working from the joint level down through the single components; this also reflects a common heritage, at least of ideas. Second, the definitions used tend to be consistent with NATO. That said, a simple search across the internet using common terms does not produce similar answers for French or German aerospace power doctrine – if any at all. Beyond the similarities, why should the student of air warfare even look at these manuals? The first, and easiest, answer is that for study into those air forces which do produce formal, written doctrine it is the easiest way to find an authoritative view on almost any particular military aerospace topic from leadership and command through to the operation of remotely piloted systems. One can also attempt to deduce something of the ethos of a particular service, and the political and cultural environment in which it exists, by the way its doctrine is presented. For example, the USAF is comparatively bullish in the quotation that it uses on the primacy of air, thinking:

> Our doctrine does not mirror the Navy's, nor the Marine's, nor the Army's ... it is aerospace doctrine ... our best practices ... and we should not be bashful about how we write it or what it says.[12]

This contrasts with other nations' doctrine in which the emphasis is extremely heavily placed on joint operations.

For the historian of air warfare, doctrine is often taken in the wider sense of including such evidence of formal thinking as Air Staff Memoranda (ASM), articles in formal air force publications such as the interwar *RAF Quarterly*, *The Hawk* (the annual journal of the RAF Staff College) and the *Journal of the Royal United Services Institute*.[13] Using the formal doctrine publications themselves has to be done with care and a critical eye. In the first place, the production of formal doctrine has been something of a cyclical process. For example, doctrine in the RAF went into hibernation from 1968 when the fourth edition of AP 1300 *RAF War Manual* was last amended and then subsequently withdrawn as 'obsolete' in the early 1970s; doctrinal thinking did not re-emerge until 1990.[14]

A further issue is more political and that is the question of why the doctrine has been produced in the first place. It is often too simplistic just to accept the 'guidance of the military' rhetoric. This may be true, but there may also be an element of 'influence' as well as 'inform' or 'educate'. For much of its early years RAF air power thinking was based on the importance of maintaining the air force as an independent service. This was for operational reasons as well as financial. The theory on the operational side was that air warfare was best fought by airmen who understood the benefits of air power and its limitations. It was not a question of ownership of assets, but of operating them such that the utmost flexibility could be derived. That in turn meant that command and control had to be exercised at the highest possible levels and air power assets not frittered away in penny packets. Some of these tenets had been established through what had worked in practice, but others were added to ensure both that the RAF continued in existence and that it received what the senior airmen perceived to be their share of the budget. If this was a general issue in the interwar years, it was especially true of strategic bombing and the line that the bomber would always get through.[15]

More recently, the staff work supporting the UK Strategic Defence Review of 1997 was characterized by extensive reliance by the British army on their doctrine. At the time, neither the RAF nor the RN had equivalent tomes, so were less able to counter assertions for each of the scenarios that were war-gamed to generate force levels. The third edition of AP3000 and BR1806 followed shortly afterwards along with a comprehensive collection of supporting documents. Coincident with this, and announced as part of Strategic Defence Review (SDR), was the setting up of the Joint Doctrine Centre (JDC) which was the forerunner of the extant Development, Concepts and Doctrine Centre (DCDC).

The historian may also choose to examine the various secondary sources of doctrinal thinking including those produced by organizations such as the USAF Air University; examples include the two-volume *Ideas, Concepts, Doctrine: Basic Thinking in the United States Air Force 1907-1960* and *1961-1984*.[16]

Secondary literature and sources

At its simplest, primary sources are (usually) archival materials in their original state and unaltered by later generations. Published material provides the bulk of the secondary literature. There are, inevitably, grey areas between these demarcations including in the production of official histories and where files have been sifted. These will be discussed below. There is a further complication in that what is primary, and what is secondary, can sometimes depend on the research question under consideration. For a piece of research into conditions on Royal Flying Corps (RFC) airfields in 1914, reprints of fragments of letters appearing many years later would constitute secondary source material. But if the research question centred on how the conditions had been depicted by later generations of authors, they would be primary materials as they would have illustrated the thought processes in memorialization.

Official histories

For the students of air warfare seeking to research some earlier campaign, the Official History seems to be a natural starting point in their quest. Indeed, it may well be. But on the other hand it may not be a godsend as it first appears. As air power historian Christina Goulter has written, 'All good military historians go through a *rite de passage* the point at which they realise that the Official Histories are not necessarily gospel.'[17] That said, they are still essential sources which have to be considered, albeit with a critical eye. The first issue that has to be confronted is that these versions of history are 'official'. As Jeffrey Grey pointed out in his Introduction to *The Last Word*, this is 'frequently synonymous with "cover up", where not indeed with official lying'.[18] Among some university historians there is an innate suspicion as to why anyone would want to produce official history forsaking the much treasured academic freedom and independence. Part of this is based on their assumption that these authors are actually second-rate historians, if indeed they are actually historians as opposed to civil servants or just folk who can write.[19] Academics are generally aware which faction, or school of thought, their colleagues belong to and their views can be said to belong to, say, a classical or revisionist camp. But this is much more difficult with official historians because the influences on them are likely to be policy based. For example, the Air Ministry in the interwar years was obviously keen to portray the RFC, the Royal Naval Air Service (RNAS) and latterly the RAF in the First World War in the best possible light and as Noble Frankland (co-author of the official history of *The Strategic Air Offensive against Germany, 1939-1945*) has noted, Raleigh and Jones 'reflected Air Staff doctrines of the 1920s and early 1930s and made them the core of their study of the war in the air'.[20] Frankland goes on to describe this as both 'objectionable' and 'damaging'.[21] This does not, however, mean that *The War in the Air* should be consigned to a second-hand bookstore and not considered further. There is still a huge quantity of detail and analysis worthy of study; the more the researcher understands the constraints under which the official historian worked, the more useful the end product will be.

By the very nature of the task set to them, the official historians have access to official files, documents, interviews and other materials denied to other researchers until they are formally released into the public domain. In Webster and Frankland's case in writing *The Strategic Air Offensive against Germany*, they had access to the various Cabinet Office, Air Ministry and Bomber Command files and to the classified AHB Narratives.[22] As Seb Cox makes clear in his masterly chapter on the production of this official history, it was not all 'plain sailing' in terms of access to material and permission to quote from it. There was particular controversy over the use of the demi-official correspondence between Marshal of the RAF Sir Charles Portal (Chief of the Air Staff, hereafter CAS) and Commander-in-Chief (C-in-C) Bomber Command Sir Arthur Harris.[23]

Although official historians have privileged access, they are also subject to restrictions on what could be included or used. For the Second World War series of official histories, the Cabinet Office put in place a comprehensive set of rules enforced under the editorial eye of J. R. M. Butler and the scrutiny of the cabinet secretary.[24] The rules included restrictions on direct quotation from Chiefs of Staff minutes, but as Cox records, Sir Charles Webster refused to proceed and was able to gain agreement to them being lifted.[25] As it was *The Strategic Air Offensive against Germany* was able to encompass a huge range of material, but there were still exclusions such as the role of Ultra. It is also interesting to note that the Air Ministry was keen, after the Second World War, to produce a 'popular' account of the air aspect of the war without the Cabinet Office restrictions and did so with Richards and Saunders's *The Royal Air Force 1939-1945*.[26] But it is also significant that there is no overall 'air' official history and specific aspects of air warfare history such as the desert war or Normandy are wrapped up in the wider campaign histories; this may well be logical given the genuinely joint nature of these campaigns. But from a purely air perspective, the air warfare historian needs to consult the AHB Narratives.

For the student of air warfare carrying out research on the RAF, the AHB Narratives, where they exist or have been released, are of vital importance. They sit on the boundary between primary and secondary sources in that, to be pedantic, some have been published. The Branch is a small department within the RAF and part of its remit has been to produce these Narratives as stand-alone documents and in support of official histories. The more recent volumes remain classified, but many others are available for study within the Branch or in The National Archives (TNA). Some have been commercially scanned and are available on the RAFCAPS website.[27] In The National Archives, the Narratives are in the AIR 41 series. The seven-volume set covering *The RAF in the Bomber Offensive against Germany* starts at AIR 41/39 and was produced by Professor R. B. Wernham of Oxford University.[28] This first volume examines the experience of air warfare from 1914 to 1918 and how the doctrine on the 'independent' use of air power developed; it goes on to look at the interwar years and bombing policy that evolved as war loomed. Other Narratives have been commercially printed and these include the *Air Defence of Great Britain* series produced by T. C. G. James.[29] There are six volumes running in sequence plus a separate book of maps. For the student of the laws of air warfare, J. M. Spaight, who was previously a senior civil servant in the Air Ministry and a delegate at the 1923 Hague Convention was commissioned to produce a Narrative on the *International Law of the Air, 1939-1945. Confidential supplement to Air Power and War Rights*.[30] This is a highly detailed, originally classified, analysis of the bombing campaign from a lawyer's perspective. The Narratives are immaculately referenced using the original Air Ministry filing numbers for the files used and these must be cross-referenced to The National Archives AIR series.

In his Introduction to *The Last Word?*, Grey noted the comment made by Robin Higham that these works often form the first rather than the last word.[31] With their privileged access to documents that others may not see for decades, there is a fair chance that they will indeed set the historical agenda. As Cox has noted, this was true with Webster and Frankland influencing Anthony Verrier's *The Bomber Offensive* and Max Hasting's *Bomber Command*.[32] The same is obviously true with Churchill's *The Second World War* which is a memoir, rather than an official history, but which still set the wider agenda for a generation of historians.[33]

The United Kingdom has been by no means the monopoly on the production of air official histories. The USAF has a comprehensive, seven-volume history of *The Army Air Forces in World War II* edited by Craven and Cate.[34] In March 1942, President Roosevelt ordered each war agency to produce an 'accurate and objective account' of that agency's war experience. The Army Air Force set up a historical division under the Air Intelligence section of its Headquarters. At the end of the war, Lieutenant General Ira Eaker entrusted the task of writing the history to the University of Chicago stressing that it should 'meet the highest academic standards'.[35] The ensuing seven volumes were completed between 1948 and 1958. The Air Force Historical Studies Office (AFHSO) has also published a four-volume history of the *US Air Service in WWI*.[36]

The USAF AFHSO has also brought out some fifty-five special studies which were produced by their historians in 1960s and 1970s. The general theme of the 'blue book' series is the USAF in Southeast Asia, but there are other topics covered. Examples include *Tactics and Techniques of Close Air Support Operations 1961-1973* and *USAF Airborne Operations in WWII and Korea*.[37] There are also monograph series on Southeast Asia, a series on the USAF in Korea and so on. Beyond this very short summary the AFHSO has an extensive publications listing of officially produced documents and reprints.[38] At first sight, the scale of publications is rather mind boggling. It is therefore very tempting just to select one particular source as that would secure a reference or footnote. But the prudent researcher would do well to ascertain just what the source actually is, why it was commissioned and where it fits into the overall historiography.

The RAAF Air Power Development Centre also has an Office of Air Force History which has a statutory duty to maintain unit histories. At the government level, the Australian War Memorial (AWM) is responsible for sponsoring official war histories. Four distinct series have been commissioned covering the two world wars, Korea and Southeast Asia. The official historians were given unrestricted access to classified material. The AWM stresses that the histories were subject to the authors' own interpretation and do not follow a government line.[39] For the First World War, Volume VIII covers *The Australian Flying Corps in the Western and Eastern Theatres of War*.[40] The Second World War is covered by a four-volume series under the title *Australia in the War of 1939-1945. Series 3 – Air*.[41]

In Canada, the First World War is well covered in the *Official History of the Royal Canadian Air Force* with the first volume covering *Canadian Airmen and the First World War*.[42] The second covers *The Creation of a National Air Force* and is followed by *The Crucible of War 1939-1945*.[43] Further to this, there is a three-volume history of the *R. C. A. F. Overseas*.[44]

New Zealand has a single volume on the Royal New Zealand Air Force (RNZAF) in the *Official History of New Zealand in the Second World War 1939-1945* series.[45] This is supplemented by three volumes on New Zealanders serving with the RAF.[46]

Secondary literature

At its simplest, secondary material has been published. But some published sources may actually be primary with letters and diaries being instant examples of this. Some archival materials such as papers or Narratives have also been published. There are other grey areas between primary and secondary, but it is not worth expending too much energy on the precise definitions. In practice, secondary sources are books, journal articles and some online materials. Other secondary sources go beyond the standard list to include artefacts, art, literary works, film and television. Media materials could also be added to this list. Here the nature and phrasing of the research question is vital as the primary/secondary boundaries will blur very quickly. Michael Paris' book *Winged Warfare* is a classic example of this.[47]

In working through, or even just identifying, secondary literature, a number of key questions will cycle through the mind of the researcher. These questions do not necessarily form a shopping list, but most will be relevant to most pieces of work. The first is to try and identify why a particular piece may have been written. In some instances, it may be simply to make money or to cash in on a particular anniversary. In conversation, one (unfortunately late) military historian admitted producing and marketing books of a particular genre with the explicit intention of trying to get them into the *Sunday Times'* best-sellers list in the run up to Christmas; part of the motivation was to finance his daughters' weddings. The vagaries of work and contracts in the academic world also act as a stimulus for publishing. One cannot make sweeping generalizations about materials mainly produced for financial gain, but there is a tendency for authors to be content to rely on other secondary sources without as much archival material as would be evident in a piece designed for an academic audience.

Academics in virtually every country are under considerable pressure to publish their research; in most, this is balanced by the need to teach and to carry out some form of academic administration such as convening programmes, administering student admission and so on. In the UK, part of the government funding for higher education is based on peer assessment of academics' publications. In general, they are expected to produce a monograph plus about three high-quality journal articles. Without venturing into the world of academic snobbery, there is a 'pecking order' of the prestige of publishers, academic journals and the types of material that are in vogue at any particular time. This system is further complicated by recent trends that show that academic work and research are having an impact on wider society.[48] This may be easy to show if one's research delivers a cure for cancer, but the air power researcher must be looking to influence, directly or indirectly, politicians (such as through the House of Commons Defence Committee), policymakers or practitioners. For the last category, the obvious place to publish will then be in professional journals such as the *USAF Aerospace Power Journal,* or the *RAF Air Power Review.*

Conference papers and proceedings are generally rather low on the prestige league tables, but again can score highly on impact. All of these issues influence academics in the material they choose to research along with what and where they publish. In turn, these impact on later individual researchers and what is available for them to study.

There are many wider reasons why academics and members of the public choose to research a given topic and to publish the fruits of their labours. One of these is linked to family members and the dedications of many books will reflect this.[49] In other cases, the research represents a culmination of life-long ambitions or fascination with the subject.[50] Other motivations for researching and publishing involve factors such as exoneration, blame or castigation.[51]

In surveying the field of published material the researcher has to identify who has published the material and where are the gaps in the literature. These gaps could be there because there is neither a story nor sufficient controversy. Or possibly there is a gap because there are very few primary source materials. An example of this was when a student wanted to contrast RAF interwar anti-submarine policy with that of the RN; as neither service had much of a policy he faced a conundrum. Gaps in the literature can either be based on the narrative, on sources or on the approach taken. In this latter category, the approach may be to use a social science analytical tool or a philosophical approach such as Foucault. As discussed in the previous chapter, subjects as rich as air warfare can be approached from many different angles; some aspects have arguably been thrashed to death, others are still awaiting research as archives open.

Whether the research is being conducted for the award of a degree, purely for publication or for personal interest, the benefit in conducting a thorough review of the secondary literature helps the author to become a master of the subject. It also helps to avoid the pitfalls of having to admit that one had missed a key work which covered the same ground. In addition to being an exercise in critical analysis, the author is constantly reviewing how others have not just approached his or her subject, but more importantly, how they have tackled the research question in mind.

Many subjects in air warfare, and in military history more broadly, fall into a cycle of early work, new research, revisionism, reinvigorating to the classical view. The Alan Clark *Donkeys* thesis and the contrasting work of Gary Sheffield on Haig's competence as a commander makes an instant example.[52] The cycle can either be fairly flat, or the whole debate may be multifaceted and complex. The researcher has to position his or her research question somewhere in this debate to be able to add something new to it and this can only be done by a thorough review.

In starting a review of the literature and existing research the author needs to take in books, journal articles and unpublished research such as doctoral theses. Care has to be taken with the provenance of online material which may have been submitted as part of a course requirement somewhere, but may not have been moderated or supervised. It is therefore worth identifying, in a brief meta-analysis, who the main scholars are in a given field. Concentrating then on a nucleus of key texts helps the researcher to position the rest of literature in a fairly secure framework. Careful study of these texts will also help to identify gaps, assess the nature of the debate and start to note possible locations of primary sources.

Secondary literature – an international perspective

As stated in the introduction, this text has tended to focus on British, American and Commonwealth air forces and their use of air power. It would be remiss not to broaden the context somewhat to embrace other countries. Given the nature and status of military history in some countries, the literature may not be extensive, or necessarily written by nationals of the country involved. The following paragraphs deal with a number of major countries and outline some of the key texts that are readily available, albeit predominantly in English. It is very much a summary of some of the available literature.

For Germany, the First World War has its almost inevitable literature of the tales of aces and aeroplanes.[53] Other accounts such as Hans Ritter's *Der Luftkrieg* are also worth consulting.[54] The rise of the Luftwaffe in the interwar years has attracted considerable scholarly attention with E. R. Hooton's *Phoenix Triumphant* covering the period from November 1918 through to June 1940.[55] In turn, James Corum's *The Luftwaffe: Creating the Operational War* covers the same period while Williamson Murray's *Strategy for Defeat* covers 1933–1945.[56] Depending on the research question at hand, work on the interwar Luftwaffe is likely to embrace the German Army doctrine and the rise of the Blitzkrieg concept; there is a sizeable literature on this field.[57] A useful overview of German thinking on air power can be gleaned from Boyne's *The Influence of Air Power on History*.[58] International comparisons on air warfare in the Second World War are uncommon and the work edited by Horst Boog in 1992 is extremely valuable (both in terms of content and secondhand cost).[59] If the research question involves work on conditions in Germany during the Second World War, the series edited by Jeremy Noakes is worth consulting for material such as the SD Reports produced in Germany on the state of morale.[60] There is a growing literature, in many languages, on the experiences of life under air bombardment and from the German perspective examples including Friedrich's *The Fire* and the wider literature on Dresden and Hamburg.[61] For much of the Cold War, German air power was very much under the NATO umbrella and it is covered in that literature. More recently the changing nature of the use of air power (covered below) has meant that work such as the chapter by Holger Mey on German air power has become increasingly relevant.[62]

Given its early predominance in designing, and demonstrating, aircraft it is not surprising that France is well covered in First World War literature, again with its stock of works on aces and aircraft.[63] Interwar thinking on air power in France is again well covered by Boyne and is the subject of a comparative study by Robin Higham.[64] French air power in Vietnam has been briefly examined in a comparative study published by the US Department of Defense which should be read in conjunction with the much wider literature on Dien Bien Phu.[65] More recently, work has been done on French air power in Africa, Libya and in the context of European air power.[66]

Russian Aviation and Air Power in the Twentieth Century edited by Higham, Greenwood and Hardesty provides an excellent introduction to the subject with contributions covering subjects from early flight through to the Cold War.[67] Beyond the coverage in Boyne, Russian air power theory is dealt with in detail by James Sterret.[68] For the Second World War, O'Brien's *How the War was Won* takes the arguments over mass armies (particularly on the Eastern Front) and the operational level of war to a higher plane arguing that the economic and technological developments in sea and air power effectively 'broke' the German and Japanese war machines and that these contributions more than made up for the late second front.[69] More recent times have coverage by Kainikara, Gordon and De Haas.[70] The end of the Cold War and the impact on air power has also been the subject of a RAND study by Ben Lambeth.[71]

Given the prominence of Pearl Harbor, it is not surprising that Japanese air power has tended to concentrate on naval aviation with Mark Peattie's *Sunburst: The Rise of Japanese Naval Air Power*, a useful source.[72] John Buckley's chapter on the war in the Far East in *Air Power in the Age of Total War* is also very comprehensive.[73] Inevitably, there are a number of official US sources on the air war with Japan including offerings from the USAF History Office.[74] In common with these cited works, there are a number of others which take the air war from an allied perspective including Peter Preston-Hough and, of course, Henry Probert.[75]

Primary sources and their use

Oral materials

Oral, or spoken, history is an immediate and vital source for historians. This can take the form of live interviews with participants or witnesses. Using interviews can be very time consuming in preparation, execution, transcription and analysis.[76] Care has to be taken to analyse critically the story that unfolds for the veracity of the account, any exaggeration (not that aircrew in particular are prone to this), self-justification or self-depreciation. The interviewer also has to be suitably trained in the process and must avoid pitfalls in 'leading' the veterans with careless language. Use may also be made of sound archives where museums such as the Imperial War Museum and the RAF Museum have carried out, and recorded, a wide range of interviews.[77] There is a middle area which includes witness seminars where testimony is taken orally and subsequently presented in published format.[78]

Printed materials

Primary source materials are the lifeblood of original research. They take on many forms from printed collections of diary entries through original files to original notebooks and artefacts. In most countries, there are national repositories for official files in addition to various collections. Some are available for access and for quotation; others remain in owners (normally family members) possession and their use may be restricted. As has been briefly discussed above, the nature of the research question under investigation will influence what is actually a primary source.

Collections of diaries or letters are the most common form of printed primary source material. These can be the material generated by commanding generals down to the musings of the private soldier or airman. They may be about the conflict in question, or writing to take their mind away from the troubles. Again, the relative importance to the researcher will depend on the research question. At first sight, it would seem relatively straightforward to transcribe the original material and simply then go to print. But if one takes the war diaries of Douglas Haig as a case study, it immediately becomes apparent that it is more complex.[79] The first issue that Gary Sheffield and John Bourne as editors had to contend with was what to leave out as space available meant that 'only a selection of entries could be reproduced'.[80] As is evident from their title, they also decided to include some private correspondence (as opposed to 'official' material). The next major problem was that the diary exists in two forms, a contemporary manuscript and later typescript version, and there are differences between the two. The editors chose to work with the manuscript version because of its 'accuracy, immediacy and authenticity'.[81] Both versions, however, have their own 'legends' with the second in particular seen as an attempt to 'rewrite history' especially as it was made available to the official historians in the UK and Australia.[82]

The next issue to be considered is the motivation for keeping a diary at all. Most editors of diaries concur that their authors continued out of habit.[83] Many also kept them for their wives and for the later amusement of their children.[84] But in Haig's case each completed section was sent home to his wife who in turn sent extracts to the king's assistant private secretary, at the king's request.[85] The diary entries therefore had the potential to be very powerful tools in assisting Haig's standing at the time and again in later life when his conduct in command was under scrutiny.

Similar challenges face the editors of collections of correspondence with issues around selection and capacity. It is worth noting that some correspondents deliberately wrote to family members where there was a prohibition on keeping a diary for security reasons, or in place of the diary. In others, the diary was something of a confessional and allowed the author to reveal his or her feelings, at least to some extent.[86] Some collections contain only the letters sent and omit the responses.[87] Others include both sides of the correspondence.[88] These collections provide an easily accessible place to find appropriate references to support a text. But it still may be necessary to return to the original files to seek out the supporting arguments of, say, the staff in the Air Ministry in assisting the Central Authentication Service or the Secretary of State formulate their notes and letters.

The natural progression from diaries and letters is into memoirs and autobiographies. Obviously the closer the events are to the date of publication, the more immediate the impact of the subject's message. Whatever the timescale involved, the students have to allow for self-justification, exoneration, the imperative to make money and the need to get their version – or their side of the story – told first and thereby shape our initial perceptions; two immediate examples include Churchill's six-volume history of the Second World War and 'Bomber' Harris's autobiography.[89] Comments in autobiographies or memoirs that are not supported by documentary evidence, or even worse are reported second hand are dangerous. A classic example here is Haig's supposed antipathy to aviation which comes from Sir Frederick Sykes's *From Many Angles*.[90] Haig's remarks have been seized upon, especially by the *Donkey* school as evidence of his prejudices and reluctance to embrace technology. Yet there is a considerable amount of painstaking research showing the contrary, but once lodged it is difficult to shake out a myth.[91]

Like diaries, memoirs come with a range of authors and reasons for writing. Some may be of interest because the authors may have been Secretaries of State for Air and their writings give an insight into a politicians view of, say, Trenchard.[92] Equally important, depending on the research question, reminiscences of bird-watching 'adventures' with the RAF provide a vital insight into the social history of the service which is much under-researched.[93] A major drawback in this area is where senior individuals in pivotal posts do not leave either diaries or memoirs with Marshal of the Royal Air Force (MRAF) Sir Charles Portal as a classic example; where Alanbrooke's diaries have been published, there is nothing at all from his air counterpart.

Archival materials

Most countries have their own selections of archives and a few will be covered in this section. National archives are often the first place to start depending on what clues the researcher has found in the bibliographies of existing works. In the UK, The National Archives are at Kew in west

London. With them, as with almost any archives, libraries or museum research departments, the visitor must check beforehand what is available digitally, what the opening times for visits are, what forms of identity are required, what the rules are on photographing or copying documents, the vagaries of document ordering and reading and what is allowed and forbidden in terms of note taking.[94] It is worth allowing at least one day to do a reconnaissance of the archive concerned to get used to the system. It is also worth thoroughly exploring the archive's website and search engine – some are better than others. Beyond that, it is almost impossible to provide real guidance as to how long the research may take. If the researcher is just looking for a couple of references for simple footnoting and knows where to look, the experience can be fairly brief. If, however, the research is more detailed, it can be a time-consuming and frustrating occupation. Unless the search engine used by the archive in question, and the database behind it, has been loaded with comprehensive keywords, there is often no alternative but to wade through the files until the nugget of the material is found.

In trying to piece together the story that will help answer the research question, it may be necessary to examine the files of several parts of an organization. For example, for the debate on attacking oil targets in the winter of 1944–5 between Portal and the Air Ministry on one side and 'Bomber' Harris on the other, a simple set of references may be gained just from the CAS's files in the Air Ministry.[95] But with such a complex interchange of correspondence it is also worth looking at what was recorded on the Bomber Command files in the AIR 14 series. The letters themselves are of considerable interest, but the intra-departmental correspondence, such as a minute from the director of Bomber Operations (Air Commodore Sydney Bufton) to Portal as the CAS sheds real light on the thinking in London and, at first sight, easily squashes the question as to whether Harris was disobeying orders over not attacking oil targets as there was 'no doubt that Bomber Command have done excellently in the attack on oil'.[96] But they go on to cast doubt saying 'and the C-in-C may well feel convinced that he is attacking it to the best of his ability', and then go further questioning whether every opportunity had been taken.[97] By reproducing these two fragments, this incident shows that recourse to primary material is essential in gaining a real understanding of what had been discussed. The temptation just to 'lift' part of the quote from secondary literature should be avoided wherever possible.

It is also tempting to just take the minutes of the meeting of, say, the Chiefs of Staff as being a suitable reference for the debate on a given subject; these are available online at CAB 25. But a fuller picture may be obtained by looking through the supporting memoranda in CAB 24.[98] If the subject matter is a thorny debate over allocation of resources between services, it is also worth going back to the internal department's files used for preparing their ministers or officials. For minutes of meetings, it is worth searching through early drafts of those meetings to see what has been changed and ideally why. Where the meetings are chaired by a senior official from another government department, such as with the award of medals in wartime during the Second World War, it is worth using the Treasury files as the master set, in this case T300 as the meetings were run by the Permanent Under-Secretary to the Treasury (PUS).[99] It is also worth cross-checking correspondence in these examples with the Prime Minister's files (PREM) or even the monarch. The bulk of these National Archive files are only available to inspect at Kew, although they can be ordered digitally at considerable cost.

In some cases, the original files have been preserved complete with minute sheets, marginal handwritten comments and so forth. If the researcher is not familiar with this process, it is worth working through a couple of files to see how that particular organization was working then. Other file categories in The National Archive are compilations of fragments of files which have been collected and retained where the material has been used in AHB Narratives and in Official Histories or are of sufficient importance to have been kept in their own right. For example, the AIR 1 series contains material mostly; from 1914 to 1918 and AIR 2 covers 1887–1985! Air 9 covers the Directorate of Operations and Intelligence from 1914 to 1947. A key source for many researchers will be the Operations Record Books known as Forms 540 and 541. Those for RAF Commands are at AIR 24; for Groups at AIR 25; for Wings at AIR 26; and for Squadrons at AIR 27.[100]

Although Kew is a natural starting point for many researchers into air warfare, it is not the only one. The Department of Research and Information at the RAF Museum at Hendon holds an extensive collection of personal papers including those of Lord Trenchard, 'Bomber' Harris and Amy Johnson.[101] The Museum also has an extensive collection of Air Publications as well as the archives of a number of famous British aircraft companies including Supermarine, Handley Page and Fairey.[102] Work on aircraft design may also necessitate the use of BAE Systems' Heritage archive and collection which also has extensive holdings.[103] Other archives include the Imperial War Museum, the Fleet Air Arm Museum, the Liddell Hart Centre for Military Archives, the India Office Collection in the British Library and some records retained in the AHB. Many archival resources remain in the collections of private individuals ranging from parents' flying logbooks and personal papers through to those still retained by Viscount Trenchard. Yet others are in smaller libraries and museums; access may be on an appointment basis or may necessitate family permission to use or to quote from. The nature of the research may be a key factor in the permission being given.

In Australia, over 250 series of RAAF records are held in the National Australian Archive (NAA), including those of the Air Board, squadron and unit histories and Commanding Officer's reports.[104] If visiting the NAA either virtually or in person in Canberra it is also worth looking at the Australian War Memorial Unit histories for a range of conflicts.[105]

The Military Heritage section within the Library and Archives Canada holds a range of records covering the early years of North West Mounted Police through to recent campaigns. These include unit war diaries, military service files and so on. The Department of Defence Directorate of History and Heritage has an Archives and Library section which includes biographical files and Permanent Record Files created for Canadian units at home and abroad.[106] They also hold an extensive set of files copied from those at Kew and this highlights the shared experiences of the Canadian, Australian and New Zealand air forces with the UK in the world wars.

Library and Archives Canada holds a range of private and government records covering the early years of European exploration through to present day. Although there is a Military Heritage section within which you may find information such as unit war diaries, military service files and so on, additional information is located within thematic record groups (RGs) such as RG 24, Records of the Department of National Defence. The Department of National Defence's Directorate of History and Heritage (DHH) has an Archives and Library section that may be accessed by the general public. It contains biographical files, historical reports, files generated by Canadian units at home and abroad and so on. The DHH also holds an extensive set of files copied from archival holdings overseas, such as those at Kew, highlighting the shared experiences of Canadian and allied air forces from First World War to modern coalition operations.

In the United States, a useful starting point is again the National Archives based in Washington DC.[107] Its website is comprehensive and easily searched. The Air Force Historical Research Agency (AFHRA) holds an impressive selection of personal papers and oral history records.[108] In addition to a long section of fact sheets, the agency has a large number of historical studies, ranging from research on recent operations to studies on women in Minutemen crews.[109] Its holdings are searchable online at Air Force History website.[110] A useful summary of the AFHRA, which is based at Maxwell AFB in Alabama, has been published by the Society of Military History.[111] One must not forget the more 'social history' aspects, like African Americans.[112] Finally, the National Museum of the Air Force in Dayton, Ohio, has an archival collection.[113]

A case study: The Bomber Command medal saga

It is worth attempting to pull together some of the details contained in this chapter into a case study in order to illustrate the use of some of the sources and resources that have been outlined. In the first instance the researcher, or student, has to come up with a research question. Writing an essay during a course is relatively straightforward because the module convenor, or member of staff, will have set the question quite specifically seeking to elicit certain facts and, more importantly, arguments and analysis; frequently there will be debate among historians or strategists on the topic. A research question requires the individual to do this question setting independently. The research in question could range from family history through to complex interdisciplinary questions examining the interrelationship between the use of armed force and society over a long time period. Arriving at the research question is usually a process of cyclical, or iterative, development where the researcher seeks to ensure that it has not been done before and that it can be satisfactorily answered within the constraints of time and space allowed. In some cases the researcher will be limited by the organizational constraints of the sponsor of the research; this may be a time and word limit on a thesis or dissertation set by the university, or a word length stipulated by a journal or book publisher.

Research questions can be formed by approaching the topic from a variety of viewpoints which may depend on the intended audience; the availability of source material; the nature of the debate on the subject; what has been covered before; and the preferences of the researcher. The last two points are important. Most research takes time, effort and concentration and it really does help if the researcher is passionate about the subject; the converse is equally true. The requirement for originality in doctoral theses makes the question of what has been done before very relevant. The researcher needs to consider five basic questions in his or her approach to the topic. The first is to identify why the research question is interesting. In other words, why should the researcher invest the effort required? This may be the novelty of the subject, its relevance to a policy debate or may be a contribution to historiographical balance. The second question starts the cycle by asking who else thinks it is interesting; this in effect becomes a literature review encompassing books, journal articles, unpublished theses and so on. The researcher then needs to be able to identify how the fruits of his or her research will contribute to the broader body of knowledge. The fourth question involves an outline of how the answer to the research question will be structured and the final question will be to check the feasibility of tackling the research question. This could involve language skills, access to archives, security classification of materials and so on. It is highly likely that as this process evolves, the research question will change; the most obvious reason for this is that someone else has already tackled the subject.

In this case study, the interest stems from the controversy around the lack of recognition for personnel of Bomber Command following the Second World War. They, along with their C-in-C 'Bomber Harris', were seen as having been snubbed by the authorities.[114] This became regarded as 'The Great Ingratitude'.[115] The flames were fanned shortly after the war by Harris himself in his autobiography bemoaning the fact that all that his team received was the 'defence medal' while they had been engaged on offensive operations for the entire war.[116] The debate has continued ever since with a great deal of bitterness felt by the veterans themselves. After years of simmering animosity towards Whitehall, the prime minister commissioned a wide-ranging report into this and other disputes centred around medals.[117] The findings were duly reported in 2012 and the upshot of the whole was the award of a clasp to Bomber Command aircrew to wear on the 1939–45 Star. In this last sentence lies the rub of the controversy, in that the aircrew were the only personnel entitled to the recognition. Arguably, they had already received recognition with the Aircrew Europe Star. The ground crews still received nothing.

There is clearly plenty of controversy over the issue and it is worth some further research. This can be approached in a number of ways. The first port of call is the secondary literature on the subject. These include Harris's own autobiography detailed above along with biographies on him and on Portal.[118] Interestingly, much of the usual literature on the strategic air offensive is quiet on the issue which is always interesting from a researcher's point of view. The positive is that the field is relatively open. But it may also beg the question as to why; quite often this is because of the lack of source material. Fortunately for this case study, there is plenty of primary material.

The files in The National Archive and in the Churchill Papers show a lot of correspondence on the subject. Given that the main saga has already been partly examined, what else could be looked at?[119] A further research question could be to look at the nature and impact of the various Commonwealth countries' inputs into the Prime Minister's Office as each of them tried to ensure adequate recognition for their people. Another area of potential interest could centre on the role of the king in approving the various schemes and in his wider relationship with Churchill.[120]

Having established, either through a formal literature review, or just a brief survey, who else has tackled the subject and how the answer could contribute to the greater sum of knowledge, the researcher will have established a useful working knowledge of the secondary material on the subject. He or she will also have started to identify some of the primary materials that had been used by their predecessors and some of the bureaucratic processes that were at work over the period in question, and will therefore be in a reasonable position to source official files and personal papers. In this case study, the bulk of the work in London was carried out by the Committee on the Grant of Honours, Decorations and Medals in Time of War. The committee was chaired by the permanent secretary to the Treasury, Sir Richard Hopkins. Its civilian members were the permanent secretaries to the Dominions Office, India Office, Colonial Office and the three Service ministries which were also represented by the senior military personnel officers (the director-general of Personnel for the Air Ministry (DGPS)). The committee also had a representative from the Central Chancery of the Orders of Knighthood and included the private secretaries to the king and the prime minister. Because the chair of the committee was the senior official from the Treasury, they owned the core series of files.[121] It is worthy of note that they started their deliberations as early as 1943 and the permanent secretaries almost always attended rather than delegating to lower-level officials; this matter was taken very seriously.[122] But the T300 Series only tells part of the story. Each of the main departments submitted papers to the committee, argued various points and disagreed with the way in which minutes were recorded. For a research question on the Bomber Command medal saga it would, of course, be essential not only to look at the Air Ministry files, but also the Bomber Command series (AIR 14) along with Harris's papers in the RAF Museum at Hendon. It would also be necessary to consider the Admiralty and War Office files if their counter-pleading or other arguments looked likely to have influenced the process. For example, as the process continued and the discussions on 1939–45 Star evolved, it became increasingly clear that there would need to be a campaign star for Africa, the Pacific, Burma and so on. The Permanent Secretary to the Air Ministry (Sir Arthur Street) was obviously aware that RAF personnel in the respective theatres overseas would receive the star appropriate to that theatre. But he was also concerned that the aircrew based in the UK would receive 'a pretty raw deal' and wrote accordingly to the Treasury.[123] This eventually resulted in the Aircrew Europe Star which was predominantly light blue with yellow and black stripes at the edges; this represented operations by day and by night with the yellow denoting the searchlights.[124] Only RAF aircrew were eligible, and the vast majority of these were from Bomber Command; it was in effect a Bomber Command campaign medal for operations up to D-Day (after which the aircrew received the France and Germany Star).[125] It is interesting to note that Harris does not acknowledge this in his autobiography. It is also worth acknowledging that Harris himself came in very late to the debate with a lone letter to the Secretary of State for Air (Sir Archibald Sinclair) in October 1944 followed by a brief flurry of correspondence in June 1945.[126]

Depending on the research question chosen, other avenues of exploration can be opened. If the researcher is interested in the Commonwealth perspective, the Treasury files, along with Churchill's papers contain the correspondence with the prime ministers of the respective countries. Part of the contention was that where RAF ground crew were at 'home' and therefore entitled only to the defence medal, those for Canada and Australia were serving abroad. As discussed earlier, copies of various Kew files are available in the respective archives. Wider research would be required to unearth the internal staffing in Ottawa or Canberra.

From an air power perspective, there are a number of interesting additional elements to the debate. The first of these is a cultural issue. Where Harris was at extreme pains (albeit very late in the debate) to point out the bravery and arduous conditions under which his troops worked, it was clear, however, that Churchill had a very low regard for RAF airmen whom he classed as being in the 'same category as many classes of people who help to feed, clothe, and make efficient the fighter pilots'.[127] The second point is that the fundamental underpinning of the Committee on the Grant of Honours, Decorations and Medals in Time of War was that only overseas service counted for anything. A clear exception was made for Battle of Britain aircrew for obvious reasons, not least of which was their participation in combat. The same could be said for the Aircrew Europe. Harris was aggrieved that his less able staff officers whom he could afford to have seconded to headquarters in Europe after the invasion received the 1939–45 Star along with the France and Germany Star. His better officers, whom he kept at RAF High Wycombe, got nothing.[128] At the root of the problem was Churchill's attitude coupled with a complete failure of the non-airmen on the committee to understand how air power had completely changed the nature of warfare. It is significant that the Air Ministry only seemed to have caught the significance of this late in the day when in a minute to the Secretary of State for Air, the CAS and the Permanent Secretary, the Air Member for Personnel wrote:

> The Committee gave the Air Ministry representatives a sympathetic hearing. But the fact of the matter is that the Committee is comprised of senior civil servants, generals and admirals who are really incapable of war except in terms of battlefields and 'theatres of war' geographically defined, and of course everything afloat. They cannot understand that the air has changed everything.[129]

This case study has obviously not been able to cover all of the aspects of the Bomber Command campaign medal saga, but it has introduced some of the challenges and processes involved in arriving at a research question and then in dealing with various sources.

CHAPTER FOUR

Air power thinking and theory

From Douhet, Mitchell, Trenchard and de Seversky through to Boyd and Warden, the literature resonates with names, books and articles describing the potential of air power and its uses in warfare. Some of their writings are pure hypothesis; some are a distillation of experience; but some are political rhetoric designed to justify the existence of an air force or to argue for its share of the defence budget. The immediate challenge for the student of air warfare, at any level, is to ascertain what is being said by the theorist and, arguably more importantly, to analyse why it was written and who was actually influenced by the work.

This chapter cannot hope to summarize all of the trends in the writings of the various authors on air power. Even just deciding on a list of influential writers would be difficult enough. To some extent, these summaries have already been done and new biographies and thoughts on their subject's impact emerge regularly, often serving to re-emphasize the passions and 'outrage' of an earlier age. Thomas Wildenberg's *Billy Mitchell's War with the Navy* and Phil Meilinger's subsequent review in the *Journal of Military History* illustrate this point.[1] The chapter will instead seek to outline some of challenges facing the researcher. These will inevitably include thoughts on familiar names, but the chapter will attempt to put their writings into a wider context, including what was extant in land warfare and naval theory. It will outline some of the literature and point out alternative paths in the development of air power thinking.

Purpose of theory, thinking and writing

It is first worth establishing what is meant by theory and why its study is important. At its simplest, theory is a 'system of ideas explaining something' and in particular, 'one based on general principles independent of the particular things to be explained'.[2] Several elements of this dictionary definition are worth emphasizing in the context of air power. The first is that ideas have been distilled into a system, and not just assembled in a random fashion. Second, the theorist is giving his or her 'ideas explaining' how air warfare may be conducted or how aircraft may be used to advantage, say, against a conventional surface fleet in Mitchell's case. The third is the emphasis on 'general principles' which are 'independent' of the specific. This immediately gives the theorist carte blanche to explore areas of potential, if need be, divorced from the practicalities of technology, laws of war, ethics and so on. The debate surrounding genuinely autonomous aerial systems which have their own agency and volition and no human associated with decision-making illustrates the point in that the ideas can be aired without having tiresome comments about whether such systems are yet technically possible.[3] An article by Marra and McNeil is interesting not least because the authors, as American lawyers publishing in a law journal, have used Boyd's OODA (Observe, Orientate, Decide, Act) loop as an aid for their discussion on the degree to which humans are involved in decision-making in 'drone' operations.[4] The final element of the definition used is the emphasis on 'general' and, while this seem to be semantics, there is an immediate divergence from the 'fundamental principles' essential in the formulation of doctrine. This difference is important when considering the early years of air power theory, when there was insufficient experience of air warfare to be able to produce coherent doctrine but no shortage of ideas.[5]

Having discussed the doctrine in the previous chapter and now defined the theory, it is next necessary to consider the relationship between theory and strategy, not least because much of the commentary on air power theory is in volumes such as Peter Paret's *Makers of Modern Strategy*.[6] Recourse to the dictionary shows strategy to the 'art of war'.[7] Not surprisingly, as a co-translator of Clausewitz with Howard, Paret accepts the German writer's definition of strategy as being 'the use of combat, or the threat of combat, for the purpose of the war in which it takes place'.[8] But as Paret goes on to say, strategy has a higher-level meaning in that it may include 'the development, intellectual mastery, and utilisation of all of the state's resources for the purpose of implementing its policy in war'.[9] It is immediately clear, therefore, that air power is capable of contributing to this implementation of policy. Theory, thinking and writings on the subject are part of the ideas chain of how and why this may come about. At this point, it is worth pausing to consider whether the use of air power is constrained to the pursuit of policy in war. It can be argued that the government's high-level policy is, in the main, the avoidance of war. Air power, and in particular air mobility, can be used in a wide variety of humanitarian situations potentially reducing the risk of conflict.

The scope

It is tempting to limit this chapter to the main air power 'prophets' mentioned at the beginning of the section above along with their more modern counterparts. By broadening the title to encompass thinking on air warfare, it is possible to expand the scope. Douhet and Mitchell may be commonplace names in the air warfare world of today, but they were not on the reading lists for the RAF Staff College at Andover in its interwar years. Other authors such as Liddell Hart, Fuller and J. M Spaight were on these lists and did write about air warfare as will be discussed below.[10] They all, in their various guises, thought through many of the issues over the role of air power in future conflict. But they did not write in a vacuum. Liddell Hart when talking about British ways of warfare had an eye on the works of Corbett and Mahan and these must be discussed in turn as they provide a valuable backdrop. In the same way, many air force officers thought and wrote about the employment of air power. Some authors such as Slessor have stood the test of time; others have slipped from view and their work has to be sought in the *Journal of the Royal United Services Institute* (JRUSI).[11] In addition to individuals writing for a variety of audiences, it has to be remembered that routine staff work continued, as it still does today. This varies from innovative thinking on how to push the lethal envelope of a weapons system through to the highest levels of achieving real strategic effect. In the smoke-filled corridors of Trenchard's Air Ministry as well as the depths of Air Corps Tactical School at Maxwell Air Force Base, staff officers discussed, planned and publicized their thinking through ASM and the like.[12] The thinking and writing processes can be likened to schools of thought rather than just the work of the 'prophet' at their head or who inspired them from afar.

Early writing on air power and flight

Mankind's fascination with flight has been evident from the earliest Greek legends, with the story of Daedalus and Icarus's daring escape from Crete being one of the most obvious examples.[13] A quick scan of English and French literature in search of early references to air warfare will produce fairly predictable results with Jules Verne featuring strongly along H. G. Wells's *War in the Air* and Swift's *Gulliver's Travels*.[14] Over a century after Swift described the flying island of Laputa's custom of throwing rocks at rebellious cities below them, Alfred Lord Tennyson published *Locksley Hall* with the following prophetic words:

> For I dipt into the future, far as human eye could see,
> Saw the Vision of the world, and all the wonder that would be;

Saw the heavens fill with commerce, argosies of magic sails,
Pilots of the purple twilight dropping down with costly bales;

Heard the heavens fill with shouting, and there rain'd a ghastly dew
From the nations' airy navies grappling in the central blue;

Far along the world-wide whisper of the south-wind rushing warm,
With the standards of the peoples plunging thro' the thunder-storm;

Till the war-drum throbb'd no longer, and the battle-flags were furl'd
In the Parliament of man, the Federation of the world.

There the common sense of most shall hold a fretful realm in awe,
And the kindly earth shall slumber, lapt in universal law.[15]

These verses lend themselves to the analysis of a number of air-related themes including the commercial use of aircraft. The legitimacy of warfare is highlighted along with what turned out to be the League of Nations and, subsequently, the United Nations. The air power element clearly signals bombardment from the air, and the phrase 'grappling in the central blue' resonates with control of the air. The 'central blue' becomes a recurring phrase in air power literature including the title of Slessor's autobiography (with due acknowledgement!).[16] It also features as a section head in Richard Hallion's history of early flight where he describes air combat in the First World War.[17] But from a theory point of view, David MacIsaac uses the phrase for his chapter on the air power prophets in *Makers of Modern Strategy*.[18]

Wells's *War in the Air* was first serialized in the *Pall Mall Magazine* in 1908 and appeared in book format the same year.[19] Wells introduced several air warfare themes including the destruction of the US fleet en route to New York, which first surrenders and is then totally destroyed. The conflict escalates following a massive battle between air fleets and results in the total collapse of society. Wells emphasized, as others would do later, that there would be huge psychological damage in addition to the physical destruction wrought from the air; he also emphasized the inevitable contest for control of the air. At the simplest level of analysis, commentators have seen *War in the Air* as a blend of future history and science fiction. His work is widely quoted in aviation articles because of its prophetic nature. But how much it influenced the general public is hard to gauge. That said, Tami Davis Biddle quotes W. F. Kernan who in 1935 stated that 'the average citizen is inclined to believe in the reality of the menace'.[20] The implication from this is that people's views are coloured by such works and the subliminal effect becomes hard to shake off when the realities of bombing are experienced.[21]

The early prophets

As a single point of reference for work on the early power prophets, the standard piece is the MacIsaac chapter in *Makers of Modern Strategy*. Like

Tony Mason in his *Centennial Appraisal*, MacIsaac took his discussion on air power back to Major J. D. Fullerton's suggestion in 1893, at the Chicago World Columbian Exposition, that 'airships will in the future cause as great a revolution in the art of war as gunpowder did in the past'.[22] Fleets of the best battleships could be sunk within an hour and land warfare would be transformed. Fullerton in his original text went on to predict that in future wars, 'the chief work will be done in the air, and the arrival of the aerial fleet over the enemy's capital will probably conclude the campaign'.[23] MacIsaac commented that such 'far-seeing predictions' received far less attention than their prescience warranted.[24] Mason has pointed out the organizational link between Fullerton's membership of the Royal Engineers and their involvement in the formation of the British army's first air battalion in 1911. But in looking at his wider influence, he goes on to warn that just because ideas are coincident in time, the cause and effect linkages remain unproven; this is, of course, true with discussions on theory.[25] But this has also to be seen in the context of Hallion's comment that the Wright brothers 'were well aware of all previous work' and followed developments in America and internationally.[26] Furthermore, it is evident from the actual conference proceedings that it was a really major international event with many key engineers present.[27] Although the direct links may be hard to find, the air warfare researcher needs to understand that the thinkers and engineers were not working in isolation; it was a relatively small community and, despite the lack of internet and modern communications, ideas circulated quickly. The key is to question and challenge the evidence and not assume mere coincidence or rely on causal links that may not have existed.

In his chapter on air power theorists, MacIsaac built on the earlier version written by Edward Warner, published in the first edition of *Makers of Modern Strategy*.[28] Warner very cleverly made the point that the early theorists 'glibly' switched their tenses from present to future and back, and rather than offering a debate on the choice of theories, all emphasized the predominance of air power over other forms of conducting warfare.[29] Inevitably, but not necessarily logically, the first theorist to come into the frame is Douhet. Giulio Douhet was born near Naples in Italy on 30 May 1869. He came from a distinguished military family and was commissioned into the artillery in 1888, and after various junior appointments, joined the General Staff in 1900. A common theme in the biographical literature on Douhet is that his colleagues regarded him as a radical.[30] The friction between him and his superiors was exacerbated by the publication of various articles, some based on lectures and other journalistic pieces published anonymously in the Genoese daily *Caffaro*.[31] Douhet was well connected socially having married, in 1905, the daughter of a senator, and he became close friends with Giovanni Caproni (known more generally as Gianni) who went on to design and fly a range of bombers and light-transport aircraft.[32] Following Italy's aerial excursions in Libya, Douhet was tasked to write a report on the impact of the war on the future employment of air power which he completed in 1912. Douhet was then appointed head of the recently reorganized Aviation

Battalion, but the Italian establishment preferred to rely on dirigibles rather than the powered aircraft that he and Caproni were advocating, causing yet more friction. All this time, through to 1915 when he was finally banned from publishing, he wrote some 156 articles under the pseudonym 'Spectator' for a Turin-based newspaper.[33] Douhet was extremely critical of the Italians' conduct of the war and wrote many memoranda criticizing his superiors. The 'accidental' loss of one of these led to his court martial and a year-long prison sentence. After the end of the First World War, a formal government committee came to the same conclusions as Douhet had voiced; he was exonerated and promoted to major general.[34]

Douhet continued to be prolific in his writing, publishing books, novels and many articles. In 1921 he published, under War Department auspices, *The Command of the Air* for which he remains famous.[35] He also gathered many of his articles and scripts and published those in edited volumes; they have subsequently been collected for publication.[36] The critical thing to note is the volume of material that he produced over a considerable period of time. His views changed, or were moderated by experience. For example, in 1910, Douhet abhorred the prospect of attacking defenceless cities as such acts would be barbaric and 'the conscience of all the civilised world would revolt'; he went further, even advocating an international convention to prohibit air warfare.[37] But as the First World War progressed, Douhet moved through a complete reversal from what Hippler has described as pacifism to indiscriminate strategic bombing.[38] Douhet also hardened his line on the command and control of air forces from his 1912 report in which he 'slyly added' that although aviation units could be assigned at corps level, that would not prevent the 'formation of independent air units'.[39] By the time *Command of the Air* was published, Douhet was advocating an independent air force that would no longer be the Cinderella, and the older sisters would have to recognize her existence.[40] The first edition of *Command of the Air* was published in 1921 and the second in 1927. Over the intervening years Douhet again hardened his line on the use of air attacks on a country's vital centres as being of prime importance with what he called 'auxiliary aviation' set aside for army support of fighter defence as 'useless, superfluous and harmful'.[41]

The literature on Douhet has been comparatively limited, not least because *Command of the Air* was not formally translated into English until 1942. Excerpts were translated and in circulation in the US Air Service as early as 1923 and, according to Meilinger, Douhet's work was being more widely discussed in articles and military publications by the mid-1930s.[42] In the UK, Douhet's first appearance in article form was in the *RAF Quarterly* in 1933.[43] According to Mason, neither Air Marshals Slessor nor Harris had ever heard of Douhet.[44] Alan Stephens, however, has expressed his doubts as to whether Douhet had no influence at all on the formulation of RAF bombing policy.[45] Douhet's legacy is addressed in Bernard Brodie's *Strategy in the Missile Age* ensuring that his thinking continued to stimulate thought, discussion and controversy.[46] In 'Voices from the Central Blue', MacIsaac has suggested that Douhet, like naval strategist Mahan, was important not for producing original thought, but more for drawing together and structuring what was largely already there.[47]

The same collecting instinct can be said about William 'Billy' Mitchell as can be gathered from Alfred F. Hurley's biography *Billy Mitchell: Crusader for Air Power*, with the emphasis being on his collecting ideas 'from an international community of airmen' rather than his own theorizing.[48] Mitchell was, and arguably remains, one of the most controversial figures in air power thinking. He was born in Nice (his parents were there on holiday) in 1879. He was the son of a US senator and his grandfather was a wealthy businessman. Like Douhet, he had plenty of connections and he and his family were not averse to making use of them. Mitchell was a junior officer in the Signal Corps and, on the General Staff, was responsible for assessing the military potential of aviation.[49] Mitchell learnt to fly in 1916 and was subsequently sent to Europe as an observer visiting both the French and English lines and Trenchard's headquarters. According to Mark Clodfelter, Mitchell was impressed by Trenchard's commitment to a 'single, unified air command that would allow him to "hurl a mass of aviation at any one locality needing attack"'.[50] Notwithstanding a number of impassioned confrontations with his seniors, Mitchell performed well in France in command of US Army air combat units and in particular, at the Battle of St Mihiel. He was subsequently promoted to brigadier general and appointed Chief of the Air Service, Army Groups.

The problem for Mitchell in the years after the First World War was that his air-crusading spirit did little to enamour him to his army superiors and thus assistant chief of the Air Service was as high as he would be appointed.[51] But the combination of his distinguished war service, his family connections and his headquarters' location in Washington gave him ample opportunity to expound his views in Congress and in the press.[52] Mitchell, like many air warfare advocates, effectively saw air power as a means of averting another costly attritional land war and was constantly frustrated by his conservative peers and seniors, many of whom clung to outdated land-centric notions of warfare. Mitchell was also clear in his conviction that the new dreadnought-style battleships were highly vulnerable to air attack and thus poor value for the American tax payer. He was able to prove his theories, at least to his own satisfaction, with the sinking of the German ship the *Ostfriesland* off Virginia Capes in 1921. The 'battle of the narratives' between the Air Service and the US Navy was bitter, with Mitchell courting press attention and leaking his own version of events. Despite being sent on inspection tours to Europe and Asia to keep him out of the way, things came to a head in 1925 when the US Navy airship *Shenadoah* crashed killing fourteen crew; this coincided with loss of three seaplanes on a record endurance flight to Hawaii. Mitchell accused his seniors in the army and the navy, in an unauthorized press conference, of 'incompetency, criminal negligence and almost treasonable administration of the national defense'.[53] Mitchell was duly court-martialled and, notwithstanding the validity of some of his arguments, found guilty of the specific charges. He was suspended from active duty for five years on no pay; President Coolidge subsequently altered this to half pay. Mitchell resigned in 1926 to devote himself to writing and speaking on his ideas on air power.

Mitchell's air power advocacy changed over time as he became more bombardment focused and less willing to allow for direct support for troops in contact. He insisted that war from the air could paralyse an enemy nation by repeated attacks on its 'vital centres'. These would include transportation, factories, housing, stock and food supplies.[54] Mitchell was not advocating direct attack on civilians per se, but on the means of production and their will to continue to fight; he would have been content with the almost inevitable collateral damage that would have ensued, but he stopped short of recommending specific targeting of the population. From these simple steps, the logical progression, in the interests of efficiency and economy, was the formation of an independent air force, naturally built around the bomber force. How much of his thinking was original, and how much mirrored Douhet and Trenchard, is not really important. What is vital is the influence he had within the Air Service and thereafter, through the Air Corps, to the USAF. Officers on his staff who became disciples of Mitchell included Hap Arnold (who was initially taught to fly by the Wright brothers and went on to command the US Army Air Forces during the Second World War); Carl 'Tooey' Spaatz (commanded US Strategic Air Forces in Europe and became the first Chief of Staff of the USAF); and Ira C. Eaker (commanded the US Eighth Air Force in the UK). Clodfelter has emphasized that these officers and their colleagues not only went on to high command, but also became theorists in their own right.[55] Another aspect of Mitchell's legacy was his establishment of the Air Corps Tactical School, first at Langley and subsequently at Maxwell Air Force Base in Alabama. This became the centre of gravity for US Air Corps thinking in the interwar years with much of it based on Mitchell's blend of advocacy, passion and the wide knowledge base from which he drew.

Of the three air power 'prophets' that appeared in the Warner chapter in the first edition of *Makers of Modern Strategy*, Alexander de Seversky is the least well known today.[56] MacIsaac has suggested that de Seversky's inclusion in that first volume was more to do with his topicality than his prestige as a prophet.[57] De Seversky was born in Tbilisi in Georgia in 1894, went to a military school at the age of ten and graduated from the Imperial Russian Naval Academy. He became a naval aviator and his career was the stuff of schoolboy comic strips. At the end of a mission to attack German warships, his right leg was blown up and so badly damaged below the knee that it had to be amputated. Not surprisingly, the Russian authorities grounded him when he had recovered sufficiently to return to work, but he secretly substituted himself for a display pilot in front of a group of VIPs. His display was outstanding, and even more so when the identity of the pilot was discovered. He narrowly avoided court martial (a developing theme here) and was allowed to return to flying when Tsar Nicholas II approved of his heroics. De Seversky's reputation continued to grow over the war with many kills to his name and decorations to match. After the war, he was sent to America as part of a naval mission, but when the Bolsheviks took over in Russia, de Seversky remained in the US.[58]

During the interwar years, de Seversky worked as an aircraft engineer and designer, eventually setting up his own company. Unfortunately his business acumen did not match his prowess as a pilot or as an aeronautical engineer with the company not meeting its orders. In 1939, while he was abroad, his company colleagues removed him and changed the name to Republic which then went from strength to strength. De Seversky shared many of Mitchell's views and consciously took some of his lines.[59] He produced many articles, radio interviews and press releases. Because he was a civilian, he expressed controversial theories more openly than his military counterparts. He also wrote two books, of which *Victory through Air Power* was the more significant. The importance of this book was several fold; it was highly topical as he dealt with immediate Second World War issues such as the Battle of Britain. It was also highly accessible, as it was a Book of the Month Club selection, as well as controversial. De Seversky was adamant that Germany could be beaten and an isolationist stance by America was unsustainable. The whole message became even more widely aired when Walt Disney made it into a movie which opened in July 1943. Although the movie took only three months to make, it took the military censors ten months to pass it fit for public entertainment![60]

The movie, as befitting a disciple of Mitchell, shows conventional warships as inherently weak and tanks as mere targets for air power. It also exaggerates the accuracy and impact of heavy bombing.[61] Having alienated the army and the navy, and despite calling for an independent air force, the airmen were not exactly enthralled either. De Seversky maintained a deep and bitter grudge against Hap Arnold, whom he blamed for his being removed from his own firm, and did not hesitate to use every opportunity to attack him in print and in interviews.

De Seversky remains in the 'prophet' category today for a number of reasons. The first is that he neatly fills the gap between the interwar theorists and those of the Cold War and later. Like his predecessors, there is no immediate originality. Rather there was an unremitting faith in air power and relentless energy to preach its benefits. De Seversky regarded the policy and decision-makers as lost causes, but was happy to lecture to USAF junior officers and public alike and reached millions doing so.[62] As Meilinger has pointed out, de Seversky was not perfect as a designer, a businessman or as a 'prophet'; he took his disdain for maritime and land forces altogether too far and never really got to grips with the nuclear debate.[63] But he was able to communicate his ideas to a wide audience in an engaging manner; his analytical skills helped him to shape his reputation as an air power prophet and more generally, as a predictor of events.[64]

When Sir Samuel Hoare (later Viscount Templewood) took over as Secretary of State for Air in 1922 after his first meeting with Trenchard, he described the CAS as being the first 'really great man' he had ever met.[65] He continued his description with the apt words 'Whilst Trenchard spoke, I felt myself in the presence of a major prophet.'[66] The new secretary of state

> listened enthralled to the words of the prophet, and as I afterwards reflected on them, I realized that I might after all have come to the Air Ministry not to wind it up as Bonar Law had suggested, but to help establish it upon an equality with the Admiralty and the War Office, and to create a peace-time Air Force as a united and independent service in no way inferior to the Navy and Army.[67]

Hoare went on to state that his mission 'was to be the prophet's interpreter to a world that did not always understand his dark sayings'.[68] From these few lines, it is possible to distinguish Trenchard from the preceding 'prophets'. As CAS, Trenchard was in charge of his own independent air force and was not just commentating from the sidelines. Furthermore, he had a secretary of state over him which meant that the ministry in which they worked had its own budget for which they were responsible to Parliament. The constant battle to retain independence, and a steady flow of income, should not be underestimated. But it was an easier task than that facing Mitchell and his colleagues in having to arrange the separation from a parent service and establishment a new entity. There were lines of development open to the 'major prophet' and his interpreters. The first of these was to establish and fund the infrastructure for a permanent service including a cadet college, an apprentice school and its own staff college.[69] These were deemed essential tools in forging an 'Air Force spirit'.[70] Sending air force mechanics and officers to be trained in the institutions of the older services would impede this process. Trenchard did not try to hide the fact that these schools and colleges would be expensive to build and it is clear that he thought this investment was worth the sacrifices that would have to be made in terms of aircraft procurement.[71]

The central thesis behind the 'Air Force spirit' was, and arguably still is, essentially that air power, in peace and war, is best commanded and controlled by airmen who have been specifically trained, educated and have acquired the necessary experience in warfare in the third dimension. The big question, requiring the foresight and vision of the prophet, was what the air power was to be used for. During the First World War, Trenchard had been absolutely resolute in ensuring that the RFC gave full support to Haig's armies on the Western Front.[72] But the senior airmen who had fought over those trenches were adamant that the attritional warfare with its huge losses for minimal gains had to be avoided in any future conflict. Furthermore, it would not be necessary to maintain an independent service to provide close support to ground troops or to the navy. Certainly in straitened times of the peace of the interwar years, absorption of the air arm would give considerable savings. A distinct role was needed. Air power offered an alternative by going over the fronts directly to the heartland of the enemy. The theory, as expounded by Liddell Hart and others, was that a 'swift and powerful' blow, inflicted very early on in a conflict, aimed at the 'complex and interdependent fabric' of the modern state would bring the enemy state to a standstill.[73] Liddell Hart's influence as an air power theorist in his own right should not be underestimated. His writings, along with those of J. F. C. Fuller, were a regular staple on the Andover Staff College reading list.[74]

Notwithstanding his earlier scepticism on the efficacy of the Independent Force established with a view to retaliating against the German bombing raids on London, Trenchard was keen to embrace the offensive. Offensive, rather than defensive, action had been the central pillar of the RFC's approach to the air war and it remained deeply ingrained in the RAF in the interwar years and during the strategic air offensive against Germany.[75] Before the advent of radar it was extremely difficult to defend against bombers, especially at night. Going on the offensive meant that the enemy had to expend his efforts and resources in attempting to counter the attacks. Trenchard likened the defensive as playing soccer with eleven goalkeepers. He also emphasized the ratio between the effect on the morale of the enemy as being at least three times more than the actual physical damage. This thinking was consistent with Napoleon's assertion on similar lines. Trenchard, almost inevitably, took things further varying the ratio depending on the audience and the political impact desired. He was also convinced that the British could endure suffering under bombardment more than either the French or the Germans.[76] Trenchard was also adamant that control of the air was a vital prerequisite for any action.

The other theme that Trenchard was able to rely on was the use of air power in domestic and imperial policing. At home, aircraft had been used in 1917 to drop leaflets to aero engine workers urging them to end their strikes.[77] After the war, a major rail strike threatened to disrupt totally the postal system in Britain. Aircraft were used to fly urgent despatches to seventy-six administrative centres thereby ensuring that contact was maintained between the police and central government. In an early example of the use of air power in information operations (or psyops) copies of *The Times* were distributed to administrators in the provinces. This exercise was repeated during the General Strike of 1926. Bombers from 9 and 58 Squadrons delivered 1,377,000 copies of the *British Gazette*.[78] By the summer of 1920, two squadrons of aircraft had been deployed to Ireland. Mail drops were carried out along with regular patrolling duties. The presence of aircraft had something of a deterrent effect on the Irish Republican Army. Frustration over the flexibility of the terrorists was such that there were frequent calls for armed aerial intervention – Churchill had demanded the use of aircraft against Sinn Fein members involved in drills in order 'to scatter and stampede them'.[79] Such requirements were strongly resisted, not least by Trenchard himself.[80] This may have been because he could see that a successful outcome was unlikely and he was unwilling to attract the criticism for his air arm that would inevitably follow. In the event, armed patrols were eventually sanctioned, albeit under strict regulation, and few hours were actually flown.[81]

But it was overseas, in Mesopotamia and the Middle East, where the real financial savings were made. In mid-February 1920, Churchill asked Trenchard if he would be prepared 'to take Mesopotamia on'. The deal would involve the reduction of the standing garrison to 4,000 British and 10,000 Indian troops, but with an air officer as C-in-C and an extra £5 million on the air estimates, down from some £18 million.[82] Much to the chagrin of the army, this was repeated in other theatres where the speed of reaction, psychological impact and flexibility had considerable benefits to the local commanders and officials.[83]

Unlike Mitchell, de Seversky and Douhet, Trenchard and his followers chose to conduct their bureaucratic battles largely behind closed doors in the smoke-filled rooms and corridors of Whitehall and not in the press. Furthermore, once the main policy had been set in Trenchard's memorandum of 1919, it remained extant. In an address to Royal United Services Institute (RUSI) in 1931, the then Squadron Leader J. C. Slessor referred back to it several times, in effect using it as the backbone of his talk on the 'Development of the Royal Air Force'.[84] Historian, Neville Jones has described this paper as the 'clearest and most convincing statement of the doctrine of the strategic offensive as a means of securing Britain from air attack'.[85] Given that Slessor had been in the Air Plans directorate in the Air Ministry from 1928 to 1930, it can be reasonably assumed that this was official policy.[86] It endured through the period of disarmament until the spectre of German rearmament forced the Air Ministry to take note of developments in radar and the advent of the Spitfire and Hurricane.

Inevitably, the thinking behind the strategic bomber offensive has given rise to a vast amount of literature. The fact that Trenchard and his team did their work officially has meant the Air Plans and CAS files are well stocked with valuable material. This has been supplemented by several notable works by contemporary writers such as Slessor, Kingston-McCloughry and Spaight.[87] In addition to the official historians, the AHB staff and the practitioners themselves, key authors include Biddle, Jones, Tress, Robertson and Cooper.[88] The staff at the School of Advanced Air Power Studies has also produced numerous articles in addition to those contained in *The Paths of Heaven* which have been widely cited above.[89]

Post-Second World War theorists

Following the attacks on Hiroshima and Nagasaki, much of the energy on discussing theory immediately turned to nuclear issues and this is reflected in Paret's *Makers of Modern Strategy*. This contains a chapter entitled 'The First Two Generations of Nuclear Strategists' by Lawrence Freedman along with one by Michael Carver entitled 'Conventional Warfare in a Nuclear Age'.[90] This is mirrored in the wider historiography with Freedman's own volumes along with those of Bernard Brodie. Within this context, the tag of air power theorist has devolved on to John Boyd and John Warden. Both were controversial characters in their own right and warrant some attention. They feature in the chapter in *Paths of Heaven* by David S. Fadok entitled 'John Boyd and John Warden: Airpower's Quest for Strategic Paralysis'.[91] At this stage, it is worth pausing briefly to reflect that this excellent volume was specifically produced as a textbook for the USAF School of Advanced Air Power Studies and therefore has to be seen in that light.

According to his biographer, Grant T. Hammond, Boyd's ideas were highly innovative and had an enduring legacy.[92] Boyd was first and foremost a fighter pilot who first plied his trade in Korea. He was also a scholar in his own right and wrote many briefings on jet aerial combat including the official manual on the subject.[93] Boyd was also heavily involved in the design and development of the new breed of fighters in the USAF where high manoeuvrability was considered essential to counter the Soviet threat. Those aircrafts became the F-15 and the F-16. To his supporters, Boyd was absolutely revered. This included the US Marine Corps which had made him an Honorary Marine and their Commandant (General Krulak) wrote a long and emotional tribute to him following his death.[94] To many of his air force seniors he was a '24-karat pain in the ass'.[95] Beyond the fighter development, Boyd was famous, and deservedly remains so, for his formulation of the Boyd Cycle – the OODA loop. The four terms are self-explanatory, but the emphasis must be on the cyclical element of it as this must be repeated, not just taken as a solitary exercise. The feedback loop is important throughout.

Boyd developed the OODA loop from his air-to-air combat experience where the cycle would be a constant process of assessing what his opposition were doing. Inherent in this would be an intuitive understanding of his own fighter's energy state as if this was allowed to bleed away, the enemy would gain advantage. But the simple loop can be applied in a huge variety of situations at all levels of warfare. Each of the components can be broken down, examined and work set in place to improve each of them so that the overall tempo of decision-making is improved. Whether this is done from the F-86 that Boyd flew, an F-35 in the future or at the strategic level using satellite or RPA feed, the basics are the same. In *Modern Strategy*, Colin Gray has stated that 'the OODA loop may appear too humble to merit

categorization as grand theory, but that is what it is'.[96] In the debate over the
use of RPAs and the move towards increasing automation and autonomy,
Boyd's vocabulary has been deployed by international lawyers to help depict
where the person in the decision-making process should be either in the loop
or on it.[97]

Colonel John Warden was (and remains) a controversial character. He
was an F-15 fighter pilot during the Cold War and completed the usual
round of staff appointments.[98] But what makes Warden stand out from his
fellow aircrew, in blunt terms, was that he thought too much and was not
afraid to challenge conventional thinking. As a student at the National War
College, Colonel Warden applied his thinking to air power at the operational
or theatre level of war. In the slightly wider context, it must be remembered
that planning for the Cold War was essentially at the strategic level and
executed at the tactical. The operational level of war was basically considered
redundant.[99] In his War College thesis, Warden challenged this state of
affairs. His commandant, Major General Perry M. Smith enthusiastically
supported Warden and insisted that his work be published as a book under
the title of *The Air Campaign: Planning for Combat*.[100] The book remains
in print with a variety of high-level endorsements and revisions including a
Gulf War Epilogue.

Following a tour in Germany on the F-15 Wing at Bitburg, Warden joined
the Air Staff as head of *Checkmate* which had responsibility for long-range
planning and conceptual thinking.[101] This coincided with Iraq's invasion
of Kuwait and General Schwarkopf's call to the Pentagon for planning
assistance ended up on Warden's desk. He then effectively used his thesis as
the central planning theme for air operations. Although it was amended and
refined many times, Warden's work has been described as the 'conceptual
basis for the air campaign against Iraq'.[102]

It can be argued that in *The Air Campaign*, Warden does not say very
much that is new, but that he repackages, in an easily accessible way, the
thinking of the theorists covered earlier in this chapter including Fuller and
Liddell Hart.[103] But given that many military officers are slightly reluctant
to go back to original texts, especially when planning an immediate war,
some repackaging is a good thing. Warden, first of all, stresses the absolute
importance of air superiority. He is very clear that air power can act as a
supporting arm, but land and maritime may, in turn, act as the supporting
components. He is equally clear, and there is plenty of supporting historical
evidence for this, in that comprehensive joint planning is essential. Many of
Warden's compatriots saw air power as having a nuclear weapons delivery
capability (Strategic Air Command) or as providing conventional support
for land forces. Warden added to this that air power could achieve decisive
results independently. Warden was at pains to point out that technology had
remedied the deficiencies apparent in the interwar years and that multiple
centres of gravity could be attacked in parallel. He further argued that for all
states and organizations with a political presence, leadership targets would

be at the centre of five concentric rings. The next ring would be the means of production, followed by infrastructure, population and at the outside, and with lowest priority, fielded forces.

After *Checkmate*, Warden went, still as a colonel, to command the Air Command and Staff College at Maxwell, where he put many of his theories into the classroom. His ideas had a great deal of influence, albeit substantially amended, on the conduct of the air war on *Desert Storm* and his shake-up of the Air Command and Staff College has had a major impact on USAF Doctrine.[104] Warden retired from Maxwell for a second career in consultancy and remains active on the air power lecturing circuit. He has his detractors who remain willing to challenge him on his theories in public and in print. One of the more significant conceptual challenges is over the practicability of having multiple centres of gravity.[105]

Other writers and thinkers

It has been a recurring theme in this chapter that the key individuals did not necessarily originate the concepts about which they have written. In many cases they repackaged, in accessible form, work that had been carried out by others. In short, the so-called 'prophets' did not receive the final word from some air warfare deity. So where did the material and thinking come from? Whose work did the 'prophets' actually collect and distil? The simple answer to these questions is that there were, and are today, many people writing on air power and warfare in official circles and in private. If one considers the concept of air superiority, the fundamental prerequisite for all military operations, it is clear from James Pugh's PhD thesis that the staff of the RFC and RNAS had thought through the issues of the need for air superiority long before the technology became available to attain it.[106] In the same way staff officers have been behind much of the thought throughout the last century, but were either prohibited from publishing, prevented by their bureaucracies from speaking in public, or in the case of Trenchard just inarticulate. That said, J. M. Spaight was an 'insider' in the Air Ministry, albeit as a senior civil servant in charge of contracts. His writings on air warfare, both while still working and after retirement, indicate that he may well have been part of the wider discussions in the smoke-filled corridors; this will be discussed in more depth in the case study. Proving causal links, and influence, is achievable on air law and may well extend to other avenues.[107] The staff officers working in the Air Corps Tactical School (ACTS) at Langley and Maxwell will have had similar experiences. It is also clear that there was a steady interchange of ideas internationally.

There have also been ex-RAF officers who, having retired from the service, still thought about air warfare and were willing to write about the subject. P. R. C. Groves, for example, was air correspondent for *The Times* in the interwar years.[108] Similarly, Captain Norman Macmillan wrote for *Flight* and compiled many of his articles in a volume entitled *Air Strategy*.[109]

In carrying out research necessary to establish who thought what about air warfare, it is also essential to embrace the semi-official or official journals edited from time to time by the various air services. These include the *RAF Quarterly* in the interwar years; *The Hawk*, the journal of the RAF Staff College; the USAF *Aerospace Power Journal*; the RAF *Air Power Review*; *JRUSI* and so on. It is also worth examining the publications emanating from the various air power or air warfare studies centres and their staff. In addition to the *Air Power Review*, the Director of Defence Studies (RAF) has, in the past, chaired a number of Chief of the Air Staff's Air Power Workshops and published the collected papers.[110] The same applies to conference papers published as edited volumes.[111] Another useful source is doctoral theses, either unpublished or issued as books, often in series such as that produced under the editorship of Seb Cox and published by Frank Cass.

An outline case study

There is a natural tendency to take strategists, or air power prophets, in relative isolation. It is much easier to do so than to place them in their broader context. It is even more difficult to take a loose society of individuals and chart the linkages between them. If the air warfare researcher wishes, say, to analyse the extent to which Trenchard was indeed a prophet it will be essential to decide whether he was a lone voice operating in accordance with his own vision and thinking. Or it may be that, like many brilliant artists over the centuries, he presided over a 'school' – in this case of thought. This is the case study chosen to present in outline. In the first instance it is worth assessing just what Trenchard wrote himself and what he published. Slessor has recorded that Trenchard would call his writing team into his presence and give them their 'riding orders – which even Boom's personal stenographer was unable to reduce to any very consecutive record'.[112] They would produce a first draft and it would come back the next day with alterations in Lady Trenchard's handwriting.[113] It would then take several iterations to reach a final product. At first sight, this does not look to be a promising start for an influential prophet. But it is worth checking what Trenchard actually wrote or published. This search immediately comes up with very limited results beyond a small number of pamphlets and journal articles.[114] So it may be more productive to regard Trenchard as the centre point of a school of thought from which his various staff officers and so forth produced a collective wisdom which was then disseminated through lecture briefings, ASM and so on.

This chapter has already considered the possible influence of Douhet and it is far from clear if he had more than second- or third-hand influence.

Indeed Higham, having devoted an Appendix to the subject of Douhet's influence, has described his responsibility for influencing air power theory in Britain and America as a 'myth'.[115] It is, however, worth following Higham's lead to Frederick William Lanchester as having made a significant contribution to air power theory.[116] Higham has suggested that Lanchester's most significant contribution was *Aircraft in Warfare* which featured an introduction by Sir David Henderson.[117] Higham has further suggested that Trenchard had probably read Lanchester's work through the influence of Henderson and has copied a section from *Aircraft in Warfare*, for direct textual comparison with an order issued by Trenchard in 1916.[118] Higham went on to acknowledge the difficulties of attributing influence to authors who may never have been read or whom people did not know. But he thought that Lanchester's reputation as an engineer, along with his work with the Advisory Committee for Aeronautics made the likelihood of influence rather stronger.[119] This was reinforced with regular contact with other senior figures in the RFC and the RNAS. Lanchester's influence, again through Henderson, was seen with his theory on attacking enemy formations that found its way into the RFC Training Manual. This had been based on a lecture first given in 1914 and was known as the N-Square Law.[120]

It is neither possible nor desirable to attempt to trace a direct lineage of thinking. The reality of influences is more like a network or three-dimensional pattern. But the discussion above on Lanchester does help to build a picture. It also shows how individuals can be 'lost' in history as his works do not feature highly in bibliographies. Nevertheless, their influence was pertinent at the time even if its traces have largely evaporated. Other forms of influence come through in detailed research such as where Tami Davis Biddle has traced the origins of the so-called 'Gorrell plan' which actually took the work of Lord Tiverton 'virtually verbatim' into his own work.[121] In addition to straightforward plagiarism, the researcher must also keep an open mind on the possibility of work being recycled with individuals in the process being unconscious to the linkages.

It is clear from various sources that Trenchard was on good terms with J. M. Spaight who was a civil servant on his staff.[122] It is also evident that Spaight's influence extended far beyond his various roles in Accounts or Contracts. They also went beyond his undoubted influence on international legal issues and included his wide range of air power publications.[123] If one takes genuine thinkers such as Spaight, it is clear that he almost certainly had influence in a range of areas each of which could be analysed in turn. On the input side of the equation, Spaight had enjoyed an extensive legal education in Dublin where he gained a bachelor's degree and a doctorate in law. He would certainly have been influenced by the intellectual environment there and it is significant that this continued with his own writings in *War Rights*. His membership of the UK delegation to the Hague Conference in 1923 will be discussed below. Unfortunately the detailed links proving influence are hard to find with the occasional exception. These include the following explicit mentions. In a CAS submission to a Chiefs of Staff Meeting in 1928, the equivalence of naval and air bombardment was reintroduced with a specific reference to the *British Yearbook of International Law* article written in 1923 by Spaight.[124] A similar, but even more explicit, reference occurred four years later in the context of Air Ministry proposals for amendments to the Hague Rules in which a minute to the CAS confirmed that

> some help has also been given by Mr. Spaight whose book on 'Air Power and War Rights' has been considerably drawn on in framing the paper.[125]

The minute sheet was subsequently initialled with '*I agree* J.M.S.' presumably indicating Spaight's concurrence with the paper. It is clear from (then) Group Captain C. F. A. Portal's signature (as director of Operations and Intelligence) on a number of minutes in the file that the future CAS was fully conversant with the debate.[126]

None of these provide the conclusive proof that would be ideal in a criminal court of law seeking to establish a case beyond reasonable doubt. But depending on the level of proof acceptable, it is possible to build an ever stronger case that there was a school of thought originally influenced by the liberal-modernist era, by intellectual debate in the widest sense which was then heavily influenced by the First World War.[127] Pooling, as Trenchard did, intelligent individuals such Spaight, Portal, Tedder, Slessor and others, it would have been possible for them to have built upon the works of Lanchester, Tiverton, Sykes and others to produce the Trenchardian prophecy.

CHAPTER FIVE

Air warfare in practice

This chapter makes the transition from theory into the wider employment of air power, both in war and in other operations. It does not seek to replace the various excellent doctrine manuals in use with air forces around the world. Indeed the chapter has deliberately diverged from describing the use of air power in conventional doctrinal roles. It could be argued that some doctrine manuals, often in order to portray their truly joint or combined nature, have tended to gloss over differences; others are the products of committee processes designed to reach a text by consensus. This chapter will highlight some of the debating issues and contentious points at the same time providing some useful texts for the student or practitioner of air warfare to explore further.

In terms of the scope of the chapter, it will cover the origins of a particular role in air warfare and then describe how thinking developed. It will attempt to use a wide variety of case studies and texts. But it cannot attempt on its own to be an encyclopaedia on air warfare.

Aerial reconnaissance

Reconnaissance has been chosen as the first role or use of air in warfare because it was the first practical use of balloons and aircraft in a military context. The story of hot air balloons conventionally goes back to the Montgolfier brothers and their experiments in 1782.[1] Their work had its antecedents in early Chinese texts and in the demonstrations by the Brazilian Bartolomeu de Gusmão before the Portuguese Court in 1709.[2] The military potential of balloons for observation purposes and to transport personnel was immediately evident. The quest to see 'over the other side of the hill' is as old as combat whether at sea or on the land.[3] The first operational sortie was made by the French fighting the Austrian army at the Battle of Fleurus on 26 June 1794 and had a decisive impact on the nature of the fighting and outcome.[4] Balloons were then used extensively in the American Civil War and by the British in the Boer War. With the establishment of small, but enthusiastic, units in each of the major armies, it is unsurprising that balloons, supplemented by the new heavier-than-air machines found their way into army manoeuvres and into battle in the First World War.[5]

The advent of these machines was quickly accompanied by appropriate systems to exploit the intelligence gained and to ensure an appropriate level of sustainability.[6] But it also brought a degree of controversy, both at the time and in the subsequent historiography. The classic iteration of the supposed disdain felt by senior officers towards aircraft has been expressed by Sir Frederick Sykes in his autobiography *From Many Angles* in which he claimed that 'opposition by senior officers to air experiments amounted almost to mania'.[7] Accusations of Luddite thinking have entered the wider historiography of the First World War with many authors content just to cite Sykes as their source. Recourse to the original reports on the manoeuvres shows the opposite to be true.[8] Equally inevitably, Haig has frequently been criticized for being against technological progress where in fact, again, the opposite can be argued.[9] Part of the glee with which this issue has been greeted is due to the juxtaposition of modern technology with traditional cavalry and the resulting image of 'colonel blimp' type attitudes. Again the truth is more revealing with the two actually being combined in the *Field Service Regulations* of the time.[10]

By the end of the First World War, the trench lines had been photographed many times over and both senior commanders and their artillery chiefs had accurate and timely information on enemy dispositions. The processes of tasking, taking the photographs and then developing and disseminating the images were honed to near perfection and it would have been unthinkable for serious action to be contemplated without aerial reconnaissance. This applied in particular to the next logical stage in the use of the intelligence in the work with the artillery where spotting was augmented by battery direction.[11] Over the course of the First World War, this interchange of intelligence gathering linking directly to targeting was arguably one of the most vital air power roles. With the need for fighter escort it was a genuine combat intelligence, surveillance, target acquisition and reconnaissance (ISTAR) activity.

For much of the interwar period, reconnaissance was left as an additional consideration rather than being the centre of air power attention. Aircraft designed as fighters or bombers could fulfil the role as an additional duty. It was well into the Second World War that designs needed to be modified specifically for the duty with high performance, in terms of altitude and speed, at a premium for photo-reconnaissance aircraft; examples include variants of the Mosquito and the Spitfire. Other specialist types such as the Focke-Wulf Fw 200 Condor were developed as an airliner design in Germany and used for maritime (especially convoy) reconnaissance. As all belligerents made increasing use of the electromagnetic spectrum for detection, communications and countermeasures so the intelligence gathering and reconnaissance functions expanded towards the end of the war; these became extremely important during the Cold War and beyond. The historiography on the Second World War is notably silent in terms of dedicated materials although the subject occurs regularly in standard works.[12]

As the Cold War developed, visual reconnaissance was increasingly eclipsed by dedicated photo-reconnaissance aircraft operating at low and high altitudes. Some flights were conducted close to borders; others with illegal overflights.[13] As surface-to-air missiles became more sophisticated and capable, intruding aircraft had to fly under or over their engagement envelopes. The shooting down of Gary Powers and his U2 by the Soviets is very much the tip of this iceberg.[14] As Cold War politics waxed and waned, aircraft from countries other than the two superpowers were used extensively to help reduce the chances of an incident sparking a nuclear escalation.[15] Most of the research on these issues is relatively straightforward, but the odd area of interest occurs such as the use of reconnaissance aircraft for atomic cloud sampling.[16] The gathering and dissemination of information can now be done by almost any platform; the material can then be collated, shared and used in the targeting process. Platforms include manned, unoccupied and space-based assets. Many of the latter may be rented rather than owned. Most of the modern concerns over these issues occurs when 'drones' are used by civilian intelligence agencies and are armed.

Naval aviation

At first sight it may seem to be questionable as to whether naval aviation needs a separate section. The basics of control of the air, reconnaissance and attack apply equally to the maritime environment as they do to operations over land. Indeed it could be argued that the flexibility of air power allows and encourages exploitation of the third dimension in a truly joint way. But one of the major issues arising out of the employment of air power is that ownership of assets, along with the associated funding, has always been contentious in many nations. This has been particularly the case in times of defence reviews and associated budget cuts.[17] This has been compounded by the tendency for the historiography to concentrate on air forces. But the problems of operating aircraft at sea, and the operational and strategic flexibility that maritime air gives, combine to generate further debate. Naval aviation can be broadly defined to embrace all air operations carried out by, or in support of, naval units.[18] Or it can be more narrowly construed around just those operations carried out by naval units at sea. The actual definition chosen will often depend on the nature of the research question or, unfortunately, the political standpoint of the author. From an air power perspective, it is arguably better to choose the broadest definition and avoid parochialism.

The origins of naval aviation go back to the earliest days of flight when it became clear that a higher perspective than that allowed from the top of a ship's mast would allow the 'eyes' of the fleet to extend beyond the horizon. Hand in hand with the reconnaissance potential a number of early thinkers on the subject of aviation noted the possibility of aerial attack.[19] As Hallion has pointed out, those nations with a strong maritime tradition, namely America, France and Britain, were at the forefront of thinking on the subject of air power and on practical developments.[20] Particularly over the period that Churchill was First Lord, British naval aviation was deployed in the widest sense with raids on Zeppelin sheds in Cologne and Dusseldorf as early as September 1914.[21] This was duly extended into naval strategic bombing of targets in Germany.[22] As the war progressed, the RFC became more dominant in the formation of air policy, and the competition for resources intensified eventually resulting in the formation of the RAF on 1 April 1918.[23]

Following the end of the war, the resource situation became critical in many countries. In the UK in particular, this led to a fierce rivalry with the army and RN seeking disbandment of the new service and the reabsorption of its budget (and assets) into the older arms. This was equally fiercely resisted by the airmen.[24] The bitterness of the battles between services has traditionally been exacerbated by the differences within the navies themselves as to the efficacy of air power in warfare.[25] This remains the case to this day and although the debate does not always surface in the press, the issues surrounding the introduction of aircraft carriers are often at the forefront. There are often three distinct lobbying groups: those in favour of carriers; those who would prefer a large fleet of conventional warships; and the submariners. Where the controversies do emerge into the open is when they become higher-level debates over land-based air power versus carriers. These become almost immediately enmeshed in strategic defence policy discussions over how a nation should project power.[26]

Carrier aviation combines this debate on the 'way of war' at the strategic level with valuable case studies which embrace the tactical and operational levels of warfare. The need for a well-thought-out strategic plan, coupled with the long-term procurement planning of bringing carriers into service and properly equipping them, makes British involvement in Norway in 1940 worthy of study.[27] British action in the Mediterranean, including the Fleet Air Arm success at Taranto, remains popular in the literature.[28] More broadly, the Japanese attack on Pearl Harbor has a huge literature with much debate at all levels of warfare.[29] More recently, the Falklands campaign brought UK maritime air power back under the spotlight as have operations in the Adriatic and the Gulf.

The use of air power in anti-submarine warfare has traditionally been a vexed subject whether during the Falklands or in the Second World War.

Submarines can be tracked, and if necessary attacked, in a number of ways varying from autonomous depth charges which respond to particular engine acoustic signatures, through the use of hunter-killer submarines or surface vessels, to maritime patrol aircraft. The latter in 'closing the air gap' were vital in the allied battle against the German U-boat threat and, according to Buckley, their importance was underestimated both at the time and subsequently.[30] Aircraft in the anti-submarine role were crucial over the Cold War where the reinforcement of Europe depended on the Atlantic shipping lanes remaining open and for the protection of nuclear missile boats.[31]

Control of the air

From the earliest thinking on the potential of the use of aircraft in warfare, the need to prevent the enemy from gaining the advantage sought by friendly forces has made air combat – or 'grappling in the central blue' – inevitable.[32] On the face of it, this should not be a contentious subject as virtually everyone involved in combat or preparations for war would prefer not to be under aerial observation or attack. Airmen take the need for control of the air as a *sine qua non* whether in terms of defending the homeland, tactically over the battlefield or over the ocean. Part of the issue becomes more complex when one notes that there are gradations within the term 'control'. Obviously 'air supremacy' would be ideal. But in actual fact this in itself is not necessarily obvious in that this level of control may come at a disproportionate cost and risk could be taken at a lower level such as 'superiority' or even 'parity'. What may seem to be an acceptable level of risk for senior commanders juggling precious resources and judging priorities, may seem less palatable to those having to keep their heads down under enemy air attack. Inevitably this is compounded when defending fighters are out of eyeshot to those on the ground. This was evident during the First World War and acknowledged by Trenchard.[33] It was more of a factor during the evacuation of the British army from Dunkirk where the RAF was caustically referred to as the 'Royal Absent Force'.[34] The reality of the situation was that Fighter Command was flying extended patrols over northern France. As the author of the AHB Narrative has pointed out, the RAF was faced with the conflicting demands of meeting the enemy in strength and continuously. This was achieved in part by 11 Group flying 'big wings' over Dunkirk at key times when the RN was taking troops aboard their vessels at the mole.[35] The fighters were thus able to achieve of air superiority limited in time and space and a modicum of air parity for the remainder.

If one takes the short step chronologically, the Battle of Britain remains one of the most written about examples of control of the air in the whole history of air warfare.[36] In addition to the AHB Narratives (and the published versions of these works) and the standard histories, there are works covering experiences of the pilots, the Blitz and the biographies of the commanders.[37] The latter include a number of works analysing the removal from post or retirement of Dowding.[38] The battle has been subject to full-length movie treatment and a plethora of television series.[39] Works examining wider perspectives include the volume edited by Addison and Crang; an examination of the propaganda has also been produced by Garry Campion.[40]

Despite the extensive literature on the Battle of Britain, control of the air remained a vital aspect of all of the Second World War including the strategic preparation of the battlespace for *Overlord* with the heavy bombing of the Reich to grind down the German war industry and economy. This became so important to the Germans that they were forced to defend against the efforts of the allies and in so doing their fighter force was reduced to the point that the eventual invasion had air supremacy.[41] Again there is a substantial literature to this ranging through the Official Histories, the AHB Narratives and then into the wider secondary material.[42] Subsequent conflicts including Korea, Vietnam, the Falklands and the Gulf wars have emphasized the importance of control of the air.[43] In some, the lessons from these fights have resulted in significant changes in training including the introduction of Top Gun, Exercise Red Flag and the NATO Tactical Leadership Programme. The Arab–Israeli wars have also had their lessons on control of the air; these have to be taken in their own context.[44] In many instances, countries, in the absence of a clear threat, have tended to take control of the air for granted. But events like 9/11 have concentrated minds as to how to cope with asymmetric threats to the homeland. This is also evident during major events such as the Olympic Games or world summits where the threat has varied from suicide missions to drone attacks.[45]

Air–land support

Following directly from the previous section, most air power advocates and practitioners would affirm that the greatest support that air can give to their army (or marine, etc.) colleagues is to ensure control of the air, thereby preventing enemy observation or attack. But this is either taken for granted or, when that is not possible, becomes the source of much discontent. Beyond control of the air, support for land operations can take numerous forms and involve as many command and control issues. The matrix of air–land options is complicated by the differing perceptions of air warfare as seen by airmen and by soldiers. As Cox has pointed out, the soldier often views air power as being organic and on call whenever and wherever desired.[46] The problem with this viewpoint is that air power assets are far too valuable to have them sitting on readiness 'just in case'. Even more wasteful would be to have them airborne on standing patrols. This has been the case since the very earliest use of air power over the trenches of the First World War. The majority of air warfare practitioners, commanders and thinkers would prefer to see air power used where it would be most beneficial for the furtherance of the joint commander's overall mission objectives. In some cases, where air power could be used for strategic effect, the employment could be at levels above even the joint commander.

In practice, air power can be used in direct support of ground troops in contact. This can be as an aid to manoeuvre utilizing either helicopters or fixed-wing transport aircraft. The same platforms may also be used for resupply, or for aeromedical evacuation.[47] These aircrafts can be tasked at various levels and are seldom allotted to a single unit other than with special forces where dedicated, often much modified, airframes are reserved. The nature of modern warfare is such that the majority of forces train regularly with air mobility aircraft and that has certainly been the case in recent counter-insurgency operations.[48] But some nations retain specifically trained air mobile or parachute trained forces. These have certainly been part of the history of air mobility with many examples coming during the Second World War involving glider operations and parachute landings.[49] But the classic utilization of air power in direct support is with close air support. This is where combat air, either fixed wing or helicopters, is used against enemy forces that are in close proximity to friendly forces. When properly applied, close air support can have a direct and immediate effect on the tactical situation in the land battle. It has to be planned and coordinated, with good communications being of the essence. With forces in close proximity, all have to minimize the risk of friendly fire incidents. Good close air support can have a pronounced physical effect on the enemy, and can make a huge psychological impact on both hostile and friendly forces. Close air support can be used in conjunction with organic ground fire, with artillery and, if necessary, as replacements in offensive action. It can also be used to break up counter-attacks and breakthroughs.

Close air support grew up from the early days in the First World War where aircraft did little more than make a nuisance of themselves over enemy trench lines. But even these light attacks demonstrated the psychological impact of air power on ground troops. By 1918, and the last hundred days of the war, aircraft had become a serious part of commanders' plans for offensives.[50] But as Cox, along with many other writers, practitioners and air warfare thinkers, has insisted, this planning process has to involve the utilization of air power from inception and at all levels; air cannot be bolted on as an afterthought.[51] Although air power was effective during the Battle of Amiens, it is clear that the planning process was far from ideal. Close air support was arguably a key factor in the air policing actions of the interwar years, often with the RAF providing the air and the ground elements of the forces deployed.[52]

Although many soldiers, and some of their commanders, may consider close air support to be the best form of air–land support, the planning process should involve a detailed analysis of how else the joint commander's air component could best be deployed to achieve campaign aims. This could involve attacking the enemy's reserves, logistics, resupply routes and concentrations of armour and artillery. These are classic air interdiction targets and again they could have a huge impact on the course of the conflict. They may be out of sight (and sound) of friendly ground forces, but the impact may be greater than close air support. Attacks on lines of communication can be carried out on a small scale to influence the course of a short battle or offensive. But it can also be utilized over a complete campaign such as the Transportation Plan prior to and during the Normandy landings. This involved the progressive and systematic destruction of railways, marshalling yards, canals and roads in order to prevent a rapid German reinforcement of the area behind the beachheads.[53] This was later extended to the whole of Germany, greatly hindering industry and movement.[54] By extension, actually attacking industrial targets to prevent the manufacture of armaments and munitions could have a much greater impact on the war or campaign than close air support, but is obviously a much longer-term option. Interwar thinking in the United States emphasized attacking key elements of the enemy industrial system.[55] This required a level of accuracy that was difficult to achieve over Europe, especially in winter.[56] It is, however, a small step from attacks on industrial targets, to targeting the work force and their homes and morale with all of the much wider implications of a strategic air offensive.[57] For the use of such offensives, there are clearly moral and ethical issues and their planning goes beyond the remit of a simple joint commander. During the Second World War, this was the realm of the Combined Chiefs of Staff with the US president and the British prime minister at the helm.[58] The Luftwaffe has often been closely associated with blitzkrieg, but as Buckley has argued, less than 15 per cent of its aircraft were assigned to working with the armoured elements of the army.[59] Beyond this, the Luftwaffe was essentially a multipurpose force with missions matching those discussed above.

As with maritime air power, some of the greatest challenges in the air–land debate have come over budgetary issues. This has occurred in particular where there have been severe cuts such as in the interwar years. In such circumstances air forces have tended to preserve those assets, and crucially, roles which stand the greatest chance of guaranteeing survival and independence. In the case of the RAF, imperial policing and strategic bombing offered these opportunities in contrast with working closely with ground forces. The army was determined that former RFC assets should be folded back into the parent organization while the RAF was even more determined to retain its assets and its independence. As the Second World War loomed over the armed forces of many nations, the British forces started to align their war aims, but arguably too late to have a real effect when they were deployed to France in 1940.[60] Notwithstanding the failure in France, common cause, along with willing, able and broad-minded commanders, in the Western Desert ensured that air–land cooperation would reach a new high in terms of performance.[61] Part of this stemmed from coordinated central planning aided by co-located headquarters. The latter has always been part of the theory behind good air–land support, but all too often the coordination has had to rely on liaison officers.

Strategic air power

Strategic air power, and bombing in particular, has been controversial since its inception during the First World War. It continues to generate debate. Part of the heat in the issue has been the tendency for air forces to rely on the strategic role to justify independence and to secure resources. Emotions have been raised by the ethical issues as well as its effectiveness. Over the course of air power's existence, 'strategic' has had a number of meanings. In some cases strategic is lumped with bombing and again this has a range of interpretations. At its simplest, strategic air power is the use of the air to influence the course of the conflict at the strategic level of war. For this to work effectively it needs to be combined in a logical and coherent plan with the other strategic levers of power such as economics, industry, diplomacy and so on. In the early days of strategic air power, the term was used to denote the use of heavy bombers in operations beyond the immediate battlefield. More precisely, the targets would be in the enemy homeland and would be part of the war-making capability; this would include communications, industry, energy production (such as oil or coal mines) and communications.[62] By the time the theories had had the opportunity for testing, and for post-war analysis, the term was effectively coincident with the size of the aircraft and its long range.[63] During the Cold War, and thereafter, the term 'strategic' has been used to denote a nuclear capability. In time, this became synonymous in America with Strategic Air Command.[64]

Strategic air power is not limited to bombing. Arguably any aircraft could have a genuine effect at the strategic level and this is particularly the case with transport aircraft. Again there has been some confusion where the range and payload of the aircraft have led to it being accorded strategic status. There have, however, been many instances of these aircraft having a disproportionate effect at the political level whether by delivering food aid or specialist equipment, such as the UK team which sent a Scorpio unmanned midget submarine to the rescue of a Russian vessel stranded on the sea floor.[65] Both in terms of reconnaissance and targeted killings, remotely piloted air systems can also have strategic effect; they certainly have the range and endurance, but not necessarily the payload. In many ways, this is indicative of the progress in air power technology as the old algorithms seeking to establish the number of Lancaster sorties needed to destroy a target have been replaced by the number of targets that could be prosecuted during a single sortie (whether manned or not).

Generic issues

Part of the problem with the use of air power in practice has been to measure its effectiveness whether in terms of cost effectiveness or simply at the operational level. As has been discussed this has followed the strategic bombing debate since its inception. It has also been relevant in both the air–land arena and at sea. Part of this has been when opponents to air power have sought to replace it with alternatives. Ironically one of the interwar successes for air power in colonial policing was when it was used the other way around, in substitution for land forces. Operational research has been utilized on a number of occasions to try and measure effectiveness, including in Normandy.[66] In terms of effectiveness of the strategic air offensive against Germany it is worthwhile for even the most casual student of air warfare to consult wider works dealing with diplomacy, morale and internal security and, of course, the economy. Adam Tooze's analysis in *Wages of Destruction* is excellent on the latter.[67]

Another recurrent problem has been the issue over ownership. From the point of view of air forces, the issues have revolved around independence from parent services. Part of this has been the fervent belief that air power is best delivered by airmen (and women) who have a detailed understanding in its employment; they consider that it would be inappropriate to have such a potent arm under the control of amateurs. But at least in equal part is the realistic concern that if air forces were part of armies or navies, the allocation of financial resources would be squeezed in times of austerity. Air-minded folk would also be concerned that operational air power would be frittered away in 'penny packets' if not retained under firm air command and control. Against this, there is a natural tendency for soldiers in particular to want organic assets under their direct command rather than having to rely on what may be a protracted allocation system. The solution to this latter problem is to have a flexible system such as that used in the Western Desert.

How a nation decides on its priorities within air power and more broadly across defence will depend on a number of key factors. In the first instance expenditure will depend on the existence, or otherwise, of an existential threat. This will govern how the threat can best be countered. Assuming that such a threat does not exist, expenditure becomes more of a policy issue based on what can be afforded. This may be expressed as a percentage of gross domestic product or some measure of the nation's wealth. It may also be predicated on commitments to multinational treaty organizations. Within a total budget, a government will need to decide on the balance of expenditure between services, what balance of manpower and equipment needs to be achieved and how much the relationship between defence industry and the armed forces needs to be serviced. Beyond the existence of a major threat, a number of factors then come into play; these will vary over time.[68] These include a nation's traditions and its long-term approach to warfare. One country may have a long maritime tradition; another may favour large standing armies. Status and prestige also play a role in the decision-making process and this includes the possession of nuclear weapons which may well skew the defence profile. A decision around naval air power and the use of aircraft carriers, for example, may well be predicated on these considerations rather than just the merits of the systems likely to be embarked.

One of the realities of studying air warfare, whether as an academic, a practitioner or an enthusiast is that, in practice, the subject covers a vast range from the technical detail through the roles to the strategic level. It remains an inescapable fact that decisions to develop, purchase and deploy air power in furtherance of national objectives can only be made in the wider context. With air power in particular, it could be argued that the transition from tactical to strategic is more condensed than with other forms of warfare. This is apparent in considering issues around routine command and control of air power as it is in the political and ethical dimensions. These issues will be discussed in the following chapters.

CHAPTER SIX

Leadership and command of air warfare

There are a considerable number of challenges for someone seeking to research the leadership and command of air warfare. This chapter will seek to identify some of these challenges and suggest ways of making sense of this huge, and fascinating, subject area. It will then identify some of the elements of leadership literature before going on to consider issues around the command of air warfare at the military and political levels.

The American historian-turned-leadership-writer James MacGregor Burns wrote, 'Leadership is one of the most observed and least understood phenomena on earth'.[1] At face value, this seems to be a very reasonable thing to say and is often seen at the top of presentations on leadership. But there are some serious underlying issues. The first of these is that there are literally thousands of equally apt sayings, phrases and quotations that could have been used. Why has that particular one been chosen? It may have been habit, or at random; it may equally mean that it is a fundamental element in the analysis that is to follow. The first aspect of the sentence worthy of consideration is what definition of leadership is being used and why. If there are many quotations that could have been used, there are even more definitions of leadership.[2] The second part of the quotation states that leadership is that it is much observed. This is partly because everyone has experienced good and, especially, bad leadership and has plenty of views on the results. When it comes to becoming a leader oneself, it is very difficult to comprehend what is involved and to rationalize the phenomena.

For air warfare in particular, the difficulties are compounded by questions over who is leading whom to do what. Put simply, is leadership in the air the same as on the ground and does it apply across all levels of command? Obviously the context of the research will shed some light on the differences, but it has to be acknowledged that terminology and definitions vary depending on service culture and ethos both within nations and internationally. Equally some terms are used rather carelessly serving to muddle the analysis.

The third area that has to be considered is the relationship between leadership and command, and in turn, with management. Disgruntled 'followers' are apt to comment that just because so-and-so's curriculum vitae states that they have commanded at every level does not mean that they have exercised good leadership at any of them. Depending on context, management skills may well be at the forefront of the competencies needed to complete a task, but most military cultures, and arguably those involved in air warfare in particular, tend to denigrate management practices. This is most noticeable where senior 'warfighters' have to make the transition to head office, moving from the comfort zone of the cosy tactical level of war into a complex and ambiguous environment for which many do not feel adequately prepared. At the higher levels, the senior leaders (or commanders or managers) will have to exercise their skills across a number of 'silos' beyond the one in which they grew up.[3] These factors come about in the real world, but are also evident in the literature, ranging from autobiographical accounts through to descriptions of crisis management. A sound understanding and acceptance of the key definitions would help the researcher to analyse what is being said and then allow them to assess the difference between the accounts at hand and the simple definitions.

Rather than attempt to construct new definitions of leadership, management and command, this chapter will use those in use in the Defence Leadership and Management Centre (DLMC as it was from 2004 to 2008) in the UK Defence Academy.[4]

Leadership

'Leadership is visionary; it is the projection of personality and character to inspire people to achieve the desired outcome.' There is no prescription for leadership and no prescribed style of leader. Leadership is a combination of example, persuasion and compulsion dependent on the situation. It should aim to transform and be underpinned by individual skills and an enabling ethos/culture. The successful leader is an individual who understands him/herself, the organisation, the environment in which they operate and the people that they are privileged to lead. [Emphasis in original]

Management

Management is a facet of Command. It is about the allocation and control of resources (human, material and financial) to achieve objectives. Management requires the capability to deploy a range of techniques and skills to enhance and facilitate the planning, organisation and execution of the business of defence. A successful Manager combines these skills with those of leadership. A Manager with the style of management most suited to the circumstances is the most successful. (A Leader/Manager)

Command

Command is a position of authority and responsibility to which military men and women are legally appointed. Leadership and management are the key components to the successful exercise of Command. Successful management is readily measured against objective criteria but commanders are not leaders until their position has been ratified in the hearts and minds of those they command.

These definitions can be simplified further. Leadership is primarily about people, and in particular, getting ordinary people to do extraordinary things. Management is about material, process and numbers. Command is harder to caricature; at its simplest, it represents a legally enforceable chain (of command). Or it is a structure in which superior organizations relay instructions to subordinate bodies and, ultimately, to individuals. But in the UK, for example, the army uses command in the additional way of 'I commanded him when he was in ...' as opposed to a more casual 'he worked for me ...'.

What is arguably more important is the relationship between each of these entities. This will inevitably depend on context. In a complex emergency the prime functions will be command and leadership with management playing little part. The reverse would be true in setting a policy for travel expenses. Without straying too far into the world of social science models, it would be possible to portray this relationship as a Venn diagram with an overarching context. Howieson and Kahn have termed this the Officers' Trinity.[5]

If one examines the wide literature on leadership, considerable focus is given to 'strategic leadership'. This is mirrored in turn in the world of executive education. In broad terms, the literature uses strategic, executive and senior interchangeably. One of the key differences at this level is that these senior leaders are also responsible for the leadership of the organization as a whole – not just for their behaviour as leaders in direct relationships.[6] Depending on the personalities, egos and interdependencies, there is a risk that the organization could come under the sway of an individual. But far more regularly, the pinnacle of the organization will be run by a top team. Andrew and Nada Kakabadse have pointed out that the senior management team is a group of individuals who are specifically brought together for the purpose of planning and clarifying direction of the whole organization – unlike a middle management team which is primarily task orientated.[7] This is as relevant in the military environment as it is in the board room of a major company.[8]

In complex military structures, as with multinational conglomerates, it is highly unlikely that the board, or top team, will be able to act in isolation. Rather, they will have to work alongside other elements of the organization – or in a hierarchical relationship. David V. Day and Robert G. Lord have emphasized that the vast majority of practical organizations are open and must therefore interact with their environment.[9] The interfaces between these elements can be critical to the success, or otherwise, of the whole enterprise. It is the role of the senior leaders to facilitate these interfaces.[10] The interfaces may work seamlessly; alternatively they can be subject to the same frustrations and difficulties as interpersonal relationships. Causes of friction can emerge from any of the areas where senior leaders hold specific jurisdiction – especially formulation of strategy and the apportionment of resources.[11] With senior leadership in a military context, at least in democracies, there is bound to be political oversight and this interface needs especially careful management. Even a cursory examination of the memoirs and the accounts of the Chiefs of Staff meetings in the Second World War would show just how important this factor was for the chiefs in their dealings with Churchill. Alanbrooke's diaries from his time as Chief of the Imperial General Staff (CIGS) are eloquent on the subject, but it is clear that Portal as CAS was altogether more subtle and successful in getting his own way.[12]

At the strategic level, the leadership team, including the relevant politicians, is ultimately responsible (to Parliament in the UK) for the formulation and execution of strategy; the organization has to be fit for purpose; and the ethos of the organization needs to be sufficiently well understood and internalized for there to be a degree of continuity without fluctuations depending on who is senior at any one time.[13]

A further approach to the problems of senior leadership is to look at the routine nature of what the individuals and teams are likely to encounter. The vast majority of these will be complex, ambiguous and not amenable to linear solutions. They are what have been described as 'wicked problems' set against 'tame' ones.[14] The latter can be dealt with using simple or linear solutions, the former cannot. Individuals who seek to clear their in-trays (or boxes) by the end of every day are unlikely to be comfortable with 'wicked' problems. Other people thrive on the uncertainty, complexity and lack of closure.

There are potential problems for air forces in reconciling the requirements for obedience to rules and orders with the need for flexibility (the so-called key to air power). There is a similar gap between the need for rapid decision-making in the OODA loop process discussed earlier and the lack of closure inherent in the complex head-office environment. The vast majority of air forces promote their pilots, often from a particular background, to the highest positions based on their expertise in those roles usually in the hope that they will acquire, by some kind of osmosis, the competence to run the organization when they reach the top team.[15] There are also issues around the differences between training and education in the services, especially in preparing officers for senior appointments. For example, many advanced staff colleges place a huge emphasis on campaign planning, which, in the way that it is carried out is essentially a linear process. In seeking a clearly defined 'military end state' for campaigns, such as the ones in Libya, Kosovo or Afghanistan, the result is bound to be divorced from the more strategic realities of the situation.[16] This was reflected in the UK Chief of Defence Staff annual Christmas address to RUSI in 2009:

> We seem to have lost an institutionalised capacity for, and culture of, strategic thought. I'm not saying that we don't have people who can think strategically, or that we haven't evolved a proper strategic basis for our actions. But we've seized on ability where we've found it, and as a result our formulation of strategy has been much harder than should have been the case. We've been hunter/gatherers of strategic talent, rather than nurturers and husbandmen.[17]

If defence ministries more generally have problems with educating, selecting and employing strategic thinkers, they also have a perennial debate over whether peace, war and the complete spectrum in between requires different leaders and different styles of leadership. Account also needs to be taken of the impact of the experience of combat on leaders. There is still a culture of denial when it comes to combat stress. In carrying out almost any high-level research into personalities or success in campaigns, some account has to be taken of all of these factors.

Literature on leadership

The literature on leadership is vast and increasing daily. Some material is good and represents a useful background. There are some key texts, depending on what exactly the researcher is seeking. But there is also an awful lot of material not worthy of consideration. The literature falls into five broad categories. The first of these can be described as 'airport terminal bookstore' material with either little academic rigour or any practical value. These works often include the name of a major warrior or military thinker, such as Sun Tzu or Clausewitz, and attempt to apply their work to the boardroom. The experiences of senior businessmen who have been successful in their field fall into a similar category. The next category can be loosely described as the 'self-help school' in which the reader is given a number of steps towards enhancing his or her leadership.

The third area sees a marked increase in academic rigour with the behavioural or occupational psychology disciplines, often situated in business schools and the associated literature. Many of these works have already been cited and they can be a very useful source of models for the analysis of leadership. There are, however, a number of challenges in using this body of work. The first is to recall that they are just models and therefore come with limitations and exceptions. The user has to be able to decide critically which model to use and why others have been excluded. Then the researcher has to be able to explain how suitable the methodology is to his chosen area. For example, many models are based on certain industries and use lower or middle managerial levels because the original study team were able to get representative samples sizes;

this may not be suitable for more strategic-level analysis. Finally, the researcher has to be able to justify any read across from the model and its original study to the work in hand. None of these challenges are insurmountable, but they do require genuine research skills.

The fourth area worthy of note is the broad field of historical research. Traditionally, this area covered the 'great man' school of history (and they were usually by and about men). As has been discussed earlier, this school covered great battles, heroic deeds and often hagiographic accounts of the main participants. This has evolved considerably, although a lot is still biographical. More work has been done on situating the leaders in the wider context. Some have also mirrored developments in the business and consulting world by using a 360-degree approach and recognizing the views of the subordinates. Such works can offer value to the researcher providing they are used in a rigorous and critical manner. They must not be cherry-picked for loose evidence.

The final category on literature focuses on the work on leadership produced by various militaries around the world, both historically and today. The older works may not use the same terminology, but the essentials remain the same. For example, the relationship between leadership and morale was first expounded in an official RAF document with the issue of *Air Publication 1300, Royal Air Force War Manual* which included a short chapter entitled 'Command Leadership and Morale'.[18] Leadership was defined as 'the power to influence and inspire men'.[19] The section on morale built on this explaining that high morale would allow greater heights to be achieved than was possible through the exercise of professional skill alone.[20] The early RAF Staff College courses at Andover tended to use the word 'morale' for the broader subject area on leadership. The covering keynote lectures were delivered by the commandant himself.[21] The students on these early courses wrote essays on the subject of morale and the best of these were published for general education and especially for those who hoped to attend Staff College themselves. These essays include one by Squadron Leader C. F. A. Portal in which he examined the morale in the forces of Cromwell, Nelson and Garibaldi.[22] More recently, as leadership centres have proliferated around the world, their staffs have produced reading lists, organized conferences and produced useful texts.[23]

Command and control of air power

It seems to have become traditional, certainly in the UK, to start sections of text on the command and control of air power with a quotation from Tedder.[24] The third edition of AP 3000 uses the following quote:

> Air warfare cannot be separated into little packets: it knows no boundaries on land or sea other than those imposed by the radius of action of the aircraft; it is a unity and demands unity of command.[25]

It is worthy of note that this quotation was taken from his Lees Knowles Lectures at the University of Cambridge in 1947 under the broad heading of *Air Power and War*; he was still serving as CAS at the time.[26] As with all such quotations, and especially those that are not referenced, it is always worth trying to track down the original source in order to check the wider context in which the statement was made. In this case Tedder was drawing on his experience as deputy commander in SHAEF and from his time in the desert with Montgomery. The quotation is from the chapter entitled 'The Exercise of Air Power'; on the preceding pages he discusses the flexibility of air power; its ability to attack across a 'target system' (shades of Warden here); the need to use air power properly; and the importance of 'centralised control'.[27]

In his lecture, Tedder usefully compared unity of command in the Middle East with that in the UK. He pointed out that all his aircraft including day and night fighters, fighter bombers, day and night bombers, reconnaissance assets (over land and sea) and torpedo bombers 'all came under one centralised command'.[28] In contrast, it was 'inevitable that the Government itself should take a close interest in the bomber operations'.[29] He goes on to list the contributors to the strategic arena as including the Ministry of Economic Warfare, Ministry of Home Security, British and US intelligence committees and the Chiefs of Staff themselves.[30] Add to this mix the Joint Chiefs of Staff including Churchill and the US president, and the importance of coping with complexity and working the interfaces discussed above is clearly evident. The discussions over bomber priorities and so on, and the ambiguity of some directives, show that command, for real, may be unified in name, but not necessarily in practice.[31] The other lesson to emerge is that high-level command is more difficult than merely issuing a set of orders even though the commander has the authority to do so.

Whether air power is a unique case, or the comments on command and control apply equally to all environments is a matter for discussion in joint doctrine centres. The important, and arguably overriding point, is that effective air command and control are essential. Inherent in this is the need to retain command at the highest possible level in order to ensure the unity of effort detailed by Tedder above.[32] But this tenet goes well beyond Tedder's Lees Knowles Lectures; it is engraved on the soul of all senior airmen. It could be argued that this is basically common sense, but it is also true that adherence to this principle prevents air assets being distributed to lower-level army formations where ownership is an issue of contention. Avoiding partition into 'penny packets' is key to allowing air assets to operate over the whole battlespace and not just the sector of a given division or brigade.

The issues around command and control give rise to another potential area of dispute and of confusion for those involved in research into air warfare. In the discussion on doctrine earlier in this book, we looked at Corbett and the need for senior commanders and politicians to be able to share a common vocabulary. To some extent this vocabulary has become specialized, often to the point of seeming tortuous. Words that have an everyday meaning in English take on more specific definitions, seem more nuanced or just serve to confuse. For example, the *Concise Oxford Dictionary* defines 'culminate' as being able to reach a 'highest or final point'.[33] Yet Clausewitz uses the phrase 'culminating point' to describe the situation where the attackers' force has been so diminished that neither the defenders nor the attackers can achieve a decisive victory; they essentially grind to a halt.[34] This may or may not be the final point and it may be the best that could be achieved, but the Clausewitzian interpretation is altogether more complicated than the simple dictionary definition. Some definitions or concepts are worth further examination.

Mission command is a much vaunted subject in the doctrine manuals and is widely taught in staff colleges. In general terms, mission command is taken as being an extension of *Auftragstaktik* which is opposite to *Befehlstaktik*; the latter loosely translates to 'detailed order tactics'.[35] In contrast, *Auftragstaktik* is based on task instructions, essentially what effect is to be achieved and why, but without the detailed step-by-step instructions. It depends on an 'unbroken chain of trust and mutual respect running from the controlling operational commander to the tank or section commander'.[36] In order to maintain this trust, and achieve the overall effect desired, the subordinate must understand what his commander's *intent* is and how that sits within the wider context at all levels of warfare (strategic, operational and tactical); the subordinate must also understand his or her own mission.[37] The wider context is important because it explains why the effect is important or necessary. The commander should make available sufficient resources to permit the mission to be carried out.[38] The commander should exercise the minimum of control over the subordinates 'consistent with their experience and ability, while retaining responsibility for their actions'.[39] It is then up to the subordinate to get the job done in their own way; that is, without detailed instructions.

With the nature of communications in Nelson's time, this sort of command system was inevitable. But in modern warfare, with real-time information, video footage and excellent communications it is tempting for senior commanders and decision-makers to indulge in meddling in tactical detail – or what is known colloquially as exercising the 'long screwdriver'.

From the UK perspective, mission command has historically featured prominently in the air doctrine manuals, not least because they are conceptually derived from *British Defence Doctrine*.[40] But there must be questions over how unity of command at the highest level is compatible with mission command. In particular, with modern air operations, conducted in a coalition, the detailed Air Tasking Order (ATO) is a vast document consisting of many serials and lines of activity. These have had to be coordinated with the activities of other components (land, maritime and so on – see below) and dovetailed into the air campaign. At least as important is the need to deconflict times over target, airspace and other weapons systems such as friendly air defences. There may therefore be scope for mission command in the Combined Air Operations planning process, but not below that.

US doctrine effectively states that the Joint Force Commander (JFC) will delegate to the

> JFACC the authority necessary to accomplish assigned missions and tasks. The JFACC will normally exercise tactical control (TACON) over forces made available for tasking.[41]

This, in practical terms, gives the Joint Force Air Component Commander (JFACC) the complete span of command and control of air assets and operations possibly excepting special forces' operations or those conducted by clandestine civilian entities. There may be scope in conflict where the situation is changing rapidly, such as in irregular warfare or personnel recovery, for classic 'decentralised execution', but less so in large-scale conventional operations.[42]

In most modern operations the overall command and control function will be exercised by the JFC who will have responsibility for all forces under command for a given area of operations. He or she will have a number of components under him or her, normally functionally based and almost invariably including air, land and maritime and possibly special forces, logistics and so on. Each component will have its own commander. This person may, or may not, be co-located depending on the region involved and pre-existing facilities. From an American perspective, the commander may be appointed from one of combatant commands. Given that most major operations will be joint (including other services) and combined (including those of other countries), the practical side of the planning and execution will be complex. In addition to their practical planning contributions to the air campaign, the national contingents will have their own commander with sovereign (and political links back to capitals) responsibilities. In terms of influencing the planning and the subsequent execution of the overall air campaign, the degree of influence will depend on a range of factors including the size of the national commitment; the personalities involved at the political level; the personalities and interrelationships between the commanders involved; and the historical precedents and understanding of working together. At a more formal level, it is understood that each nation may have a different understanding of the legal basis for the campaign and different rules of engagement. There may also be differing political policy imperatives depending on, for example, national priorities in the region. The national contingent commanders therefore have a 'red card' which will allow them to ensure that their forces will remain within the nationally agreed constraints.[43] The command and control structure may also be further complicated if the campaign has to be conducted under a regional alliance framework, such as the Libyan campaign, *Unified Protector*, with a NATO command structure and the need for consensus agreement in Brussels. The pre-existing command structure may not necessarily be fit for purpose.[44] The situation may also be complicated by the addition of a non-Alliance member when there would be issues over the sharing of intelligence. In addition to potential problems with media handling, the most contentious issues are usually political.

The political control of air power

Clausewitz, like Machiavelli, took it as a given that war was essentially a tool of politics. In his own words, 'War is simply a continuation of political intercourse, with the addition of other means.'[45] Clausewitz made it clear that war does 'not suspend political intercourse', because this continues irrespective of the means employed; the grammar may be different, but not the logic.[46] He went on to state that as war was part of policy, the policy would determine the character of the conflict.[47] Clausewitz makes it clear that political control does not extend down to the tactical level in such things as the posting of guards. But in practice, it does extend down to the rules of engagement issued and, in air warfare, quite often to target clearance, weapons to be used and approach path followed to a target. Furthermore the technology used for relaying information, particularly visual images, has a high appeal to many in the command chain almost to the point of voyeurism.[48] The temptation then to intervene with advice and instructions may make the Clausewitzian separation harder to enforce in practice. It may seem to be axiomatic, especially in parliamentary democracies, that there would be political control over the military, but it is worth the researcher regularly checking the political context under which operations have been conducted. Changes to everything from announced threat levels to acceptable terms of surrender may be due as much to domestic, or international, political imperatives as to the nature of the conflict. As Clodfelter makes clear in *The Limits of Air Power*, 'American political resolve influenced the effectiveness of air power as a political instrument' in the Second World War, in Korea and certainly in Vietnam.[49]

In order to make sense of the political, diplomatic and other drivers affecting the execution of warfare, it will almost certainly be necessary to understand the machinery in place at each level of the conflict. This will likely include the United Nations Security Council (UNSC), not least for reasons of legality; possibly the North Atlantic Council for NATO operations; and of course, the national decision-making structure in capitals and their outlying headquarters. How much detail the researcher needs on this front will depend on the research question, but in real life, it is always present. In all of these areas, it is also important to acknowledge that decisions have to be made as part of an open system and cannot just be hermetically sealed in a bubble.

Most nations are likely to have something resembling a cabinet system such as is present in the UK (albeit under different titles). In most cases this will be too cumbersome to handle all business, especially during crises and the management, prevention and handling of this work is delegated to lower-level committees. In the UK, the National Security Council (NSC) 'is the main forum for collective discussion of the government's objectives for national security and about how best to deliver them in the current financial climate'.[50] The Secretary of State for Defence is a member of the NSC. When necessary, the Chief of Defence Staff attends (as opposed to sits as a member in his own right) meetings of the NSC as do heads of the intelligence agencies. Following strategic analysis of the issues at stake, the NSC should be able to gain a broad appreciation of the situation and then to discern the main options open to it and to the wider international community. Following, in very short order, the analysis will need to match the ends desired with the ways and means. The latter will encompass the necessary assets for the campaign and the likely costs to be borne by the Treasury or finance ministry. The role of the finance ministry is interesting. In the lead up to the Falklands operation in 1982, Prime Minister Margaret Thatcher excluded the Chancellor of the Exchequer from her war cabinet, much against the Treasury's wishes.[51]

Implicit in this overall analysis is the need to ensure that the means are available in depth and that the enablers are all in place. For air warfare in particular, it is essential that all necessary reconnaissance assets are available along with air-to-air refuelling, electronic support and air transport. With long lead times on high-technology munitions, coupled with a reluctance to stockpile such expensive equipment, the analysis needs to ensure that course of action under consideration can be executed. The analysis should also encompass a risk assessment covering likely eventualities along with low probability, but high-impact threats. All of this needs to be done across the spectrum of strategic pillars including diplomatic, costs and practicalities of reconstruction and the longer-term effects. The military staffs, in conjunction with colleagues in other departments can then begin the detailed planning process.[52]

In examining the processes at work, either for current operations or historically, it should not be assumed that just because the analysis has to be done, the enabling structures are replicated. In the lead up to the Gulf War in 2003, it was evident that US Central Command would work closely with the UK Permanent Joint Headquarters (PJHQ) in planning the campaign. The key difference was that PJHQ had to work through the Ministry of Defence Crisis Management Organisation where Central Command reported directly to the Secretary of Defence.

Beyond the need for an understanding of the structures in place, it is important to attempt to grasp the politics of the time within political parties, across capitals and internationally. It is also necessary to understand what impact the media is having and how likely the government is to act in response to calls that 'something must be done'. Here the speed of reaction of air power, and its inherent flexibility, combines to make an air response very appealing at the political level. Furthermore, the visual images of aircraft deploying can turn hearts and minds beyond the immediate media impact to embrace the political and enemy dimensions. The impermanence of air power also means that the duration of the political effect can be much more accurately fine-tuned than a maritime deployment or the prospect of 'boots on the ground'. How much these issues are recorded in Cabinet minutes, or those of the various sub-committees, will very much depend on the personalities in power at the time and their willingness to leave a record. For example, Freedman has recorded that Thatcher was 'a punctilious traditionalist in her dealings with both her Cabinet and with Parliament even when her Boadicea qualities were most in demand'.[53] When prime ministers are 'punctilious' in this way, the chances are much higher of later researchers having access to the Cabinet or Committee preparatory papers, the record of decisions and the subsequent actions and reactions from the relevant players. The converse is of course true where decision-making is done informally, with special advisers, white boards and scant official representation. In such circumstances the researcher may have to fall back on memoirs of dubious value.

A case study: Portal and Harris

Strategic leadership is, as has been discussed, characterized by complexity and ambiguity. The best senior leaders (and the terms senior, strategic and top are used interchangeably) have the ability, and intellect, to be able to see 'the big picture'. They are able to look over a number of diverse areas in their organization even when they do not have the detailed, tactical knowledge of each of them. Their less gifted colleagues tend to concentrate on the silo in which they developed and prefer to revel in the tactical minutiae. It has been suggested that Portal was very much one of the former with Harris as being parochial in his outlook.[54] The genuine strategic leader has the capacity to be able take a longer-term view for the benefit of the organization as a whole. This case study will look at the controversy late in the Second World War over targeting German oil production. This had consistently been recognized as a potential bottleneck in the German war economy, but was difficult to target.[55] Historians over the years have latched on to this aspect of the offensive for various reasons. First, oil was vital to the German war effort and reducing supplies were seen as a clear way of shortening the conflict in Europe. Second, it has provided fuel for debate as to whether Churchill, Sinclair or Portal should have removed Harris for disobedience of orders.

The command and control scenario under which the orders were issued was complex. The preparations for *Overlord* had seen the British and American bombers under the control of Eisenhower and Tedder, a period Harris referred to as the

only one period of calm sailing in the 3½ bitter years – a veritable centre of the hurricane – when all went well, when all pulled together, when there was at last continuity of contact between the compass course required and the lubber line – and that was during the all too short period when Eisenhower was Admiral and Tedder the Captain on the bridge.[56]

During this period he consistently rebuffed letters and direction from the Air Ministry reminding that command rested with Eisenhower. Once it had shifted back to the Air Ministry in September 1944, the pressure was mounting for a concerted attack on oil targets.[57] Harris contrasted this control situation with the *Overlord* period as producing 'an extraordinary lack of continuity and with responsibility so uncertainly poised the natural result was a multiplicity of directives embodying one change of plan after another and so cautiously worded at the end with so many provisos and such wide conditions that the authors were in effect guarded against any and every outcome of the orders issued'.[58] A first line of defence from Harris would have been to question the clarity of his orders in line with his quotation above.

Notwithstanding Harris's objections, the Directives that was issued on 25 September 1944 was unequivocal in its placement of the 'Petroleum industry, with special emphasis on petrol (gasoline) including storage' as first priority.[59] The German transportation system was at the head of the target systems listed as second priority. The Directive allowed the designated commanders latitude due to 'the exigencies of weather and tactical feasibility'.[60] This discretion allowed the operational commanders as much room for manoeuvre as it did those writing the orders so maligned in Harris's earlier quotation. The catalyst for what became a bitter debate came from Harris's response to Tedder's note on 'Air Policy to be Adopted with a View to Rapid Defeat of Germany', dated 25 October 1944.[61] Coincident with Harris's receipt of a copy of Tedder's note, he had been challenged as to why Bomber Command had attacked Cologne on the night of 31 October.[62] In a detailed defence of his decision to bomb Cologne, Harris listed eight reasons which included weather and tactical considerations; he also stated that the target was of direct value to the land offensive and 'generally in line with the Directive'.[63] Harris also commented in great detail on Tedder's paper and made an impassioned appeal for a continuation of the area offensive.[64] The official historians have described his letter as 'unrepentant defence of his grounds for neglecting the bombing directive of 25 September 1944, but also a defiant challenge to any further directives of that nature'.[65]

Harris's constant railing against the Directorate of Bomber Operations and the Deputy Chief of the Air Staff could, when emanating from a successful commander in the field, be seen as eccentric and, given the personalities involved on both sides, almost understandable. But Harris's letter of 1 November marked a direct challenge to the authority of the CAS and the Combined Chiefs. It was also clear that he did not share, or had ever admitted to, any expression of the vision and purpose of the bomber offensive that did not match his own interpretation. It was also evident that Portal had failed to convince

Harris of either the strategic considerations or the real merits of alternative strategies. While it was by then too late in the war to sack Harris without causing uproar in the Command and the wider public, it was also arguably late in the day to try and win Harris around. Nevertheless, Portal attempted to do so. In his response on 5 November, Portal informed Harris that his requests for information were made not because 'I am ipso facto exhibiting lack of confidence in Bomber Command's operations', but that he may have to 'explain, and if necessary defend' what had been going on.[66] Portal accepted that he was risking being dubbed by the C-in-C as 'another panacea merchant', but went on to state his belief that 'the air offensive against oil gives us the best hope of complete victory in the next few months'. Although Portal admitted that there may be occasions when the re-emerging U-boat threat would need to be addressed, or the land campaign would require support, he considered that the bomber offensive must seize absolutely every opportunity to maintain a positive balance between their destruction of the industry and German efforts to repair it. On the basis of the 'available intelligence' (including Ultra) the CAS believed that the 'whole war situation is poised on "oil" as on a knife edge'.[67] What had previously been a debate between 'directed letters' and appropriate 'Sir, I have the honour to refer' responses had now become a battle of will between two of the most senior leaders in the service couched in demi-official language. The sensitivity of the correspondence was still evident some years later when the official historians sought to use the material and were initially refused.[68] As a result the whole Official History project was either nearly 'emasculated', or driven to extinction.[69]

Harris replied with yet another defence of his decisions to attack cities rather than oil targets, and then challenged the accuracy of the intelligence upon which the plan was based.[70] He also regretted the suggestion that it was thought that he did not 'understand the importance of the oil war, because that is entirely wrong'.[71] Portal's response returned to the issue of the devastation of cities to which Harris had referred in his letter of 1 November:

> I know that you have long felt that such a plan to be the most effective way of bringing about the collapse of Germany. Knowing this, I have, I must confess, at times wondered whether the magnetism of the remaining German cities has not in the past tended as much to deflect our bombers from their primary objectives as the tactical and weather difficulties which you described so fully in your letter of 1st November. I would like you to reassure me that this is not so. If I knew you to be as wholehearted in the attack on oil as in the past you have been in the matter of attacking cities I would have little to worry about.[72]

Notwithstanding the vagaries of the language used in the various Air Staff communications there could be absolutely no doubt as to the higher commander's intent on this matter. Portal's language was firm, to the point and personal. At this point, it is suggested that, under an objective test, it would have been reasonable for Harris either to do what he had been directed, in the spirit in which it was intended, or at least return to 'consent and evade'. But Harris chose to resort to a battle of the experts and forwarded an appreciation carried out by his Operational Research Section who had calculated a huge required sortie and bomb load rate to destroy the key targets.[73] He berated the 'MEW experts' for having 'never failed to overstate their case on "panaceas", e.g. ball-bearings, molybdenum, locomotives etc'. Harris considered that the oil plan was already following the path of previous schemes with the inclusion of Benzol plants.[74]

Richards has stated that this missive 'disturbed Portal more than the earlier ones'.[75] Certainly, Portal's pencil annotations to Harris's letter confirm that he spent a considerable period going through the detail.[76] Nevertheless, he responded patiently by stating that he was 'profoundly disappointed that you still feel that the oil plan is just another "panacea"'.[77] Portal went on to confirm that Bomber Command's load in attacking these targets was shared with the Americans (thereby spreading the risk of attrition against which Harris had complained) and that 'immobilisation and the continued immobilisation of the remaining producers' was the 'greatest and most certain contribution that our strategic bombers could make'. In response to Harris's challenge on the competence of the Ministry of Economic Warfare (MEW), Portal suggested that greater efforts might have produced the results predicted. Portal also expressed his doubts that Harris's staff would not give their best in the 'accomplishment of your first priority task if you yourself are not whole heartedly in support of it'.[78] Harris responded by reiterating his distrust of the MEW and defended his Command's efforts against the target sets which Portal had said had not been prosecuted with due diligence.[79] The official historians have described Harris's response to this next letter as 'extraordinary' and suggested that further attempts to persuade him 'would be useless'.[80] They also alluded to Portal's unwillingness to replace Harris at this stage.[81] But what is arguably a key paragraph in this letter, from which they do not quote, is where Harris admits that where he leaves 'no stone unturned to get my views across, but, when the decision is made I carry it out to the utmost and best of my ability'.[82] Nor did the Air Staff seriously challenge this saying that there was 'no doubt that Bomber Command have done excellently in the attack on oil and the C-in-C may well feel convinced that he is attacking it to the best of his ability'; they did, however, doubt that every opportunity had been taken.[83] In support of the contention that Bomber Command had made progress against oil targets, Cox in his introduction to Harris's *Despatch on War Operations*, has made the point that Bomber Command's performance was acceptable given the weather, moon conditions and so forth.[84] What continued to concern the Air Staff was Harris's lack of enthusiasm and the effect that this would have on his staff and the wider prosecution of the campaign.[85] But Harris refuted

Portal's accusation that his views may well have influenced his staff for the worse. His words were classic Harris and are an interesting cameo, depicting him as very much an 'old school', or traditional, military commander:

> I do not give my staff views. I give them orders. They do and always have done exactly what I tell them to. I have told them to miss no opportunity of prosecuting the oil plan, and they have missed no worth while (sic) opportunity.[86]

The correspondence therefore continued and Portal's next letter, of eight pages and produced after lengthy discussions with his staff, contained what the official historians have called 'a most significant passage' which is worthy of repetition at length:

> While area bombing, if it could have been continued long enough and in sufficient weight, might in the end have forced the enemy to capitulate, his counter-measures would have prevented us from maintaining such a policy to decisive point. We would have been forced to precision attack to maintain the air situation needed to continue the offensive at all. The Americans did this for themselves in 1943/44 with a little help from Bomber Command. Under cover of the favourable air situation which was created 'OVERLORD' was launched successfully, and the advance to the German frontier gave night bombing a new lease of life. But for this it is possible that the night blitzing of German cities would by now have been too costly to sustain upon a heavy scale. These factors must not be overlooked when considering the post and future results of area attack.[87]

In many ways, this passage is actually the most significant, even extraordinary, of the whole chain of correspondence and could only have been conducted in the less formal demi-official manner. The key element was that it was the United States Army Air Forces that had won the vital air superiority necessary for *Overlord* without which the bomber offensive would have ground to a costly halt. *Overlord* had, in turn, allowed the ground forces to overrun the early warning sites, and Bomber Command was thus able to operate more freely. The official historians challenged Portal's understanding of the situation, or at least his 'oversimplification'.[88] But it could be argued that this is beside the point. The demi-official correspondence had, by its personal nature, a degree of subjectivity to it that would not otherwise be evident and that was behind the two leaders' reluctance to have it quoted from and refusal to allow its publication. Regardless of whether Webster and Frankland's subsequent analysis was more correct, the critical issue is whether that is what Portal actually believed.[89] If it was, and he had decided to remove Harris, it would have all the appearances of the C-in-C being sacked because Portal and the Air Staff thought that the area offensive had failed; they could hardly have published the letters as evidence of Harris's intransigence. Had Harris been sacked for the perceived failure of such a costly campaign, the wider impact on morale in the RAF would have been considerable.

Harris duly responded, albeit with regret, that the debate had been widened beyond the merits of the oil plan.[90] Harris outlined, again, his objections to any form of selective bombing and to the oil plan in particular. He also vigorously defended himself against any charge of disloyalty, but likened the situation to a case of 'heads I lose, tails you win'; if the policy in which he had no faith failed, the blame would lie at his door for not prosecuting it with sufficient vigour. Harris went on to ask the CAS 'to consider whether it is best for the prosecution of the war and our success of arms, which alone matters, that I should remain in this situation'.[91] As Richards has stated, 'Portal in the pleasantest possible way brushed aside Harris's offer of resignation':

> I willingly accept your assurance that you will continue to do your utmost to ensure the successful execution of the policy laid down. I am sorry that you do not believe in it but it is no use my craving for the unattainable. We must wait until the end of the war before we can know for certain who was right and I sincerely hope that until then you will continue in command of the force which has done so much towards defeating the enemy and has brought such credit and renown to yourself and the Air Force.[92]

In many ways Portal was either naive, suffering from wishful thinking or merely being placatory in his hope that the end of the war would see one or the other proved right. The literature suggests that the debate is still healthy and contentious.[93] It is certainly outside the scope of this study to examine the merits or pass judgement on the success of the bomber offensive. From the leadership perspective, however, it is instructive to note Sinclair's comment when he was shown the trail of correspondence; he concluded that Portal was 'exquisitely right' against one of the CAS's replies to Harris and that 'I see what troubles his soul – our failure to go nap on the policy of obliteration and that the laurels he is receiving are for successes – e.g. the pathfinders, incendiary attack, the oil plan – which are not of his design.'[94] As Sinclair also noted, Harris was obviously 'under considerable mental stress' which is less than surprising given his role for so long. But then the same could be said for Portal who had to endure numerous overseas trips as well as Churchill's 'midnight follies'.[95] Senior leadership is, and has always been, mentally and physically taxing.

Having justified his request for information on the grounds that he may either have to explain, or defend, Bomber Command's operations, it is worthy of note that Churchill's sole minute to Portal on the subject of oil came at the end of January 1945.[96] In this minute, Churchill noted that three times as many bombs had been dropped on transportation targets compared with oil. He went on to say that 'in view of the great success of attacks on oil targets and of their immediate effects, I trust they will not be neglected in favour of the long term attrition of German communications'.[97] Portal assured him that all 'the Air Authorities, RAF and American, are agreed that oil has top priority'.[98] The prime minister appeared to have been oblivious to the turbulent correspondence at the interface between the military strategic level and the operational. From this, it is not unreasonable to infer that Portal had no intention of escalating matters by attempting to remove Harris and was content to weather the storm.

This case study is valuable for a number of reasons. The first of these is the pure entertainment value of being allowed to witness such a spat between senior leaders and to join the debate on whether Harris should have been sacked. More importantly, it illustrates the tensions between political control from Churchill (or the lack of it at this stage in the war) and Sinclair and the relationship between the two officers and their staffs. The case study also shows the value in utilizing and combining a range of primary sources including the AHB Narratives (cited as AIR 41) along with appropriate secondary material. Although the Portal Papers were cited extensively, the research was actually done with them, and then with TNA AIR files for both the CAS and Bomber Command. The file minutes cited in AIR 8/1020 give a fascinating insight into the workings of the Directorate of Bomber Operations in the Air Ministry. At first sight, the workings of a bureaucracy may appear dull in comparison with the day-to-day fight over Germany, but the importance of the oil debate was so great that it is an essential part of the picture.

CHAPTER SEVEN

Legality, legitimacy and ethics of air warfare

Most step changes in the technology of warfare have resulted in outcries of unfairness, illegality and simple horror over the consequences of the latest innovation in Hobbesian brutality. This has been true over the introduction of gunpowder, the crossbow, industrial scale artillery and chemical weapons. But, for various reasons, air power has attracted specific angst from the earliest attempts to master the third dimension. Part of the reasoning behind this has already been explored in the section on how air power was romanticized by the public, the press and popular writers. There is also an element of unease over warriors withdrawing from close combat in favour of ever more remote warfare; this has become particularly evident in contemporary debates over the use of remotely piloted air vehicles or drones.[1] Many of the attempts to limit technological progress have come from nations whose own research, development and industrial base have been unable to keep pace with more advanced countries. This was certainly evident in the rationale for the early Hague Conferences of 1899 and 1907 where the czar of Russia was concerned over Western progress.[2]

The early conferences were part of a trend towards codification of broad principles, unwritten rules, custom and practice, tacit agreements between states, in the early military texts and in religious teaching.[3] In some ways it seems counter-intuitive for potential belligerents to seek to limit the reasons for going to war (traditionally known as *ius ad bellum*) and then how it is conducted (*ius in bello*). After all, Clausewitz started his first chapter in *On War* with the classic definition of war as 'an act of force to compel our enemy to do our will' and dismissed 'certain self-imposed, imperceptible limitations hardly worth mentioning, known as international law and custom, but they scarcely weaken it' (force).[4] Professor Howard, however, has changed the complexion of the discussion completely asserting first that the military use 'violence with great *deliberation*' (emphasis in the original).[5] Howard then goes on to confirm that this violence is 'purposeful, deliberate and legitimized' and that this constitutes '*force*'; when used between states, this defines war.[6] It is significant for the study of air warfare to note that Howard chose to cite 'area' bombing [*sic*] as an example of random destruction demonstrating the readiness of many authors to choose such examples. It is also important to note the use of the word 'legitimized' as this is reflected in a government's decision to go to war (or use force outside conventional conflict – see below), its rules of engagement and both general and individual targeting decisions. The complexity of the need for deliberation and legitimization is, in part, due to the need to maintain a moral high ground and especially so for democracies where the will to fight could be undermined by public revulsion. But Howard also acknowledged that humanity in warfare does not always coincide with military necessity.[7]

In modern warfare commanders and politicians are increasingly held to account by their publics, the press and in most cases the democratic process. There is an increasing requirement for collateral damage to be reduced to zero; for the maximum discrimination between combatants and non-combatants; and for the minimum force to be used commensurate with a demonstrable military necessity. This is particularly the case with air warfare where the immediacy of the engagement can be relayed to home audience in very near real time. In short, humanity and military necessity are being forced onto a converging path. This is in marked contrast to some campaigns where enemy regimes have been subject to long attritional air bombardments accompanied by descriptions such as 'shock and awe'.[8]

This chapter will examine the overarching system of international law and international humanitarian law, but can only hope to highlight some of the debates and to outline some key sources. The same applies to the wider ethical debate and this has been used to analyse previous air campaigns. Part of the issue here is the need for the air power practitioner or student to understand the vocabulary in use; the linkages with the development of international law and the importance of the wider debate.

The laws of war and air warfare

The development, and application of international law of armed conflict has long been problematic in that states have consistently sought to avoid the incorporation of laws that they consider likely to impinge upon their national interests; this is compounded by the absence of any real enforcement mechanism beyond the utterances of the International Court of Justice.[9] In his detailed review of *Air War and the Law of War*, American military lawyer Hays Parks has cited one of the most pre-eminent international lawyers of the twentieth century, Sir Hersch Lauterpacht, as stating: 'If international law is the weakest point of all law, then the law of war is its vanishing point.'[10] It is, however, suggested that this is an overly cynical viewpoint, especially if one considers the amount of materials published on the subject. There is an extensive literature on the international law of armed conflict and of air warfare. Some texts are aimed specifically at international lawyers and their students; others are for more general audiences including international relations students, strategists, military staff college students and practitioners.[11] Beyond the general texts which provide an excellent background to the development of the laws of war and how they have been interpreted over the years, it is also worth referring to texts on specific areas. The first of these acknowledges the reality that military force often has to be applied in conflicts other than conventional war. These scenarios include countering international terrorism, counter-insurgency operations and peacekeeping operations. These are covered under the broad heading of international humanitarian law.[12] More detailed studies include works examining targeting generally and targeted killing in particular.[13] In law schools the world over there is a standard adage which notes that an out-of-date legal text is positively dangerous as the law changes through legislation and case law. The same is true with international law. One of the key factors in this is that 'the writings of jurists' is an established source of international law so a number of academic ideas can gain a foothold relatively rapidly. This has certainly been the case since the end of the Cold War, the first Gulf War and onwards through the collapse of Yugoslavia.[14] Concepts such humanitarian intervention and the duty to protect come under this category. This rapid change also highlights the dangers of differing interpretations of modern developments. This can be exacerbated if administrations in various countries are seeking an interpretation of international law to justify a chosen course of action.

The basics of the modern international laws of armed conflict are based on the fundamental assertion in the United Nations Charter that

> all Members shall refrain in their international relations from the threat or use of force against the territorial integrity or political independence of any state, or in any other manner inconsistent with the Purposes of the United Nations.[15]

There are a number of exceptions to this basic rule. The first, and arguably most important for the legitimization of the use of armed conflict, is Chapter VII UN Security Council Resolution (UNSCR) authorizing the use of force if there is a 'threat to the peace, breach of the peace, or act of aggression'.[16] Beyond this, states have an inherent right to self-defence which may be as individual states or collective entities (such as NATO).[17] Although there is an extensive debate on the merits of customary international law of self-defence set against Article 51, the basics of imminence of the threat and the need for a proportional response remain extant.[18] The political realities of the UNSC are that gaining authorization for the use of force is not always possible as one or more of the permanent members may exercise their right to veto the proposed Resolution. In this event, and if the situation in question may lead to a humanitarian disaster, states may be able to justify military action.[19]

The international law of armed conflict is part of international humanitarian law and is essentially based on customary law and on treaties. Customary law is, as the name implies, based on state practice which has become accepted as legally binding. It does not necessarily have to have been unanimous in its application, but the practice will have usually been widespread.[20] Most, but not all, elements of the law of armed conflict have been codified into treaty law. In most cases, treaties are only binding on those states that are party to the treaties. Some elements of treaty law, however, are considered to be so fundamental that they have been considered to have universal application under customary law.

One of the first significant attempts at the codification of the rules of warfare was completed by Dr Francis Lieber of Columbia University for issue to the Union Army on 24 April 1863.[21] The 'Lieber Code' became the model for many national manuals and for the Hague Peace Conferences of 1899 and 1907.[22] Due to its relative infancy, air warfare was not high on the agenda at the Hague Conference of 1899, but Commission I of the conference agreed to a five-year moratorium on the discharge of explosives or projectiles from balloons.[23] This prohibition on the utilization of balloons duly expired, but was renewed by the 1907 Hague Convention.[24] Article 25 also prohibited the bombardment 'by whatever means' of undefended towns and villages.[25] This prohibition did not, however, prevent the Germans from launching airship and aircraft attacks on the UK during the First World War and nor did it prevent naval bombardment of coastal towns. Despite assertions that all targets were military in nature it was evident that considerable damage was done beyond this. Along with a range of other limitations sought by the international community, attempts were made to limit air bombardment.

The Hague Commission of Jurists commenced on 11 December 1922 under the chairmanship of John Bassett Moore of the United States and consisted of representatives of the United States, Great Britain, France, Italy, Japan and the Netherlands; each delegation consisted of legal and technical experts.[26] The delegation from Britain included J. M. Spaight, a senior official from the newly formed Air Ministry.[27] The Hague Conference finished on 19 February 1923 with the unanimous adoption of a two-part report; the first part covered *Rules for the Control of Radio in Time of War* and the second *Rules of Aerial Warfare*.[28] The 1923 Hague Rules were not ratified by any of the nations, with France, the Netherlands and Great Britain particularly opposed to their adoption.[29] The conventional view, therefore, was (and remains) that they were a political and legal failure.[30] That said, the Hague Rules were a valid attempt to align air warfare with other forms of war. Spaight was an influential figure on UK thinking on air power and the constraints that could be applied.[31] His work was studied for the RAF Staff College entrance examination and he advised widely within the Air Ministry.[32] The basic principles of the Hague Rules were cited by Neville Chamberlain in the House of Commons in 1938.[33] Chamberlain admitted that 'no international code of law with respect to aerial warfare which is the subject of international agreement', but that the underlying principles of the law as it applied to sea and land warfare were applicable to the air 'and are not only admitted but insisted upon by this Government'. These principles included that it was

> against international law to bomb civilians as such, and to make deliberate attacks upon civilian populations.
>
> In the second place, targets which are aimed at from the air must be legitimate military objectives and must be capable of identification.
>
> In the third place, reasonable care must be taken in attacking those military objectives so that by carelessness a civilian population in the neighbourhood is not bombed.[34]

So despite never having been ratified, the rules provided guidance for politicians and military planners until Churchill took power from Chamberlain.[35]

The Second World War was a significant turning point for international law across the spectrum. In particular, the 'total' nature of the war in which virtually the whole of the populations of the major combatants were involved in the war effort to some extent. The various bombing campaigns went far beyond the ambitious principles described above. Although the subsequent Nuremberg trials have been described as 'victors' justice', the tribunal held that the Hague Rules (across the board) were declaratory of customary international law.[36] Subsequent codification and extensive revision of laws of war took place in Geneva and are laid out in the four Conventions.[37] These were supplemented by the Additional Protocols of 1977 with Protocol I covering international armed conflicts and Protocol II dealing with internal conflicts. Protocol I sets out detailed rules on targeting and the methods and means of warfare.[38] Article 35 specifically states that these are not unlimited and must not cause 'superfluous injury or unnecessary suffering'.[39]

The international law of armed conflict has thus evolved, been refined and revisited in the light of the norms of society and from the experiences of warfare. Nevertheless, there are four fundamental principles at the core: military necessity, humanity, distinction and proportionality. These clearly apply to air warfare as well as any other form, but arguably have a greater application or visibility when it comes to formulation of rules of engagement or targeting criteria.

Military necessity allows only the 'degree and kind of force, not otherwise prohibited by the law of armed conflict, required for the partial or complete submission of the enemy with a minimum expenditure of time, life and physical resources'.[40] There are several key issues within this. The use of force, as covered by Howard above, must be deliberate and controlled. The wording is clear, as is the intent, that military necessity cannot be used to excuse breaches of the law. But if certain means or techniques are not prohibited, they can be used if necessary to achieve aims quickly and effectively. Unnecessary force is, by definition, illegal as it implies wanton destruction or killing. For a full discussion on this, it is worth consulting the UK's JSP 383 *Manual of the Law of Armed Conflict*.[41]

Humanity builds on military necessity by directly outlawing destruction, killing, injury and the infliction of suffering as ends in themselves. The principle of humanity effectively also confers non-combatant immunity for civilians and their property as they are not part of the military effort. But it is not a blanket prohibition in that it allows for accidental or incidental damage to civilian property if it has occurred in an otherwise legitimate attack on genuinely military objectives. This is collateral damage and is an essential aspect of targeting decision-making. Humanity also embraces centuries-old concepts of chivalry and the humane treatment of the wounded. Perfidy and dishonourable or treacherous behaviour are also outlawed.[42]

Distinction follows from the basic requirement for wars only to be fought between military forces. It therefore requires there to be clear discrimination between military targets and civilians and between combatants and non-combatants. This is covered in detail in Articles 48 and 49 of Additional Protocol I and is enshrined in customary law.[43] Non-combatants are not permitted to take part in hostilities and should they do so, lose the right to protection from attack.[44] The presence of civilians in target areas that are clearly military in nature does not confer immunity on those installations. These can include command and control facilities and munitions factories. It should be noted that these rules apply to international armed conflicts where states are at war with each other; other conflicts will be discussed below and in the literature already cited. That said, the provisions on discrimination are vitally important in the intelligence-gathering phase and in assessing and clearing targets for attack. JSP 383 states that the commander should make

> reasonable efforts to gather intelligence, reviews the intelligence available to him and concludes in good faith that he is attacking a legitimate military target, he does not automatically violate the principle of distinction if the target turns out to be of a different and civilian nature.[45]

An important point to note in this is that what may be considered to be 'reasonable' is not defined. In practice, this test is becoming more stringent with each conflict to the point where targets may not be prosecuted unless discrimination is near perfect. It should also be noted that in coalitions, there may be differing interpretations of the expression 'in good faith'.

Proportionality covers two issues. The first of these provides a link between *ius ad bellum* and *ius in bello* ensuring that the rationale for going to war is in proportion to the force subsequently used; minor incursions cannot be used to justify mass retaliation. The second element is that the force to be applied, and the potential losses, has to be in proportion to the gains expected.[46] Additional Protocol I also refers to proportionality in the context of commanders having to avoid indiscriminate attacks and where civilian losses would be out of proportion with the military advantage gained.[47] For modern air power, applying the principles of proportionality and distinction requires careful consideration of a number of factors. These are invariably discussed as part of the target clearance procedures. One issue is that minimizing civilian casualties may only be possible at the cost of increasing risk to one's own crews. The law does not cover this angle and in practice it will be for commanders and governments to balance this, partly depending on the possible strategic benefits against possible damage to domestic centres of gravity if aircrew are lost. The principle of proportionality also applies in cases where military are close to civilian risk areas, or have been deliberately placed in the proximity. This was certainly true in both Gulf wars with the use of human shields and Saddam Hussein's positioning of forces close to mosques.

Laws of armed conflict outside of war

The Geneva Conventions and the Additional Protocol I, along with the bulk of international law, regulate behaviour between states. But this only represents part of the picture of modern conflict. There are a number of terms for non-interstate conflicts including internal conflicts, civil war or more generally non-international armed conflicts.[48] Operations involving counter-insurgency and counterterrorism also fall outside classic interstate conflict. There must obviously be a dividing line somewhere between mere disturbances and violence that has reached the level of 'armed conflict'. This dividing line is not always clear, especially as many states are reluctant to admit that the line has been crossed.[49] Once reached, the laws covering non-international armed conflicts stem first of all from Common Article 3 of the Geneva Conventions; this is, as the name suggests, common to each of the four conventions and specifically addresses internal conflicts.[50] This is supplemented by Additional Protocol II of the Conventions.[51] The nature of these conflicts has been such that there is little agreement between states over definitions and terminology.[52] Case law, state practice and academic writing on the subject have, however, continued to develop. The law of non-international armed conflict is synonymous with international humanitarian law, with the latter term in more regular use.[53] This, in turn, is supplemented by international human rights law, adherence to which does not cease in the event of armed conflict occurring.[54]

Conflicts in Afghanistan and Iraq and operations in Yemen and Pakistan have all complicated the environment with the added impetus of addressing issues around the use of remotely piloted systems. For most proponents of air warfare, adherence to the basic principles of military necessity, proportionality, distinction and humanity would be a useful starting point. The problems then escalate in terms of distinguishing between combatants and non-combatants and actually defining what constitutes a military target. It should also be noted that those taking part in these conflicts cannot be accorded prisoner-of-war status, but should be treated humanely.

Ethics and air warfare

Thus far, this chapter has dealt with relatively straightforward treaties and conventions. But it has also had recourse to the underlying principles and guidelines for behaviour that have grown up over the centuries. International humanitarian law and human rights law have stemmed from these principles. The various chivalrous codes that have also arisen have found their way into the laws of war and how, in particular, belligerents should treat each other. The philosophical discipline of ethics lies at the heart of the various debates that have led to the formulation of laws and the codes to which warriors have adhered. Ethics is essentially the science of morals in human conduct.[55] The study of ethics is essential for warriors for a number of reasons. The first of these is the requirement for commanders, and war fighters more generally, to be able to explain the rights and wrongs of a particular course of action. It should be relatively simple just to have recourse to legal opinion and quote a specific cause and say this action is lawful. But very often this is just not possible, or is insufficient to convince. Legal opinions, over the Gulf War in 2003 for example, differ widely. Furthermore, merely because a legal justification can be found does not allow escape from the more fundamental question as to whether it is actually right to do something, or wrong not to take action. To be able to make up one's mind what is right or wrong, it could be argued that one should have the mental apparatus to be able to do so. To explain it to others requires at least a basic vocabulary without necessarily immersing oneself in philosophical treatises.

This is a discipline that has specific interest for air warfare students as many of the uses of air power have generated often heated debate and recriminations. These have included air policing, the strategic air offensive against Germany and the more recent discussions on remotely piloted air vehicles.[56] In his work on Churchill as a warlord, Carlo D'Este described the bombing of cities in the Second World War as the 'most savagely debated military aspect' of the conflict.[57] This has occurred for several reasons. The first is that the simple recourse to a legal justification remains impossible because the 1923 Hague Rules were never ratified (as discussed above). The second complication is that the nature of conflict has often been described as a total war in which whole populations were involved. Finally, the subject has been attacked by commentators from many disciplines including historians, moral philosophers, economists and political scientists.[58] The debate goes beyond what was right or wrong about the various offensives, but includes consideration of their respective effectiveness and strategic impact. A further set of debates centres on academic rigour, cherry-picking of historical evidence and the applicability of contemporary values to a previous generation. Similar, multidimensional debates could be had over many conflicts including Vietnam and the Middle East.

An ethical underpinning for military action obviously goes beyond mere debate, however important that may be. As a starting point, it has long been recognized that a moral justification is an essential aspect of leadership at all levels. It is invaluable to be able to convince those fighting that the cause is just. General Viscount Wolseley in his *Life of John Churchill*, writing in 1894, stated that

> history proves that it [the army] has seldom fought well in what it believed to be an unrighteous cause. Unless the Rank and File are interested in their work, there will be no enthusiasm, and from an army without enthusiasm little can be expected.[59]

The essence of this, written as it was by a distinguished soldier, was that the need for a just cause was paramount for military forces to be expected to function (presumably in the absence of prevailing laws of armed conflict which were then just being formulated).[60]

It will not be possible, nor desirable, for this chapter to explore philosophical theories in real detail. It is worth, however, mentioning utilitarianism, deontology and then spending a little longer examining Just War Theory. Jeremy Bentham (1748–1832) is generally regarded as the originator of this theory which is based on the 'greatest happiness of the greatest number'.[61] His work was subsequently developed by John Stuart Mill.[62] Bentham stated that the only fundamental moral value was the balance between human happiness and the avoidance of pain; humanity was governed by 'pain and pleasure'.[63] All other values are derived from this and that all actions should have maximizing human happiness as their aim. Each person counts as an equal in this theory and it concentrates on the ends to be achieved, not the means. From a military commander's perspective, this last element of utilitarianism could have a certain appeal, because it may allow for considerations such as rights to be swept aside.

Deontology, in contrast, is the ethics of rights. Some of these rights, which resonate with human rights law, are fundamental and unalienable. They include the right to life, liberty, security, freedom from torture and so on.[64] Rights are considered to be absolute and have been called 'trumps'. Although rights have to be guaranteed, they do generate correlating responsibilities. If these responsibilities are not honoured, the rights may be forfeit. So, in the military context, an individual, or a state, may forfeit the right to life by himself or itself killing someone. This contractual element of deontology provides an explanation of why intentional killing may not necessarily be wrong. In turn, this may help to determine acceptable reasons for using force or going to war. It provides a useful basis for debate on self-defence at all levels and helps to justify humanitarian intervention. The principles of necessity, proportionality and discrimination are also consistent with a deontological approach.

Realism is a term more appropriate to a discussion on international relations theory than moral philosophy. But in practical terms, the reality of a situation may be such that deontological and utilitarian discussion is swept aside. Realism essentially works at the state level and has a long intellectual history from the Greek city-states onwards.[65] It finds more recent expression in comments made in a lecture by W. V. Herbert to a meeting in the Royal United Service Institute in February 1898. He doubted whether it was possible to have an ethical side to warfare. Herbert went on to discount the arguments germane to the professional philosopher who 'will argue a soul into a stone, and beauty into the earthworm', preferring to align the discussion with 'the ordinary fight-your-daily-battle individual like you and me'.[66] Herbert dealt with *ius ad bellum* as concomitant with nationhood and therefore inevitable.[67] But he saw *ius in bello* as having changed, or developed, with 'women and children not molested – at least, not officially'; 'open towns are not shelled and poison gas is held in abhorrence'.[68] Herbert concluded with the suggestion that warfare had developed, and needed to continue to develop, a 'universally-accepted code to regulate its conduct'.[69] But he then went on to stress the primacy of actually winning:

> All said and done, 'Win your war' is the most important, and it is the most primitive, maxim of the science of strategy – that is drive your opponent into such a corner that he is content to have the terms of peace dictated to him. The rest comes a long way after.[70]

In an answer to a question from the floor, Herbert explained that a code of ethics could only be relevant between nations of an equal state of civilization and that it could not reasonably be expected to apply between the English and the Zulus.[71]

The realist approach, however, only provides a one-dimensional justification for action or the use of force. It does not answer more nuanced or fundamental questions about whether it is actually right to do something. It is also clear that neither utilitarianism nor deontology can act as stand-alone theories. Just War Theory helps to bridge the gaps between the three approaches already discussed. It dates back to the letters of St Augustine. The theory builds on the work of early Christian writers who, acknowledging the sanctity of human life, tried to impose a degree of rationalism and discipline on the inevitable exercise of violence and taking of life. In 418, St Augustine wrote a short treatise on military morality to a senior Roman official charged with keeping tribesmen from the Sahara out of Roman (Christian) Africa. St Augustine advised that war should only be conducted when necessary and then with the minimum force necessary; he added that mercy should be shown to the enemy.[72] The theory has continued to have widespread appeal since then with notable exponents including Thomas Aquinas who, for war to be lawful, insisted on sovereign authority, just cause and rightful intention.[73] More recent authors have added that war should only be fought as a last resort, that there should be a reasonable prospect of success and echo the principles of proportionality in that the gains should not be outweighed by the costs and implications of fighting.[74]

Just War Theory had a major resurgence in the world of philosophy and more widely as scholars attempted to make sense of the American involvement in Vietnam.[75] Michael Walzer's *Just and Unjust Wars* is a key text for the theory and has been widely discussed and debated in the literature.[76] It builds on the historical antecedents and usefully bridges the gaps. It uses very similar terminology to international law and care has to be taken not to mix the two. The theory therefore uses *ius ad bellum* to cover the reasons why a state could resort to war. These include the need for a just cause such as self-defence or humanitarian intervention. War must also be a last resort and must be capable of being fought in a just manner with a reasonable prospect of success. For a state to go to war, it should be for the right motives and the justification used must be the real one and not just as an excuse. The principles of proportionality also apply. Just War Theory mirrors international law again in that it is the purview of states and of individuals.

Once war has been started, Just War Theory goes to *ius in bello*, again following international law (or vice versa). A key point here is that individuals are responsible for their actions in battle and cannot rely on orders. *Ius in bello* emphasizes discrimination between combatants and non-combatants and immunity for the sick and injured. It also insists on necessity, military utility and proportionality.

Just War Theory also acknowledges the realities of warfare and international relations whereby in order for a state to survive it has to suspend its adherence to the rules of *ius in bello*. Walzer has used the term 'supreme emergency' echoing Churchill at the start of Second World War.[77] Walzer has argued that the threat from Nazism was so radical and imminent that Europe did face a supreme emergency; he stressed that there had to be danger and imminence.[78] Walzer was therefore able to argue that from the fall of France in 1940 through to the end of 1942, Britain was in a state of supreme emergency and that the bomber offensive against Germany was justified. However, Walzer contended that once the United States entered the war following the attack on Pearl Harbor, other means had become available to beat Germany and the rules of discrimination within *ius in bello* again applied. It should also be noted that Walzer condemned the bombing offensive against Germany for reasons of revenge or reprisal at all stages of the conflict.[79]

Concluding comments

The last 150 years have seen warfare develop almost exponentially in scale and lethality as technology, industry and national wealth have, in many cases, combined. Air warfare has been an integral part of this development. Two of the wars that have been fought have been on such a scale as to warrant a global epithet and a third, although 'Cold' in definition and title, always ran the risk of worldwide devastation. The horrors of war have long been recognized and scholars have sought over the centuries to restrict recourse to war and to limit, or regulate, the destruction. The recurring themes which have underpinned the development of the international law of armed conflict and international humanitarian law resonate closely with philosophical thinking. In some instances, the linkages are more important where academic discussions in the universities on philosophical issues of war are translated relatively quickly into the writings of jurists and thence into international law. This certainly occurred with concepts of humanitarian intervention. Following Iraq and Afghanistan it may well be repeated with an extension of individual culpability in *ius ad bellum*.

This chapter has sought to introduce some of the basic concepts of international law and philosophical thinking on warfare. Much of it is general and applies to all war. But it is notable that much of the fiercest debate has come over air power issues such as the strategic air offensive against Germany, the American bombing of Tokyo and subsequently Hiroshima and Nagasaki and currently remotely piloted air vehicles.[80] International law is by no means perfect and there is obviously no way of enforcing it should states choose not to comply or withdraw from acceptance of the jurisdiction of the international court of justice.[81] Although there are conventions that require states only to develop weapons that if used, would be lawful, it is evident that a number do carry out research and development on so-called 'black' programmes in secret. But international law as part of the wider international community and the United Nations does have a beneficial effect with many countries seeking peaceful or legal ways to resolve differences. The annual reports of the ICJ attest to this.[82]

Over the period in question, the debates on warfare, and many other subjects, have moved beyond face-to-face discussions and letters to editors to embrace all kinds of social media and internet fora. Likewise, the media is far more engaged in all issues of public life including those around air warfare. The various debates on 'drones' are a clear evidence of this. There is a natural reticence for governments to prefer to work outside direct scrutiny, but this is rarely possible. An ability to show accountability, openness and to engage in debate is essential as is an understanding of the ethical issues at stake.[83] It is evident that the theories discussed in the chapter all have their limitations. Just War Theory has unashamed roots in early Christianity and does not necessarily chime with other religions or societal values. But as Charles Guthrie and Michael Quinlan point out, there are more linkages with early Islamic and Judaic texts.[84] Many of the issues in international law and in the morality of going to war have universal application. It is therefore incumbent on all students of air power and air warfare not only to follow and understand the rules of engagement and targeting criteria, but also have an appreciation of the wider sources and debates.

A case study: The road to strategic bombing

As has been discussed, the UK never ratified the Hague Rules of 1923, but it was clear that Neville Chamberlain did his utmost to ensure that the Air Ministry adhered to the principles enshrined therein. This case study will examine the gradual process through which the decisions were taken to move towards unrestricted bombing.

The use of air power in Spain (and in particular in Barcelona in March 1938 where bombardment had been used with the threat that it would be repeated every three hours until the city surrendered) and by the Japanese in China was cited as evidence that 'the only way to humanise war is to abolish it'.[85] The prime minister admitted that the advent of air warfare had introduced 'new methods, new scope and new horrors which have, in fact materially changed its character'.[86] He went on to admit that there was 'no international code of law with respect to aerial warfare which is the subject of international agreement', but that the underlying principles of the law as it applied to sea and land warfare were applicable to the air 'and are not only admitted but insisted upon by this Government'.[87] These principles included that it was

> against international law to bomb civilians as such, and to make deliberate attacks upon civilian populations.
>
> In the second place, targets which are aimed at from the air must be legitimate military objectives and must be capable of identification.
>
> In the third place, reasonable care must be taken in attacking those military objectives so that by carelessness a civilian population in the neighbourhood is not bombed.[88]

This expression of formal government policy was reiterated to Bomber Command in response to a query from the C-in-C on 30 August 1938 that in attacking German aircraft factories, a proportion of bombs would fall outside the immediate designated target area causing serious casualties among the civilian population.[89] The Air Council replied on 15 September 1938 having taken advice from Malkin.[90] The Air Council admitted that 'there are certain objectives, particularly among aircraft factories, which it would be impossible to attack, even by day, without causing loss of life to the civilian population in the neighbourhood'. The operational limitations were again acknowledged, but

> for reasons of policy, however, which the Council feel sure you will readily understand, it is essential that in the opening stages of a war your action should be rigorously restricted to attack on objectives which are manifestly and unmistakably military on the narrowest interpretation of the term; and that even such objectives should not be attacked initially unless they can be clearly identified and attacked with a reasonable expectation of damage being confined to them.

The policy was based on the need not to alienate neutral opinion (not stated, but presumably America as Roosevelt had appealed for such restraint) and to avoid giving any 'genuine pretext for retaliatory action'. Attacks would therefore have to be concentrated on targets such as railways (but not trains unless positively identified as military), formed bodies of troops and concentrations of transport. Newall, in submitting this directive to Swinton for approval concluded that these restrictions were unlikely to last long stating 'But we obviously cannot be the first "to take the gloves off".'[91]

Chamberlain's acknowledgement of the parallel nature of some of the laws of war came into focus in 1939 when the Admiralty raised the question of bombardment of targets on the shore including coastal defence works and docks.[92] The CAS wrote to his naval counterpart (Admiral Dudley Pound) suggesting that Malkin chair a meeting with representation from each of the services to discuss setting rules to prevent loss of civilian life.[93] The meeting went into considerable detail and outlined a two-stage approach with first restricting bombardment to a very narrow interpretation of military objectives and the second allowing a broader approach consistent with the lines agreed with the French in Staff Conversations.[94] The instructions, which Army commanders were to be required to obey in spirit, reiterated the key principles of bombardment of civilians being illegal.[95] In the event, foreign policy issues intervened with Lord Halifax of the opinion that the original 'Stage One was too restrictive and would alarm our allies'.[96] These were duly issued by the Air Council to air officers commanding at home and overseas on 22 August 1939, followed by a further letter enclosing 'Air Ministry Instructions and Notes on the Rules to be observed by the Royal Air Force in War'.[97] In setting the foundations for the future direction of war, the Air Ministry letter included the following general statement:

> The policy governing the selection of targets for air attack is a matter for decision by the government. This policy will be made known, through the Air Ministry, to Commanders-in-Chief and will be reflected in operation orders'.[98]

The practicalities of who would be allowed to do what and when were discussed by the Chiefs of Staff and subsequently in the CID on 1 September 1939. The essence of the discussion was that if Germany initiated unrestricted air attacks at the outset of hostilities, Bomber Command would be used to attack the German oil resources. If, however, Germany was to restrict attacks to military objectives, the RAF would attack the German fleet at Wilhelmshaven; attack warships at sea when found within range; undertake widespread propaganda (leaflet) drops at night; and 'conserve resources until our hands are freed'.[99]

Bomber Command therefore went to war with bombing policy predicated on the foreign policy requirements consistent with President Roosevelt's message to all potential belligerents that their 'armed forces shall in no event and under no circumstances undertake bombardment from the air of civilian populations or unfortified cities, upon the understanding that the same rules of warfare shall be scrupulously observed by all their opponents'.[100] The other constraint (imposed by Halifax) was that the rules should not appear overly restrictive lest allies (France, in particular) think that Britain was being overly cautious in the interests of its own defence. But throughout the process, it is clear that the serving officers, at least from group captain and above, were prepared to follow a restrictive approach. It could be argued that this was a merely mechanical reaction based on the, admittedly high, likelihood that the gloves would indeed have to come off at some stage. But the evidence suggests that if those in the Air Ministry were cynical about the whole issue, they had the sense to not confide their doubts to the files destined for the archives! But as Parks has pointed out, even the international lawyers of the day doubted the applicability of the international law of war to the modern means at the disposal of nations on an unprecedented scale.[101] Interestingly, Parks acknowledges the failures in diplomacy, but has hard words for the failure of international lawyers and moral philosophers of the time 'who failed to adjust international law and moral thinking to major technological changes in society and warfare'.[102] Nor could the scholars claim that the issues had not been raised.[103] That said, neither the government nor the private citizens had much faith in international agreements providing them with protection.[104] The reality of the international experience of the 1930s where Britain had attempted to set the example by unilaterally disarming had been shown to be false logic. International agreements appeared to mean little to the new breed of dictators as events were proving. And the ready examples of the use of air power in Abyssinia, Spain and China suggested that the analogy of 'removing gloves' was mild in the extreme.

The raw reality of the first months of the war was that the RAF was not technologically capable of carrying heavy bombing raids into German territory irrespective of the rights or wrongs; in the words of the official historians, 'Bomber Command was small, ill equipped and ineffective.'[105] This was recognized within the COS as was the need to build up strength in what became known as the 'phoney war'.[106] Within the Air Ministry, the director of Plans (Slessor), as early as 7 September 1939, carried out a detailed review of German actions in Poland working on the basis that Germany had set the precedent for unrestricted attack.[107] The official historians point out that it was 'Air Commodore Slessor's duty to examine this question from every side, and his memorandum should not be taken as an indication that he or the Air Staff were at this time definitely opposed to the policy of restricted bombing'.[108] Nevertheless, they added that the policy was as much a matter of expediency as of morality.[109] This view was directly reflected in the words used by Newall in a telegram to Barratt in France some weeks later in which he said:

> Owing to German action in Poland, we are no longer bound by restrictions under the instructions governing naval and air bombardment S.46239/S.6 of 22/8 nor by our acceptance of Roosevelt's appeal. Our action is now governed entirely by expediency i.e. what it suits us to do having regard to (a) the need to conserve our resources; (b) probable enemy retaliatory action, and (c) our need still to take into account to some extent influential neutral opinion.[110]

At face value, this would appear as if Slessor's appreciation of the situation had been accepted by the CAS and policy had changed formally. The reality, however, is that the strategic air offensive was held in check for many months and prohibition on indiscriminate bombing remained in place until 1942 and explicitly reinforced on a number of occasions as will be covered below. From the wording used by the Air Staff, including in formal directives, it is clear that while Newall would have liked to change RAF policy, government policy had not moved at all.[111] Chamberlain clearly believed that the war would 'fizzle out with the collapse of the Nazi regime' and an escalation in the use of air power may have exacerbated the situation.[112] He had also seen the bombing force primarily as a deterrent from the beginning of the rearmament phase.[113] Chamberlain also fundamentally believed that Britain should have the 'moral right' on her side as it would be a 'tremendous force on our side' and that if bombing started it would be 'worth a lot for us to be able to blame them for it'.[114] It is possible that Chamberlain's mindset over countries far away prevented him from agreeing with Slessor's establishment of the precedent.

The question of expediency and morality had to be reviewed, first in the light of the invasion of Denmark and Norway on 9 April 1940 and then the Low Countries in May 1940. Following consideration by the COS, fresh instructions were issued on 4 June 1940 in which the term 'military' was to be interpreted in the broadest sense; lines of communication which were usable for military purposes were included.[115] From this point, there was a gradual escalation in what Bomber Command was being asked to carry out, and what it sought permission to attempt.[116] For example, in part in retaliation for the bombing attacks on London, the C-in-C sought permission to attack the 'middle of Berlin' citing the German War Office and Air Ministry as appropriate aiming points.[117] Newall's response was to substitute 'Railway Communications' and not mention the former targets![118] Nevertheless it is clear from a minute sent by SASO Bomber Command (AVM Bottomley) to the Groups which reminded them that the behaviour of aircrews from 'another Command' in jettisoning their bombs through cloud without being able to identify the target was not acceptable; the minute concluded unequivocally that 'bombs are not to be dropped indiscriminately'.[119]

The retaliatory nature of the escalation is apparent from the directive issued to the Command at the end of October 1940. This included the need to attack the morale of the German people 'when they can no longer expect an early victory'.[120] In addition to attacks on oil, and aluminium and component factories, there should be raids to cause 'heavy material destruction in large towns and centres of industry' as a demonstration 'to the enemy of the power and severity of air bombardment and the hardships and dislocation that will result'.[121] These attacks were to include high explosives, incendiaries, delayed action bombs and 'the occasional mine'.[122] Part of the rationale was to impose pressure on the fire services.[123] These instructions clearly mirror the experiences of London over the period and again echo the place of retaliatory action in the culture of the times (which had been present since the German Zeppelin raids of 1916). After an interlude, which was planned to be about four months, where the directives focused on anti-submarine activities, a 'comprehensive review of the enemy's present political, economic and military situation' disclosed that the 'weakest points in his armour lie in the morale of the civilian population and in his inland transportation system'.[124] Although barely mentioned in the directive, the aim of the review was to see what could be done to assist Russia.[125] The other important milestone in this directive was the inclusion of '*Targets on water suitable for concentrated and continuous area attacks on moonless nights*' (emphasis in the original); these targets were 'congested industrial towns where the psychological effect will be the greatest' and included Cologne, Dusseldorf, Duisburg and Duisburg-Ruhrort.[126] The section on Duisburg, almost certainly inadvertent considering the emotive tones it would later carry, included the word 'area'.[127]

This period saw the Chiefs of Staff conclude that, after 'meeting the needs of our own security', the heavy bomber would receive top priority in production in order to destroy the 'foundations upon which the [German] war machine rests – the economy which sustains it, the morale which sustains it, the supplies which nourish it and the hopes of victory which inspire it'.[128] The Directorate of Bomber Operations worked up this plan and the CAS (Sir Charles Portal) submitted it to Churchill who was doubtful, to say the least.[129] The prime minister was clearly concerned that the required resources, based on the extant woeful lack of accuracy, would not produce the effects that the Air Ministry predicted.[130] The situation was compounded by depressingly high casualty figures among the aircrews that, if sustained, would prevent the force from ever generating sufficient crews to man the expanded force.[131] Accordingly, directives were issued emphasizing the conservation of forces 'in order to build a strong force to be available by the spring of next year [1942]'.[132] This recuperative lull, and the impending introduction of navigation aids such as Gee, enabled the Air Ministry to issue the Directive of 14 February 1942 (notably to Air Marshal Baldwin who was acting C-in-C prior to the arrival of Harris) in which he was 'accordingly authorised to employ your effort *without restriction*' (emphasis added).[133] The directive acknowledged that this renewal of the offensive 'on a heavy scale' would 'enhearten [*sic*] and support the Russians'.[134] Furthermore, the directive of 9 July 1941 was modified because it had been decided that the 'primary object' of Bomber Command operations 'should now be focused on the morale of the enemy civil population and in particular, of the industrial workers'.[135] It would be all too easy to take the critical words 'without restriction' out of context and imply that this meant the formal institution of terror bombing.

   Throughout the first three years of the war, the legality and morality of the strategic air offensive were inextricably interlinked with what was technically possible. It is clear from Churchill's frustration over the lack of urgency in carrying out reprisals included an element of moral argument.[136] For much of the period, Britain fought without effective allies with whom a coalition strategy could have offered an alternative to bombing. In efforts to have some real effect on the German war machine, the march towards unrestricted area bombing was inevitable. The unthinkable option of coming to terms with Germany passed and the focus of those charged with the conduct of the war moved to come up with strategy that offered a credible way to win. W. V. Herbert's 1898 RUSI lecture had stressed the importance of winning 'with all of the rest coming a long way after' and was arguably increasingly relevant as the war became 'more total'.[137] In many ways, it was easier for those charged with decision-making if the movement (one would hardly call it progress) towards totality in warfare and was gradual and the decisions could be taken incrementally rather than in a single step.[138] This incremental process, and the central role played by Portal as C-in-C and then CAS, must be acknowledged. The Directive of 1942 was in place before Harris arrived as C-in-C. Although he had been involved in policy formulation when he was DCAS, this was earlier in the war and although he was subsequently an advocate of the Offensive, he was not its sole author or architect.

CHAPTER EIGHT

Air warfare strategy, operations and tactics

Each of the previous chapters in this book in its own way sets the scene and contributes to this chapter on the history, theory and practice of air warfare at the strategic, operational and tactical levels. History, air power theory, leadership, command, law and ethics all fuse to deliver fighting power in the air. This chapter will review the traditional levels of warfare before analysing the use of air power at each level. A key factor in all discussions of levels of warfare is the interrelationship between them. This is often blurred by casual expressions such as 'the strategic corporal' which emanated from the opportunities that exist in peacekeeping operations for the simple tactical actions of squads or platoons to have repercussions at the strategic level. A more classical or rigorous description would see direction, exercised through command and leadership, being passed down through each level with outcomes being fed back up through the levels.[1] It could be argued that this model is rather simplistic in that although it is perfectly feasible at an official level, there have been many instances of the linkages being bypassed. In modern times, outcomes can be transmitted back through social media, emails, by mobile phone, through the media, or by diverse means such as personnel in the field communicating directly with their elected representative (member of Parliament, congressman or senator). Equally, direction and guidance can come direct from the prime minister to a commander at the field at wing commander or group captain level.[2] Theoretically, the wording should be consistent through the command chain, but there is always scope for differing interpretations and nuances. None of this is new. Haig used to send his diaries back to his wife from the Western Front and she in turn forwarded segments to King George V. Similarly, Churchill was very free in his exercise of his powers as Minister of Defence to communicate with subordinates without going through the Chiefs of Staff.[3]

Air warfare, with the inherent flexibility of air power, is arguably more able than other forms of warfare to cross the theoretical boundaries between the levels of warfare. This is of course aided by the tendency to command and control air power at the highest possible levels thereby creating the conditions for its flexible use. Furthermore, throughout the history of air warfare, the range and speed of aircraft have allowed them to be deployed between theatres of operation with considerable rapidity. This was certainly true in the Second World War with Bomber Command operating over Germany one night and then being deployed to the Mediterranean theatre.[4] The same is true in modern uses of air warfare, considerably enhanced by 'reachback' in which intelligence, imagery and other time-sensitive material is sent back to a home station by satellite link for analysis and further action.

Levels of warfare

The *grand strategic* level of warfare appears in some doctrinal manuals, but not in others. For example, it was noted in the second edition of British defence doctrine, but is missing from the fifth.[5] One only has to examine the black-and-white photographs of Churchill, Roosevelt and Stalin at conferences such as Yalta where they were deciding on the shape of the post-war world to believe that this exalted level of warfare does exist. It may not be in place all of the time in practice, but it remains there to be occupied. Examination of proceedings of these conferences and of the recollections of those present reveals the momentous nature of the material under discussion. An early example of the workings of the Combined Chiefs of Staff in the Second World War adds more colour to concept with the president and the prime minister along their national Chiefs of Staff at Casablanca (minus General Brooke). The stakes at the conference were high in the immediate aftermath of Pearl Harbor as the British were deeply concerned that their new allies (especially Admiral King) would wish to change war priorities from 'Germany first' to the Pacific.[6] The Americans were equally concerned that, following victory in Europe, the British interest in the war effort would wane, leaving them to shoulder even more of the Pacific burden. Overlap with the strategic level is shown in that the US Navy owned the bulk of the landing craft and was averse to transferring them from the Pacific.[7]

More modern examples of the relationships at the grand strategic level include that between President Reagan and Prime Minister Margaret Thatcher with help for the UK over the Falklands campaign and over Operation *Eldorado Canyon* (the US bombing of Libya in 1986).[8] Grand strategic level discussions are normally the preserve of the prime minister or president of the countries concerned, but heads of defence or even lower-level officers may be crucial. The same of course applies with civil servants. An example of senior officers, but below Chief of Defence Staff level, operating at the grand strategic level arguably occurred in the planning for the second Gulf War. Because of the Goldwater-Nichols legislation in the United States, General Tommy Franks dealt with the Defense Secretary directly, bypassing the Pentagon. This caused considerable frustration in the MoD because they could not find out what was happening. The real linkage was between Franks and (then Lieutenant General) Sir John Reith who was running the Permanent Joint Headquarters as Chief of Joint Operations.[9] It could be argued that this was a genuinely strategic level interface rather than grand strategic. But given the political sensitivity of the planning for the 2003 invasion, the opposite view is more valid.

The *strategic level* is rather more straightforward. In the latest version of *UK Defence Policy*, strategy is defined as the creation and orchestration of the instruments of power in support of long-term policy objectives.[10] The instruments of power should be duly exercised at governmental level and include the military, economic, diplomatic, intelligence, information and so on. This requires some form of mechanism for coordination, particularly of top-level guidance. In the ideal world, this should be linked across a matrix of departments at international level. The so-called Phase 4 operations in the aftermath of the second Gulf War show the confusion that can ensue when this is put together piecemeal.[11] One of the key issues with strategic planning is the need to separate a coordinated, long-term vision of an outcome to a particular problem from short-term policy imperatives. This ideal is further complicated by the realities that the vision has to be affordable. Another important factor at the strategic level is to acknowledge that all of the problems potentially facing a government or coalition are interlinked. Actions in one theatre may have significant consequences in another. Managing the interfaces is therefore hugely important and requires leadership of the highest order.

In both an air warfare context and in the wider military field, care has to be taken in the use of vocabulary. Strategic has been used to indicate long range of aircraft such as with airlift. It has also been regularly used in the context of nuclear weapons delivery. The term has also been used to describe operations across conventional theatre boundaries.

For advocates of effects-based warfare (see below), the use of *air power for strategic effect* is important. This is a concept that is employed regularly in practice, but is in and out of favour in doctrinal publications.[12] In the UK, for example, strategic effect was quoted as a distinct role of air power in Edition 3 of AP 3000, but had disappeared by the time the next was published.[13] The former defined air operations for strategic effect as being 'aimed to destroy or disrupt the defined strategic centre of gravity of an opponent'.[14] The key challenge in this is actually arriving at the definition. It would be all too easy just to come up with a list of military or infrastructure targets that would fit into an air-tasking order and then be legally cleared. The problem, however, is that for many potential enemy leaders, military targets may not be of any strategic significance. An analysis of Operation

Allied Force during which NATO targeted many facilities in Serbia has shown that field forces were difficult to find and largely irrelevant to Milosevic.[15] Given that at least part of the ethnic cleansing, which had spurred the international community into undertaking action, was being conducted by paramilitary forces, attacking regular Serbian Army units was not a particularly relevant course of action. More importantly, it was irrelevant to Milosevic's perceptions of his own centre of gravity which was his hold on power. The practical aspects of this had been well covered over the previous years, especially in relation to the sanctions regimes in place. The bottom line, in all senses of the phrase, was the economic interests of Milosevic's cronies in controlling hard currency exchange (sent home by the Serbian diaspora), energy supplies, tobacco and so on. Lieutenant General Mike Short as air component commander took a more conventional air power planner's perspective on attacking more strategic targets.[16] From a strict intelligence assessment perspective this would have come closer to Milosevic's own centre of gravity, but in the early stages of the campaign would have given NATO authorities a difficult task to approve targets. If one adds what Lambeth describes as Clark's 'aggressive micromanagement' to the mix, one may be forgiven for concluding that air operations should be left to those who understand them – airmen.[17]

Several factors come from this. The first is the intelligence preparation in which the opponent's own view of his strategic centre of gravity is analysed. The second is an assessment of the means that would have to be employed to have an effect on it. This will almost invariably have serious legal and ethical problems associated as identifying the military necessity of attacking dual- and civilian-use facilities can be difficult. Similarly ensuring that collateral damage is minimized is difficult, especially where power systems have been deliberately arranged to ensure that military facilities are on the same grid as civilian hospitals; Milosevic had clearly learnt from Saddam Hussein in this respect. Third, post-attack assessment has to go beyond a statistical survey of damage done and must include an analysis of the impact of the attacks on the opponent's centre of gravity. Finally, the spat between the senior leaders over targeting and micromanagement leads to the conclusion that the exercise of air power is best left to professional airmen experienced in its delivery and practised in its art. In reality, this can only be done by airmen from an independent air force.

Air power can be projected for strategic effect in a number of ways. The most obvious is very specific targeting of key installations with either conventional or, possibly, tactical nuclear weapons with the aim of denying or destroying extremely high-value assets. But a similar effect could be had indirectly just by demonstrating a military capability as had occurred with the Vulcan raids on Port Stanley airfield during the 1982 Falklands campaign. The Argentine government moved air defence assets to the north to protect Buenos Aires.[18] But strategic effect can be achieved by other means beyond the attack role of air power. Air transport can have real impact by delivering aid, evacuating nationals or doing casualty evacuation. Although controversial for a number of reasons, including that it was just a reaction to media criticism, Operation *Irma* arguably did have a strategic effect. This involved the medical evacuation of the five-year-old Irma Hadžimuratović from Sarajevo in August 1993 after the personal intervention of Prime Minister John Major. Notwithstanding the various debates on being reactive to the media, and not using the equivalent money to aid people locally, the RAF Hercules airlift had a major impact on British public opinion and, more importantly, marked a turning point in wider Western attitudes to the conflict; the Bosnian Serbs certainly saw it as a hardening of resolve.[19] Air power can also have strategic effect when used in conjunction with special forces, either in direct support or used in parallel. On a large scale, the Berlin airlift was a classic example of non-kinetic air power for strategic effect.[20]

The *operational level* of war is the level at which operations are planned, conducted, monitored and sustained; this has to be done in accordance with the strategic aims.[21] In practice, the operational level of war sits between the strategic and the tactical. But the conflicts in Iraq and Afghanistan have arguably taken the operational level of warfare to either a higher or a more sophisticated level. With the first Gulf War giving way to no-fly zone operations over northern and southern Iraq and then the second Gulf War, along with well over a decade in Afghanistan, flying on operations has become the norm for many airmen and women. Does the J. F. C. Fuller description of 'grand tactics' adequately reflect what has been going on?[22] It may well be that the phrase has just entered the military subconscious mind whereby all understand what it means and are content to leave it at that. But over the course of the use of the term it has come to mean much more. In some cases this level has denoted a particular theatre of operations. In other cases, it is an area in which a commander of a given status or rank has had responsibility for a segment of the wider battle. Similarly it has been construed as a particular campaign. For Lieutenant General John Kizley, it is determined by 'where operational art is practised'.[23] Major General David Zabecki, late of the US Army, also has described operational art as being the link between tactics and strategy. He has likened it to the chain linking the handle (strategy) of a medieval morning star to the spiked ball used to inflict the blow (tactics).[24]

The literature on the operational level of war, and operational art, has tended to reflect that for much of the last century certainly UK armed forces were content to rely on tactics, training and procedures, leaving all higher levels to one side. That has certainly been true of air power during the Cold War where doctrinal thinking went into hibernation with units relying exclusively on NATO material.[25] Again in the Cold War context, Edward Luttwak has described as 'a major eccentricity in the modern Anglo-Saxon experience of war' in which officers engaged in conducting warfare not only do 'not *speak* the word [operational], but rather that they do not *think* or practice war in operational terms' (emphasis in the original).[26] Mackenzie and Holden Reid in the preface to an edited volume of essays taken from the first of the UK Higher Command and Staff College (HCSC) courses held in 1988 stated that for the British army, doctrine above the tactical level had 'always been an anathema'.[27]

That was a prime reason for the introduction of the course. Now its students come to the course with extensive operational experience.[28] Shimon Naveh has reflected these sentiments, stating that 'Western failure to coin a term to cover the operational field indicates, first and foremost, the lack of cognition regarding that field'.[29]

The historical backdrop therefore suggests that many Western style forces were late in thinking about the operational level of war, in marked contrast to the Soviets who invested a lot of time and intellectual energy in the interwar years.[30] But it is suggested that a combination of factors such as the AirLand Battle doctrine introduced by the United States in the 1980s and the Bagnall Reforms leading to the creation of the HCSC changed the understanding of this landscape. Particularly for air warfare, the operational level is not a closed environment; it is open to external influences and no theatre can be hermetically sealed.[31] The important key for success at the operational level, or true operational art, is the management of the interfaces between the core elements essential for tactical success and the wider factors and entities. One of the more important interfaces to be considered is between theatres of operations, and a deep understanding of the competing demands and priorities is essential. A classic example of this was Tedder's intuitive understanding of the pressures on Portal as CAS for the priorities on the provision of bombers either to the strategic air offensive against Germany or to the Middle East. Tedder's attitudes stood in marked contrast to the unequivocal stance taken by Harris.[32] Portal indeed had frequent cause to remonstrate with Harris; in one such letter, Portal wrote:

> I feel bound to tell you frankly that I do not regard it as either a credit to your intelligence or a contribution to the winning of the war. It is in my opinion wrong in both tone and substance and calculated to promote unnecessary and useless friction between your Headquarters, the Air Ministry, and Headquarters Middle East.[33]

In contrast, Tedder having requested, as opposed to demanded, the loan of three Wellington squadrons in 1943 wrote that he 'understood how difficult it must be to adjudicate between rival claims, and how hard it was once units had been transferred from one theatre to another to secure their recall'.[34] It is equally important for there to be a close cooperation between the components within the operational theatre, ideally with co-located headquarters. The modern disposition of Combat Air Operations Centres makes this exceptionally difficult to achieve. The deployment of high-quality liaison officers between commanders' headquarters is as essential as a backup.

Most operations are not just joint, but are combined with those of other nations. These can be within a standing alliance such as NATO or ad hoc depending on the operational theatre. It is essential again that this interface is properly managed. Operations in Iraq, Afghanistan and Libya have all shown the difficulties, and vital need, to be able to operate alongside and in support of indigenous forces. While many of these understand land power, they are less comfortable understanding air power or maritime operations. This is especially true when there is a collateral damage situation and explanations have to be forthcoming. The final interface to be mentioned, and there are undoubtedly others, is that which exists between the military and other government departments in the operational theatre. This could be diplomatic, or equally as likely with organizations such as the Department for International Development (DfID). They in turn provide an interface with non-governmental organizations and charities, many of which are antithetical to the military.

All of the interfaces detailed have inherent problems. In the first instance, there may be differences in priorities at the strategic level in capitals over where money and effort should be directed. Where intelligence agencies are involved, there are often issues between source protection and using the information for tactical success. There are always resource challenges both in theatre and between theatres. Less obvious, but equally important, there are cultural issues between allies and indigenous force; among allies; between other government departments; and still between the different components. Managing these interfaces requires operational staff and their commanders to be willing to look upwards and outwards and not merely focus on their own tactical silos, however much of a comfort zone they represents. Processes may help, but reliance on them or on the doctrine is unlikely to be sufficient.

The final area worthy of discussion under operational art is the relationship between operations and the wider society on whose behalf they are conducted. This may, at first sight, appear to be a strategic-level responsibility. It may well be, but the realities of news media, social media and so on make the operational level especially important. This is true whether it is just getting across the broad air power message, or constructing the narrative. The experiences again of the last twenty-five years suggest that any message from theatre is more dynamic, immediate and convincing than from spokespersons in London, or other capitals, in suits or dress uniforms. Perceptions can be all-important and it can be particularly important for air power to have a human face, especially in remotely piloted air operations. Probably the bottom line is that when the public are fed a diet of gloom, high expenditure, unconvincing rationale for involvement and, worst of all, coffins returning home, an operational focus may be essential in restoring balance.

In summary, the operational level is not just a simple linkage between tactics and strategy. Operational art has its own unique challenges and requires a high standard of leadership. The environment is complex and ambiguous; it is multifaceted and does not lend itself to simple solutions.

The *tactical level* of air warfare, and indeed any form of warfare, is where most operators, and many students, are most comfortable. The tactical level is where individuals and groups are in contact with the enemy and execute the instructions from higher levels of war. This is the level at which ordnance is discharged, loads delivered, fuel transferred, information gathered and airspace secured. In his *Ten Propositions Regarding Air Power*, Phil Meilinger wrote: 'In essence, airpower is targeting, targeting is intelligence, and intelligence is analyzing the effect of air operations.'[35] Each element of this is worth analysing starting with intelligence.

As an academic discipline, intelligence is something of a Cinderella subject, not least because the primary source material is difficult to obtain. Without wishing to enter the so-called wilderness of mirrors, a problem with intelligence is that the researcher never really knows what has been withheld. R. V. Jones has written that the 'ultimate object of Intelligence is to enable action to be optimized'.[36] It has to be collected, sifted, collated, analysed and then published in some way appropriate to its end use. Intelligence for subsequent use by air forces, airmen and for targeting can be gained in a number of ways. Open-source material from maps, charts, guide books or material from air shows, aircraft trade shows and so on can all be collated.[37] More traditional material can come from signals traffic analysis, signals and communications interception, human intelligence, aerial and satellite imagery, from prisoner-of-war debriefings, from various technical sources such as bugging and so on. Intelligence is graded at particular security classification levels often with code words such as Ultra. As with academic research, one source may be vital for one piece of work, but useless for the other. The sifting and analysis process can only be done with the end product in mind. This can take several forms including orders of battle, troop and equipment dispositions, weapons stocks and capabilities, tactics and procedures, means of concealment and so on. Some materials will be more carefully guarded than others with cryptographic and similar means of security. That said it is often possible to gain a reasonable picture just from signals traffic pattern analysis.[38]

Building orders of battle and so forth is relatively straightforward in comparison to the softer aspects of generating an intelligence picture. It is, for example, possible to determine that an enemy is moving from place to place, but much more difficult to determine the commander's intentions unless his orders can be intercepted and read. This was one of the key benefits of the Ultra product during the Second World War. Similarly assessing the morale, leadership or stamina of individuals is difficult. Given the importance that was attached to breaking the morale of the German people through the strategic air offensive, it is surprising that more was not done to assess it.

With the exception of a Joint Intelligence Committee Report in October 1943, very little intelligence work had been done on the subject since at least before America entered the war.[39] For air power to be effective, it is essential for the intelligence preparation be of the highest order. This applies throughout the levels of warfare from aiding the decision to go to war such as the dossier on Iraq's weapons of mass destruction, through the whereabouts of key leaders to basic tactical deployments.[40]

Having carried out the necessary intelligence preparation, it is then necessary to ascertain what effect on the enemy is required and to balance this with the resources available. The resource equation, at the higher levels, has to be done with the competing demands of other theatres in mind as discussed above. Military staffs have various campaign-planning tools available and it is not the place of this book to replace or repeat these. But it is worth taking Meilinger's comment on 'the effect of air operations' a little further. Much ink has been spilt on concepts such as 'effects based operations', and again a full review of the literature is not appropriate here.[41] Like many theories, effects-based operations has waned in its popularity, but some of the key issues remain valid. In planning and executing the air campaign, it has to be a reasonable assumption that weapon stocks are finite and need to be conserved for fiscal as well as for tactical and operational reasons. Furthermore, the principles of international law discussed earlier in this book prohibit destruction for its own sake. The classic approach in drawing up a target list may be to decide that the target nation's war economy is wholly dependent on oil and that attacks on this commodity would weaken the industrial base, slow down production, deprive fielded forces of fuel and demoralize the population; this was effectively the basis for the oil directives given to Bomber Command in 1944.[42] For Harris and his American colleagues in the Second World War, complete destruction of the whole plant was the only real option. As weapons delivery systems have become more accurate and precise, individual elements of the production and distribution systems can be targeted; these may include control facilities or distribution points. This is the basic level of achieving effect. The higher level is then to check on whether the attacks have had the desired effect on the war economy, the industrial base and so on. This, in turn, then needs to be weighed against whether the aims of the campaign, conflict or war are being achieved.

An analysis of air campaigns over the years will almost certainly indicate that this approach has not been followed. Rather, target lists have been drawn up on the basis of a campaign of destruction and attrition. The early phases of Operation *Allied Force* showed this characteristic until the increase in the tempo of the air campaign allowed for more suitable targets to be attacked. It should also be accepted that tactical targeting may have been undertaken for reasons obscure than purist effects-based operations would require. Military planners have a penchant for needing an 'end state' to be achieved in their campaign in order for success to be achieved. This end state is usually artificial in nature and may bear no resemblance to political reality. An end state constructed for the air campaigns over Kosovo or Libya would have been widely at variance with the political landscape that has endured in both areas. A key factor in this is that military campaign planning is, by necessity, a linear and mechanical process. The real problems in such campaigns are not amenable to simple solutions: they are complex and ambiguous. Tying the target list for the campaign into the wider military campaign and then into the political realm requires a great deal of agility, understanding and intellectual capacity.

Concluding thoughts

One of the key issues that emerges from discussions on air power at the various levels of warfare is the open question as to how valid the traditional models are now, and possibly have been over the last century. The ability of air power to range over different theatres of war on consecutive days has changed the complexion of warfare. The Second World War was probably a watershed in this regard with conventional leaders at the political level (Churchill) and senior officers in the other services not really grasping how much warfare had changed. The airmen certainly understood, but probably did not do enough to educate their colleagues. A simple manifestation of this occurred in the context of the Bomber Command campaign medal saga where the Air Member for Personnel, in August 1945 wrote to the PUS, the CAS and the Secretary of State as follows:

> The Committee gave the Air Ministry representatives a sympathetic hearing. But the fact of the matter is that the Committee is comprised of senior civil servants, generals and admirals who are really incapable of war except in terms of battlefields and 'theatres of war' geographically defined, and of course everything afloat. They cannot understand that the air has changed everything.[43]

The ability of aircraft to cross conventional theatre boundaries and influence the course of warfare while returning to home base in Britain had completely changed the paradigm.[44] Arguably the boundaries have continued to blur for the student and practitioner of air power. But, as has been demonstrated, the traditional descriptions are still in current doctrinal publications, continue to be taught and the words themselves are in common usage.

This discussion has been based largely on conventional warfare and has drawn on historical examples from the Second World War, Kosovo War and Libyan Civil War. Many of the principles hold together over the spectrum. It is, however, worth considering the use of air power in conflicts and operations where the political requirements are diffuse or unstated. Air power, not least because of its impermanence, and because of its high media profile has the capacity to allow politicians to demonstrate to an audience clamouring for something to be done, that action has indeed been taken. The initial motives may be sound and honourable such as in the Baby Irma case and evacuation from Sarajevo. But they could equally be no more than a cynical ploy to change headlines. The command chain at the time, as well as subsequent analysts, has to keep this in mind.

When it comes to operations short of war, such as countering terrorism or counter-insurgency, other factors also have to be considered across the span of the levels of warfare. The use of remotely piloted vehicles is a particularly relevant example as the consequences of their use have had repercussions far beyond the tactical gains made in theatre. The whole issue has been considerably complicated by the CIA's use of this technology for targeted killings prompting questions over legality, transparency and complicity between military and non-military personnel. Assertions that they are just ordinary platforms subject to the same targeting criteria have hardly placated the critics. Longer-term considerations also apply with concerns over whether air power generally does more harm than good in the communities over which operations take place. Just as the bombing of Dresden had significant strategic consequences beyond its tactical value, air operations over Afghanistan may have a lasting legacy. To what extent these should be factors for commanders and practitioners at the time is debatable. What is clear, however, is that these issues will remain at the forefront for generations of scholars.

A case study: Operation *Allied Force*

NATO's air operations over Serbia in 1999 provide an interesting case study in the use of air power for coercive political ends. It was, inevitable given the nature of affairs in the Balkans, a complex operation with the focus switching from the tactical to the grand strategic with alarming rapidity. It was not the sort of operation where the traditional campaign-planning tools provide a war-winning solution. Instead of dealing in levels of warfare, the strategic overtones were evident at all levels. This may beg the question as to whether levels of warfare remain relevant; they probably do as discussed earlier in this chapter, but the realities of the situation suggest that one cannot be overly rigid in their application.

At the very highest levels, the personalities involved were interesting. On the Serbian side, President Slobodan Milosevic had been in power since 1987 when he latched onto the plight of the Kosovo Serbs as a vehicle for his own rise to power.[45] He stripped Kosovo, and the Hungarian majority area of Vojvodina, of their status as autonomous provinces and vainly attempted in the former to redress the population balance by importing Serbs who had been displaced from other regions. The ethnic Albanian population still outnumbered the Serbs by a huge margin. Their 'shadow' economy

and political system functioned well; while Sarajevo was under siege and
Belgrade was in the grip of economic sanctions, Pristina appeared almost
prosperous in comparison with other parts of the Balkans – not least because
the Kosovo Albanian economy was supported by hard-currency remittances
from the diaspora. Milosevic was able to maintain his power and influence
by playing on the nationalistic traits of his countrymen and, through the
Serbian Socialist Party (SPS), by controlling elections and the black market.
The fragile stability in Kosovo was maintained under the benign rule of
Ibrahim Rugova whose pacifist stance tended to reduce the possibility of
strife.[46] But no one was naïve enough to doubt that Milosevic would not
hesitate to inflame the situation if domestic politics required a diversion,
or if the Albanians openly espoused independence. The subsequent (but
unconnected) collapse into anarchy of Albania in 1997 resulted in an
almost unlimited supply of weapons becoming available, and the scope
for armed insurrection suddenly opened. This mounting frustration, along
with a massive influx of light weaponry, resulted in the Kosovo Liberation
Army (KLA) growing from a minor bunch of disillusioned expatriates into a
serious threat to the Serbian authorities. The cycle of violence expanded with
the inevitable counteroffensives through 1998. The spectre of massacres,
ethnic cleansing and other atrocities prompted the international community
into the Rambouillet talks process.[47] Milosevic could not accept the terms
on offer, not least because they would have allowed NATO unbridled access
to any part of Yugoslavia, and was therefore an excessive infringement
of sovereignty.[48] Having come to, and maintained, power on the basis of
rabid nationalism, he could not back down without some semblance of a
fight. There was a clear risk of secession, and the details of the agreement
contained, from Belgrade's perspective, serious erosions of Serbia's
sovereignty.[49] Acceptance would have been political suicide for Milosevic –
not a trait for which he was renowned.

On the Allied side, a key player in the plot was Madeleine Albright, the
United States secretary of state under President Clinton. She was born in
Czechoslovakia and was the daughter of a Czech diplomat who at one stage
was stationed in Belgrade. She considered Milosevic to be a bully, and that
he would only understand the use of force against him as had occurred
previously over Bosnia in Operation *Deliberate Force*.[50] The application of
force would only need to be as short as three to five days. Air power was
to be the weapon of first political choice, especially as there was absolutely
no appetite for any ground intervention. NATO authorities agreed this
assessment. This was an overly optimistic assessment based more on policy
aspirations than on an analytical study of Milosevic, his associates including
his wife and the secretive SPS, and the lessons they were likely to have drawn
from *Deliberate Force* and Operation *Desert Fox* over Iraq.[51] The other
significant difference between *Deliberate Force* and *Allied Force* was that
the former concentrated on military targets, primarily in Bosnia, where as
this new campaign was specifically focused on coercing the Serbian regime.[52]

Air power doctrine consistently emphasizes the importance of intelligence in planning air operations and this as true at the strategic level as it is in choosing specific target sets. It is significant that, at the time, there was no open dissent from the three-to-five-days duration assessment in Washington, London or NATO.

The second factor in intelligence preparation became apparent once the campaign was under way and in subsequent debriefs of senior commander after the event. It is clear that General Wes Clark (SACEUR) regarded the Serbian troops in Kosovo as being a top-priority target set.[53] Given that at least part of the ethnic cleansing was being conducted by paramilitary forces, this was not a particularly feasible course of action. More importantly, it was irrelevant to Milosevic's perceptions of his own centre of gravity which was his hold on power. The practical aspects of this had been well covered over the previous years, especially in relation to the sanctions regimes in place. The bottom line, in all senses of the phrase, was the economic interests of Milosevic's cronies in controlling hard currency exchange (sent home by the Serbian diaspora), energy supplies, tobacco and so on. Lieutenant General Mike Short as air component commander took a more conventional air power planners' perspective on attacking more strategic targets.[54] From a strict intelligence assessment perspective this would have come closer to Milosevic's own centre of gravity, but in the early stages of the campaign would have given NATO authorities a difficult task to approve targets. If one adds what Lambeth describes as Clark's 'aggressive micromanagement' to the mix, one may be forgiven for concluding that air operations should be left to those who understand them – airmen.[55]

Taking the question of the identification of centres of gravity a stage further it is instructive to note that both Milosevic and the NATO nations fully understood the importance of Alliance solidarity.[56] It is therefore highly ironic that when he ramped up the ethnic cleansing, Milosevic did the one thing most likely to outrage the international community and kill any protests. The air campaign started on 24 March and as Easter approached, there were calls, especially from Greece and Italy for a suspension in operations, both to respect the Christian festival and in the hope that negotiations could be resumed, but these were to no avail.

It is not for this book to detail the unfolding of the air campaign, not least because others have already done so. It is, however, worth making some general comments. The first of these is that Milosevic and his regime were capable and able to defend themselves.[57] The NATO forces were therefore confronted by wily opponents who were very circumspect about betraying their positions by using their radars and were also constrained by the allied concerns over friendly casualties weakening resolve (especially after US experiences in Somalia).The other constraint from which Milosevic would have taken solace was the very clear message that the air campaign would not be conducted in concert with a ground offensive. The initial attacks were designed to demonstrate the seriousness of NATO's determination to prevent the aggression in Kosovo and to degrade the defences, very much along the *Desert Storm* line.

Once it became clear that the 'bully' was not only resistant to force but was not going to fold within a few days, NATO was faced with the problem of increasing the pressure. The problem then was in the various constraints being imposed by nations' capitals. These ranged from restrictive rules of engagement, considerable dispute over attacking dual-use facilities (such as power supplies from the same source to hospitals and to command and control facilities) and the wider avoidance of collateral damage. Poor weather in the early period was compounded by the need to attack from over 10,000 feet to prevent losses to anti-aircraft artillery. Nevertheless, spurred on by Milosevic's continued brutality in Kosovo, the Alliance arguably became stronger, more resolute and more willing to expand its target portfolio eventually encompassing many of the facilities Short would have preferred to attack from the beginning.

So what did air power do?

Over the period from 24 March through to 9 June 1999, NATO succeeded in maintaining a 78-day offensive against Milosevic and the Serbian regime. It flew 38,004 sorties out of a planned 45,935 of which 10,484 were strikes.[58] From a UK perspective, it is interesting to note that many of the strike sorties were flown from home bases (in RAF Germany) with air-to-air refuelling support and the crews returning home to their families. This has echoes of the Second World War strategic air offensive as well as modern operations with remotely piloted vehicles. Indeed, as the USAF Historical Studies Office has pointed out, *Allied Force* saw the first significant employment of these vehicles.[59] The air campaign did not do much in the way of damage to the fielded forces and other ground military targets, many of which were well concealed and dispersed. As the campaign increased in intensity, NATO attacked a wider range of target sets and showed no sign whatsoever of relenting or abating their efforts. It can therefore be reasonably concluded that the air campaign, in concert with a range of other factors, and in no sense 'alone', created a political atmosphere conducive to a return to the negotiating table.

So why did Milosevic return
to the negotiating table?

As with Operation *Deliberate Force*, NATO nations showed that, however reluctant they may have been initially to use military force, once engaged, they were prepared to see the respective campaigns through to their logical conclusions. Milosevic's experiences at Dayton (Wright Patterson AFB) should have left him in no doubt whatsoever that NATO under US leadership had more than enough materiel to maintain a prolonged air operation. Although Milosevic had doubted NATO nations' resolve, the fragility of the Alliance was considerably strengthened by his ethnic cleansing tactics in Kosovo. The scale of the executions and expulsions was such that the stability of neighbouring states was threatened with potential long-term problems looming; NATO nations had no real alternative but to find a way of getting the displaced population home.[60] Where there may have been doubts over the legality and legitimacy of the air campaign at its outset, the international responsibility to halt the atrocities was overwhelming.[61] Although a long way from Milosevic's thinking, he inadvertently provided a platform for the international community to take punitive (or protective depending on the choice of language) action in the absence of a United Nations Security Council Chapter VII Resolution (which would have been vetoed by Russia and probably China); in doing so he advanced the cause of the Responsibility to Protect doctrine.[62]

Milosevic had also counted on support from Russia and while this may have been forthcoming in the United Nations, there was little or no prospect of them providing military support to Serbia.[63] Pan-Slavic support and anti-NATO rhetoric were all very well, but the Russian government under Yeltsin had wider diplomatic and especially economic interests to pursue. Furthermore, it was not in the interests of either Russia or NATO for the friction to escalate into conflict. Both sides were well aware that trouble in Yugoslavia had been a regular flashpoint for scenarios in Cold War exercise planning. The Russians had also convinced themselves that NATO was contemplating ground operations which would have increased the risk of the conflict spreading.[64] Russia's diplomatic support ebbed away to the point that they were willing to endorse NATO's terms when they were tabled in June 1999. That Russia was so convinced of this possibility would have also swayed Milosevic into thinking a ground offensive likely. Russian attitudes were also affected by the new terms on offer which were undoubtedly more realistic than those on the table at Rambouillet.

On the home front in Serbia the initial exuberant support for Milosevic against NATO was ebbing away. The early days of 'rock and bomb' concerts, decking bridges with bulls-eye targets and mass demonstrations had given way to demoralization, fatigue, hunger and fear.[65] The initial anger and resentment subsided into apathy, a not untypical reaction to a sustained bombing campaign as people's focus changes to survival under the pressure. As far back as the Second World War, where morale bombing was a stated objective, psychiatrists were aware that under such pressure it was important to differentiate between routine grumbling and the actions people took as a result of bombing.[66] Serbia had been under sanctions for some years by this stage and the economy was in poor shape. Basic food provisions were under pressure and the bombing of dual-use energy systems meant that electricity, running water and all types of fuel were in short supply. Many jobs were axed, payments to pensioners cut and arguably most importantly for many Serbs, queues for cigarettes were huge.[67] The routine hardships obviously contributed to the state of demoralization, but this was intensified by the belief in Serbia that NATO was deliberately targeting them as civilians. Milosevic's own propaganda actually backfired on him. Serbs were increasingly worried about the safety and well-being of themselves and their families. This was particularly the case in regions where high percentages of troops had been deployed to Kosovo sparking anti-war demonstrations that were now seeking a settlement at almost any cost.[68] Support for the SPS and its allied political parties waned to the point that some withdrew altogether.

As the NATO air campaign increased in intensity, attacks on key infrastructure targets wreaked increasing amounts of damage. Many above-ground military installations were destroyed. More importantly, command and control and communications targets were attacked and many destroyed. Electrical power generating and distributing facilities were destroyed, as were petroleum and oil installations. Infrastructure targets such as bridges were also 'dropped'.[69] The bulk of these were located in Serbia, not Kosovo or Montengro, and as such were firmly in Milosevic's hinterland. Arguably more importantly, a number of key dual-use factories and installations were owned by colleagues of Milosevic.[70] The reality was that Milosevic had held onto power through the SPS by allowing key individuals access to lucrative jobs and ownership opportunities. The SPS had operated through the worst of the sanctions period by maintaining a stranglehold on state-owned facilities and the black market alike. It was a classic Soviet period 'party' apparatus and as long as there was money to be made, and Milosevic was in a position to distribute largesse, he was relatively safe in power. The problem for him by June 1999 was that NATO bombing had ground down the people and the economy to the point of basic poverty and there was little, if any, money to be made. As a direct result, his power base ebbed away. Whether by accident or design, NATO had attacked his strategic centre of gravity very effectively.

Air power as a weapon of first choice?

NATO went into Operation *Allied Force* with the experience of some eight years of involvement in the Balkans. Land operations, peacekeeping missions and monitoring exercises had had a chequered history with Serbian and Bosnia Serb forces proving to be well-armed, ruthless and determined foes. Furthermore, all European NATO countries had remorselessly continued the quest for peace dividends after the Cold War and defence budgets were continually being cut. From the US perspective, the situation was compounded for the Clinton administration by the humiliating experiences of Somalia. There was no appetite in any NATO nation for contested land operations in Serbia. Given that the Rambouillet terms were never going to be acceptable to the Serbs, an unacceptable stalemate resulted. Notwithstanding the institutional wishful thinking evident in the belief that a very short offensive would suffice, the only available options were a Nelsonian blind eye or the use of air power.

In reality, Kosovo was too close to home for Europe and NATO to ignore – something had to be done and had to be seen to be done. The growing refugee crisis inside Kosovo and in neighbouring states was undermining their stability and causing shock waves across Europe as refugees made their way, legally or illegally, to join relatives already living abroad. Air power was therefore the only available option. The key characteristics of air power including reach, flexibility and precision were complemented by its impermanence (normally seen as a disadvantage of air power, but invaluable in this case) were all vital in the planning and execution of this coercive operation. But the key attribute of air power evident in this operation was its ability to strike hard and repeatedly at the opponent's strategic centre of gravity. This has to be clearly identified and done so with due cognizance of the enemy perceptions of his own vulnerability. It is not completely clear from *Allied Force* whether this was done clinically and scientifically, or arrived at through a happy combination of weapons availability, weather and standard targeting lists.[71] Equally important, the gradual escalation of the use of air power allowed NATO to retain its own strategic centre of gravity. Ironically, Milosevic contributed to this cohesion with his brutal escalation in ethnic cleansing.

Lambeth has lamented this 'gradualism' and the frustration caused by the slow start, gentle escalation, restrictive rules of engagement and stringent targeting criteria centred on necessity and proportionality.[72] It is certainly contrary to the airman's natural desire to strike straight into the strategic centre of gravity epitomized by Lieutenant General Mike Short's graphic statement that he would have preferred to have 'gone for the head of the snake on the first night'.[73] But as Lambeth points out, this 'gradualism' was essential for NATO coherence in an operation fought essentially for humanitarian purposes and in a context where vital national interests were not at stake.[74] At a deeper, more philosophical level, these frustrations, particularly among air campaign planners and professional airmen are only likely to increase in any future conflict. The concept of 'shock and awe' on the first night is difficult to reconcile with Just War thinking centred on proportionality and discrimination. Trends in thinking in this field towards a Responsibility to Protect will only serve to accentuate the difficulty in 'going for the head of the snake'; it looks as if the kid-glove approach will only increase the frustration.[75]

Given the wider diplomatic, political and economic factors involved in the decision-making in entering this conflict and its eventual conclusion, there can be no question of agreeing with John Keegan's assertion that air power did it alone.[76] What does, however, come out of this operation is the importance of correct intelligence interpretation, the avoidance of policy-based wishful thinking and finally the correct identification of the opponent's strategic centre of gravity. For a ruthless and aggressive civilian leader, this was never going to be his fielded forces in Kosovo. To make matters worse, they were not suitable targets for air power on the scale necessary for campaign success. The spat between the senior leaders over this issue and over micromanagement leads to the conclusion that the exercise of air power is best left to professional airmen experienced in its delivery and practised in its art. In reality, this can only be done by airmen from an independent air force.

CHAPTER NINE

Concluding comments

This book started with a quotation taken from an air power doctrine manual citing Churchill's difficulty in defining and measuring air power. Part of the difficulty he experienced stemmed from the novelty of warfare in the third dimension. But from the intervening chapters, it is clear that Churchill's comments barely scratch the surface. Air warfare fascinated Churchill and it continues to grab the attention of both advocates and detractors. Like the broader discipline of military history and war studies, both of which have been discussed, air warfare attracts students from a wide variety of backgrounds and with a hugely diverse range of motivations for studying the subject. These include actual and potential students at all degree levels some of whom are practitioners seeking to further develop their professional expertise. Others may be seeking to put some form of structure around their interests.

One of the greatest fascinations with air warfare is the depth and intensity of the debate that it has always generated and continues to do today. There is no likelihood of this diminishing in the foreseeable future. Part of the ferocity of the debate stemmed from the separation of the RAF from its older siblings and immediately became a hungry rival for funding. It also became a beacon of hope for other air arms wishing to achieve the same level of independence. This hallowed status, and the quest to retain or achieve it, led to many claims being made in favour of warfare in the third dimension, some of which were pure speculation and wishful thinking. But once articulated they became articles of faith. All of this cyclical argument fuelled the controversies. Some of the controversies have been covered in the preceding chapters, but by no means at all. Many of the sources open to researchers have been identified; and the notes here and in the volumes mentioned open a huge cavern for those wishing to explore further.

But as was made clear in the section on deconstructing the narrative, most writing on air warfare has been done with a purpose, for a particular audience and will be relevant to a specific context. This applies even to the doctrinal manuals of the varying air arms, services and their equals in the joint world. As was made clear when examining official histories the same applies. Furthermore, some of these are excellent in quality and analysis, others are less so. There is a real need on the part of the researcher for critical analysis.

Part of the analytical process is to study, as Howard and countless teachers since have advocated, in depth, breadth and context. In examining air power theory, the context is especially important. The early air warfare theorists did not write in isolation or solely about air power. Many had extensive track records of writing on military and naval matters and these influences show through. For others, it is vitally important to follow changes in mood, tone and even basic content. Views evolved over time and the world wars in particular were often watersheds in the process. This was certainly true for the likes of Douhet, Trenchard and Mitchell. It was also true for the international community's thinking on the laws of war, with Geneva Conventions coming in 1949 in an attempt to prevent the horrors of the Second World War. Both in law and in the allied ethical thinking, the air power researcher has to be wary of those who apply today's values and standards to our predecessors. The historiographical texts are full of glib phrases about the past being a strange place where things were done differently. But it is, to some extent, true. Quite often, the only way of making sense of a particular attitude, means of theorizing, ethical standpoint or social norm is to read and study the individuals concerned, their cultural and social background and essentially what had contributed to their thought processes.

Air power has the potential to have a very real effect at all levels of war and to range across a battlespace that is global in scale. This has convinced generations of airmen that air power has to be commanded and controlled at the highest levels and with a truly strategic overview. This has inevitably caused friction between some of them and commanders in the other environments. Some of this has been about petty bickering over ownership of assets. Other causes of concern have been over identification of centres of gravity. A key theme throughout these debates has been that using air power to optimal advantage is the province of airmen who have been schooled in its uses and are experienced in its limitations and in the potential benefits. Allied to this, the dicta of Clausewitz about warfare being an extension of politics must be recognized. The impermanence of air power, and its immediate media appeal, makes it susceptible to short-term usage for the purpose of changing headlines with no immediate military necessity or utility. The student, as well as the practitioner, needs to be mindful of this.

Over the last century, air warfare has grown from fragile airframes and weak engines into a global force for good and ill. The costs have risen exponentially and the resulting potential war fighting impact followed. As

Churchill suggested, light has always attracted adventurers and those who have been fascinated by the wonder of the experience and the technical detail. But it has also attracted scholars, thinkers and theorists in far great proportions than Churchill considered. The depth of the controversies that have arisen have ensured that there is, and always will be, huge scope for study and research and it is hoped that this textbook will have provided some vectors to be followed.

NOTES

Chapter 1

1 Air Publication 3000, *British Air Power Doctrine*, 3rd edn, 1999. Introduction to ch. 2. The first sentence of the quote is from Winston Churchill, *The Second World War: The Gathering Storm* (London: Cassell, 1948), p. 87. It is noteworthy that this is a composite quote from various sources; it is always worth checking the original.

2 Martin Gilbert, *Churchill: A Life* (London: Heinemann, 1992), p. 248.

3 Martin Francis, *The Flyer: British Culture and the Royal Air Force 1939-1945* (Oxford: Oxford University Press, 2008), p. 32.

4 HC Debates 20 August 1940, Vol. 364, cc. 1132–1274 'War Situation'; the 'Few' paragraph is at c1167. This quotation has the added benefit of demonstrating the wisdom of always reading more widely from a speech than just tiny bit to be used; the context may be as important.

5 AP 3000, p. 1.2.1.

6 Joint Doctrine Publication 0–30, *UK Air and Space Doctrine*, July 2013, p. 1–1.

7 David MacIsaac, 'Voices from the Central Blue: The Air Power Theorists', in *The Makers of Modern Strategy from Machiavelli to the Nuclear Age*, ed. Peter Paret (Oxford: Clarendon Press, 1986), p. 627, fn. 6.

8 Ibid.

9 Tami Davis Biddle and Robert M. Citino, 'The role of Military History in the Contemporary Academy', Society of Military History white paper, http://www.smh-hq.org/docs/SMHWhitePaper.pdf, p. 1.

Chapter 2

1 Stephen Morillo (with Michael F. Pavkovic), *What is Military History?* (Cambridge: Polity, 2006), p. 47. The extent to which air power appeals to male audiences could do with some rigorous research. A Massive Open Online Course (MOOC) run by the University of Birmingham and Futurelearn on Aviation in the First World War had a significant, active female audience.

2 See, for example, Mark Moyar, 'The Current State of Military History', *The Historical Journal* 50, no. 1 (2007), pp. 225–40 and Peter Paret, 'The Annales School and the History of War', *The Journal of Military History* 73 (October 2009), pp. 1289–94. See also Peter W. Gray, 'Why Study Military History', in

War Studies Reader: From the Seventeenth Century to the Present Day and Beyond, ed. Gary Sheffield (London: Continuum, 2010), pp. 17–34.

3 Michael Howard, 'Military History and the History of War', in *The Past as Prologue: The Importance of History to the Military Profession*, ed. Williamson Murray and Richard Hart Sinnreich (Cambridge: Cambridge University Press, 2006), p. 13.

4 See also Joanna Bourke, 'New Military History', in *Modern Military History*, ed. Matthew Hughes and William J. Philpott (Basingstoke: MacMillan, 2006), p. 258.

5 Jeremy Black, *Rethinking Military History* (London: Routledge, 2004).

6 Howard, 'Military History', pp. 12–13.

7 Ibid.

8 Staff Colleges tend to concentrate on ranks at the major and junior lieutenant colonel level whereas War Colleges are usually for full colonels and their equivalents across other nations and services.

9 A good start on the man Cicero called 'the father of history' is Robert B. Strassler (ed.), *The Landmark Herodotus: The Histories* (London: Quercus, 2007).

10 John James, *The Paladins: The Story of the RAF up to the Outbreak of World War II* (London: Futura, 1991), p. 12. James remarks that generals have written on the art of war, poetry or painting, air marshals on what fun it was to fly when they were young, but admirals 'do not, or perhaps cannot, write'.

11 Jeremy Black and Donald M. MacRaild, *Studying History* (Basingstoke: Palgrave, 2000), p. 83 and Morillo, *What is Military History?*, p. 46.

12 Moyar, 'The Current State of Military History', p. 225.

13 Biddle and Citino, 'The Role of Military History' and Bourke, 'New Military History'.

14 See the quotation from Lucien Febvre used by Paret in which 'history that is of service is a servile history'. Paret, 'The Annales School and the History of War', p. 1289.

15 The author convenes and teaches an MA programme on the History, Theory and Practice of Air Power and has had a very wide range of ranks from the services as well as many civilians.

16 See Gray, 'Why Study Military History', p. 17.

17 Christina J. M. Goulter, 'British Official Histories of the Air War', in *The Last Word? Essays on Official History in the United States and British Commonwealth*, ed. Jeffrey Grey (Westport, CT: Praeger, 2003), p. 133. The following chapter on historiography covers this in more depth.

18 This is general practice, but the classic study in this area is E. H. Carr, *What is History?* (London: Penguin, 1990 [1961]), p. 23.

19 Michael Howard, *The Causes of War and other essays* (Hounslow: Temple Smith, 1983), p. 195. See also Michael Howard, *The Lessons of History* (Oxford: Oxford University Press, 1991).

20 Richard Overy, 'Doctrine Not Dogma: Lessons from the Past', *RAF Air Power* 3, no. 1 (2000), p. 33.

21 AP 3000, *British Air Power Doctrine*, 3rd edn, p. 3.11.1.

22 Julian S. Corbett, *Principles of Maritime Strategy* (London: Longmans, 1911), p. 3.

23 Sun Tzu (Foreword by James Clavell), *The Art of War* (London: Hodder and Stoughton, 1981); Niccolo Machiavelli, *The Art of War*, trans. Neal Wood (Cambridge, MA: Perseus, 1965).

24 See Brian Holden Reid, *Studies in British Military Thought: Debates with Fuller and Liddell Hart* (Nebraska, NE: Nebraska University Press, 1998), p. 180.

25 Ibid., p. 181.

26 Ibid., p. 106.

27 Matthew Hughes (ed.), *British Ways of Counter-insurgency: A Historical Perspective* (London: Routledge, 2013); David French, *The British Way in Counter-Insurgency 1945–1967* (Oxford: Oxford University Press, 2011) and Matthew Grant, *British Way in Cold Warfare: Intelligence, Diplomacy and the Bomb, 1945 – 1975)* (London: Continuum, 2009).

28 Morillo, *What is Military History?*, p. 48.

29 Howard, 'Military History and the History of War', pp. 13–15.

30 Claudia Baldoli, Andrew Knapp and Richard Overy (eds), *Bombing States and Peoples in Western Europe 1940-1945* (London: Continuum, 2011). See also Richard Overy, *The Bombing War: Europe 1939-1945* (London: Penguin, 2014).

31 Howard, 'Military History and the History of War', p. 14.

32 Tami Davis Biddle, *Rhetoric and Reality in Air Warfare: The Evolution of British and American Ideas about Strategic Bombing, 1914–1945* (Princeton: Princeton University Press, 2002).

33 On the one hand, see American author Stephen A. Garrett, *Ethics and Airpower in World War II: The British Bombing of German Cities* (New York: St. Martins, 1993) or David L. Bashow, *No Prouder Place: Canadians and the Bomber Command Experience, 1939-1945* (St. Catherines, ON: Vanwell, 2005).

34 H. Montgomery Hyde, *British Air Policy Between the Wars 1918-1939* (London: Heinemann, 1976), Brian Bond, *British Military Policy Between the Two World Wars* (Oxford: Clarendon, 1980) and Stephen Roskill, *Naval Policy Between the Wars* (London: Collins, 1968). As an aside, it is interesting to note the respective publication dates.

35 Howard, 'Military History and the History of War', p. 13.

36 Fred Singleton, *A Short History of the Yugoslav Peoples* (Cambridge: Cambridge University Press, 1985), p. 26.

37 Howard, 'Military History and the History of War', p. 14.

38 David French, *Military Identities: The Regimental System, the British Army & the British People c1870-2000* (Oxford: Oxford University Press, 2005). See, in particular, ch. 4, 'The Construction of the Idea of "the Regiment"'.

39 Robert D. Strassler (ed.), *The Landmark Thucydides: A Comprehensive Guide to the Peloponnesian War* (New York, NY: Touchstone, 1996). Thucydides set

out to write a neutral history and sets himself as markedly different from his predecessor Herodotus. See pp. x–xiii.

40 Howard, 'Military History and the History of War', p. 15 and Black, *Rethinking Military History*, p. 22.

41 This led the Royal Aeronautical Society to hold a competition in 2007 for a University to host an Air Power Chair or Fellowship. The University of Birmingham won this and the author was appointed in 2008. The Fellowship was funded partly by the RAF, defence industry and the University. One of the key aims was to increase the numbers of doctoral-level students.

42 See in particular, David Edgerton, *England and the Aeroplane: Militarism, Modernity and Machines* (London: Penguin, 2013). See also Richard P. Hallion, *Taking Flight: Inventing the Aerial Age from Antiquity to the First World War* (Oxford: Oxford University Press, 2003).

43 See Alfred Gollin, *The Impact of Air Power on the British People and their Government, 1909-14* (London: Macmillan, 1989); Uri Bialer, *The Shadow of the Bomber: the Fear of Air Attack and British Politics, 1932-1939* (London: RHS, 1980); for pre-First World War fiction, see H. G. Wells, 'The War in the Air: And Particularly how Mr. Bert Smallways Fared while it Lasted', *Pall Mall Magazine* 1908.

44 Carl von Clausewitz, *On War*, ed. Michael Howard and Peter Paret (London: Everyman, 1993). See other works encompassing the wider spectrum such as Paul Kennedy, *Rise and Fall of the Great Powers: Economic Change and Military Conflict from 1500-2000* (London: Fontana, 1989). For a good overview of these aspects in relation to the Second World War, see Richard J. Overy, *The Air War 1939-1945* (New York: Stein and Day, 1980).

45 Edgerton, *England and the Aeroplane*, p. 5 and more generally J. Lee Thomson, *Northcliffe: Press Baron in Politics 1865-1922* (London: Murray, 2000).

46 The introduction of a no-fly zone over Libya caused an immediate transformation in the media which had been clamouring for 'something to be done'.

47 Howard, 'Military History and the History of War', p. 20.

48 The bibliography for this period is considerable, but see Montgomery Hyde, *British Air Policy*; Lord Londonderry, *Wings of Destiny* (London: MacMillan, 1943), Major General A. C. Temperley, *The Whispering Gallery of Europe* (London: Collins, 1938), T. C. G. James, *Air Defence of Great Britain, Volume I: The Growth of Fighter Command 1936-1940* (London: Whitehall History Publishing with Cass, 2002). See also Peter Gray, *The Leadership, Direction and Legitimacy of the RAF Bomber Offensive from Inception to 1945* (London: Continuum, 2012), ch. 4. For the German perspective, see in particular Adam Tooze, *The Wages of Destruction: The Making & Breaking of the Nazi Economy* (London: Penguin, 2007), Robin Higham, *The French and British Air Arms from Versailles to Dunkirk* (Annapolis, MD: Naval Institute Press, 2012).

49 See in particular Keith Middlemass and John Barnes, *Baldwin: A Biography* (London: Weidenfeld and Nicholson, 1969).

50 See Gray, *The Leadership, Direction and Legitimacy of the RAF Bomber Offensive*, p. 130.

51 See Sebastian Ritchie, *Industry and Air Power: The Expansion of British Aircraft Production 1935-1941* (Abingdon: Routledge, 1997) and Colin Sinnott, *The Royal Air Force and Aircraft Design 1923-1939: Air Staff Operational Requirements* (London: Cass, 2001).

52 The literature is considerable on this issue, but for an introduction to the British perspective, see Peter Gray, 'The Gloves Will Have to Come Off: A Reappraisal of the Legitimacy of the RAF Bomber Offensive Against Germany', *Royal Air Force Air Power Review* 3, no. 3 (Autumn/Winter 2010), pp. 9–40.

53 Baldoli, Knapp and Overy, *Bombing States and Peoples* and Paul Addison and Jeremy A. Crang (eds), *Listening to Britain: Home Intelligence Reports on Britain's Finest Hour – May to September 1940* (London: Vintage, 2011).

54 For a bureaucratic view, see Peter Gray, 'The Air Ministry and the Formation of the Royal Air Force', in *Changing War: The British Army, The Hundred Days Campaign and the Birth of the Royal Air Force, 1918*, ed. Gary Sheffield and Peter Gray (London: Bloomsbury, 2013), p. 135.

55 See French, *Military Identities*, Timothy Bowman and Mark Connelly, *The Edwardian Army: Recruiting, Training and Deploying the British Army, 1902-1914* (Oxford: Oxford University Press, 2012), Nicholas Black, *The British Naval Staff in the First World War* (Woodbridge: Boydell, 2009), Byron Farwell, *For Queen and Country: A Social History of the Edwardian and Victorian Army* (London: Penguin 1991) and Andrew Gordon, *The Rules of the Game: Jutland and British Naval Command* (London: John Murray, 1996).

56 A possible exception is Martin Francis, *The Flyer: British Culture and the Royal Air Force 1939-1945* (Oxford: Oxford University Press, 2008).

57 See, for example, Jay Winter and Emmanuel Sivan (eds), *War and Remembrance in the Twentieth Century* (Cambridge: Cambridge University Press, 1999).

58 As a starting point, Mark K. Wells, *Courage and Air Warfare: The Allied Aircrew Experience in the Second World War* (London: Frank Cass, 1995) and Allan D. English, *The Cream of the Crop: Canadian Aircrew 1939-1945* (Montreal: McGill-Queen's University Press, 1996) are both excellent. See also A. D. English, 'A Predisposition to Cowardice? Aviation Psychology and the Genesis of "Lack of Moral Fibre"', *War & Society* 13, no. 1 (May 1995), pp.15–34. From the psychiatric treatment and diagnosis point of view, see Sydney Brandon, 'LMF in Bomber Command 1939-1945: Diagnosis or Denouncement', in *150 Years of British Psychiatry Volume II: The Aftermath*, ed. Hugh Freeman and German E. Berrios (London: Athlone Press, 1996), pp. 119–29. E. Jones and S. Wessely, *Shell Shock to PTSD* (Hove: Psychology Press, 2005). For an American perspective, see J. Rachman, *Fear and Courage* (New York: Freeman and Company, 1990). For the historical view, see N. S. Gilchrist, 'An Analysis of Causes of Breakdown in Flying', *The British Medical Journal* 12 (October 1918), pp. 401–3.

59 See Moyar, 'Current State of Military History', p. 232 in which he deals systematically with a number of Jeremy Black's criticisms of military history. See however, Hans Ritter, *La guerre aérienne* (Paris: CESA, 2012); originally published in Berlin in 1926 and translated from German to French by Horst Gorlich.

60 Ibid.

61 Group Captain A. K. Agarwal, *The Third Dimension: Air Power in Combating the Maoist Insurgency* (New Delhi: Vij Books, 2013).

62 See, for example, Lt Col (USAF) Karen U. Kwiatowski, *Expeditionary Air Operations in Africa: Challenges and Solutions* (Birmingham, AB: Fairchild Papers/Air University Press, 2012).

63 See Iain McNicholl, 'Campaigning: An Air Force Perspective', in *British Generals in Blair's Wars*, ed. Jonathan Bailey, Richard Iron and Hew Strachan (Farnham: Ashgate, 2013), pp. 265–72. For a more historical treatment, see Sebastian Ritchie, *The RAF, Small Wars and Insurgencies in the Middle East 1919-1939* (Shrivenham: Centre for Air Power Studies, 2011).

64 Not specifically mentioned hitherto, the late New Zealand-based air power specialist Vincent Orange is notable for an extensive range of biographies including those on Park, Tedder, Slessor and Dowding. Mention also must be made of works such as Alan Stephens (ed.), *The War in the Air 1914–1994* (Canberra: Air Power Studies Centre, 1994).

65 From works such as Patrick Bishop, *Bomber Boys: Fighting Back 1940-1945* (London: Harper, 2008), through Desmond Seward, *Wings over the Desert: In action with an RFC pilot in Palestine 1916-18* (Yeovil: Haynes, 2009) to Graham Pitchfork, *The Sowreys* (London: Grub Street, 2012).

66 *COD*, p. 904.

67 Hayden White, 'The Question of Narrative in Contemporary Historical Theory', *History and Theory* 23, no. 1 (February 1984), p. 1.

68 Marc Bloch, *The Historian's Craft*, trans. Peter Putman (Manchester: Manchester University Press, 1992), pp. 85–9. See also Joyce Appelby, 'Lynn Hunt and Margaret Jacob', in *Historians on History*, ed. J. Tosh (Harlow: Longman, 2000), p. 313.

69 Carr, *What is History?* p. 10.

70 Ibid., pp. 10–11.

71 Strassler, *Landmark Thucydides*, p. xvi.

72 See, for example, Ignacio Brescó de Luna, 'Memory, History and Narrative: Shifts of Meaning when (Re)constructing the Past', *Europe's Journal of Psychology* 8, no. 2 (2012), pp. 300–10; Elli P. Schachter, 'Narrative Identity Construction as a Goal-orientated Endeavour: Reframing the Issue of "big vs. Small" Story Research', *Theory and Psychology* 21, no. 1 (2011), pp. 1–7. See also the 'heroic narrative', *Beowulf*, trans. Seamus Heaney (London: Faber, 2000) and especially the Introduction.

73 See, for example, Jay Winter and Antoine Prost, *The Great War in History: Debates and Controversies, 1914 to the Present* (Cambridge: Cambridge University Press, 2005), especially ch. 8 'Agents of Memory'.

74 Jorg Echternkamp, 'North Africa: A Forgotten Theatre of War? Identity, Legitimization and the Shifts in German Memory Culture since 1945', conference paper, The Desert War: International Workshop, Madrid, 17–18 October 2014.

75 'Arthur Marwick', in John Tosh (ed.), *Historians on History* (Harlow: Longman, 2000), p. 303.

Chapter 3

1 Joint Doctrine Publication 0-01, *British Defence Doctrine*, 2nd edn, October 2001, pp. 1–1 and *AP3000*, p. 3.11.1. For the NATO definition, see North Atlantic Treaty Organization, NATO Standardization Agency, AAP-6 (2009), *NATO Glossary of Terms and Definitions* (Brussels: NATO Standardization Agency, 2009), 2-D-9.

2 Philip S. Meilinger, *Airwar: Theory and Practice* (London: Cass, 2003), p. 36.

3 Julian S. Corbett, *Principles of Maritime Strategy* (London: Longmans, 1911), p. 3.

4 MOD DCDC: *Global Strategic Trends – Out to 2045*, 5th edn, July 2014.

5 JCN 3/12, *Future air and Space Concept*, September 2012.

6 For example, see Michael Duffy, Theo Farrell and Geoffrey Sloan (eds), *Doctrine and Military Effectiveness: Proceedings of the Conference held at The Britannia Royal Naval College, January 1997* (Exeter: Strategic Policy Studies Group, 1997) and Richard Overy, 'Doctrine Not Dogma: Lessons from the Past', *RAF Air Power Review* 3, no. 1 (2000), pp. 32–47.

7 See http://airpower.airforce.gov.au/Contents/Publications/18/Publications.aspx#.U9uBueNdWk8 (accessed 1 August 2014). Australian Air Publication 1000, *The Air Power Manual*, 6th edn, September 2013.

8 See http://www.au.af.mil/au/cadre/aspc/l004/pubs/afdd1.pdf (accessed 1 August 2014). Air Force Doctrine Document 1, *Air Force Basic Doctrine, Organization and Command*, 14 October 2011.

9 See http://www.marines.mil/Portals/59/Publications/MCDP%201-0%20Marine%20Corps%20Operations.pdf (accessed 1 August 2014). MCDP 1-0, *Marine Corps Operations*, 9 August 2011.

10 See http://airforceapp.forces.gc.ca/cfawc/CDD/Doctrine/Pubs/Strategic/B-GA-400/Edition_2/B-GA-400-000-FP-000-Edition_2.pdf (accessed 1 August 2014). B-GA-400-000/FP-000, *Canadian Forces Aerospace Doctrine*, Edition 2.

11 Philip S. Meilinger (ed. for the School of Advanced Air Power Studies), *The Paths of Heaven: The Evolution of Air Power Theory* (Maxwell AFB, AL: Air University Press, 1997). Robert Frank Futtrell (ed.), *Ideas, Concepts, Doctrine: Basic Thinking in the United States Air Force, Vol.1, 1907-1960* and *Vol. 2. 1961-1984* (Birmingham, AL: Air University Press, 1999).

12 Quoting the then Brigadier General Ronald Keys, Air Force Doctrine Document 1, *Air Force Basic Doctrine, Organization and Command*, 14 October 2011, p. 1.

13 See, for example, Anon, 'The Principles of War and the R.A.F. - Security', *The Royal Air Force Quarterly* VII, no. 3 (July 1936), p. 300; Squadron Leader J. C. Slessor, 'The Development of the Royal Air Force', *Royal United Service Institute Journal* 76 (May 1931), p. 328.

14 Group Captain Andrew Vallance (ed.), *Air Power: Collected Essays on Doctrine* (Bracknell: D Def S (RAF), 1990), p. xviii. Notwithstanding the obsolescence, the manual was still used as a source in Officers' Promotion Examinations as late as 1978! See also Markus Mäder, *In Pursuit of*

Conceptual Excellence: The Evolution of British Military-Strategic Doctrine in the Post-Cold War Era, 1989–2002 (Bern: Peter Lang, 2004), p. 22. See also ch. 3.

15 Middlemass and Barnes, *Baldwin*, pp. 735–9 for a full discussion on Stanley Baldwin's famous quotation. This is another example of the benefits of searching for more than just the quote.

16 Futtrell (ed.), *Ideas, Concepts, Doctrine.*

17 Goulter, 'British Official Histories of the Air War', p. 133.

18 Jeffrey Grey, 'Introduction', in Grey (ed.), *The Last Word?*, p. ix.

19 Ibid., and Goulter, 'British Official Histories of the Air War', p. 134 where she comments on Walter Raleigh and Hilary St George Saunders with the latter providing the 'literary flourishes'. Walter Raleigh and H. A. Jones, *The War in the Air: Being the Story of the Part Played in the Great War by the Royal Air Force* (Oxford: Clarendon Press, 6 volumes, 1922–37). Denis Richards and Hilary St George Saunders, *The Royal Air Force 1939-1945* (London: HMSO, three volumes, 1953–4).

20 Noble Frankland, *History at War: The Campaigns of an Historian* (London: de la Mare, 1998), p. 4

21 Ibid.

22 For the history of its production, see especially Sebastian Cox, 'Setting the Historical Agenda: Webster and Frankland and the debate over the Strategic Bombing Offensive against Germany, 1939-1945', in Jeffrey Grey (ed.), *The Last Word:* and for sources, see the preface (pp. vi–viii) to Sir Charles Webster and Noble Frankland, *The Strategic Air Offensive against Germany, 1939-1945* (London: Her Majesty's Stationary Office, 1961).

23 Cox, 'Setting the Historical Agenda', p. 155. For a detailed treatment of the correspondence, see Gray, *The Leadership, Direction and Legitimacy of the RAF Bomber Offensive*, pp. 268–74. Demi-official letters were essentially correspondence between individuals rather than organizations, so Portal and Harris would write to each other rather than the Air Council communicating formally with the Command. Such letters would begin with personal salutations such as 'Dear Bert ...'.

24 Cox, 'Setting the Historical Agenda', p. 154.

25 Ibid.

26 Goulter, 'British Official Histories of the Air War', p. 135 and Frankland, *History at War*, p. 49.

27 See http://www.raf.mod.uk/ahb/ (accessed 5 August 2014).

28 TNA AIR 41/39, *The RAF in the Bomber Offensive against Germany.*

29 AIR 41/14, *The Growth of Fighter Command, 1936-1940*. Published as T. C. G. James, *The Growth of Fighter Command, 1936-1940* (London: Cass, 2002). The Frank Cass series which was edited by Sebastian Cox (head of the AHB) was confusingly titled 'RAF Official Histories'.

30 AIR 41/5, *International Law of the Air, 1939-1945. Confidential supplement to Air Power and War Rights*. This refers to the third edition of J. M. Spaight, *Air Power and War Rights* (London: Longmans, 1947).

31 Jeffrey Grey, 'Introduction', in Grey (ed.), *The Last Word?*, p. xi.

32 Cox, 'Setting the Historical Agenda', p. 164. Anthony Verrier, *The Bomber Offensive* (London: Batsford, 1968) and Max Hastings, *Bomber Command* (London: Pan Macmillan, 1993).

33 Winston S. Churchill, *The Second World War* (London: Cassell, six volumes, 1949). See also David Reynolds, *In Command of History: Churchill Fighting and Writing the Second World War* (London: Allen Lane, 2004).

34 Wesley Frank Craven and James Lea Cate (eds), *The Army Air Forces in World War II* (Chicago: University of Chicago Press, 1948–58; Reprinted Washington, DC: Office of Air Force History, 1983). See http://www.ibiblio. org/hyperwar/AAF/I/or http://www.afhso.af.mil/shared/media/document/AFD-101105-005.pdf accessed 4 August 2014 for full text.

35 Ibid., Foreword.

36 See, for example, Maurer Maurer (ed.), *The U.S. Air Service in WWI: Vol. I, The Final Report and a Tactical History* (Washington, DC: Office of Air Force History, 1978).

37 Lt. Col. Ralph A. Rowley, *Tactics and Techniques of Close Air Support Operations 1961-1973* (Washington, DC: Office of Air Force History, 1976) and USAF Historical Division Liaison Office, *USAF Airborne Operations in WWII and Korea* (1962). See http://www.afhso.af.mil/booksandpublications/ specialstudies-bluebooks.asp (accessed 4 August 2014).

38 http://www.afhso.af.mil/booksandpublications/titleindex.asp (accessed 4 August 2014).

39 https://www.awm.gov.au/histories/ (accessed 4 August 2014).

40 F. M. Cutlack, *Official History of Australia in the War of 1914 1918: Volume VIII, The Australian Flying Corps in the Western and Eastern Theatres of War, 1914-1918*, 11th edn (Sydney: Angus and Robertson, 1941). Available at http://www.awm.gov.au/histories/first_world_war/AWMOHWW1/AIF/Vol8/ (accessed 4 August 2014).

41 See, for example, Douglas Gillison, *Australia in the War of 1939-1945. Series 3 – Air Vol. 1: The Royal Australian Air Force 1939-1942* (Canberra: Australian War Memorial, 1962).

42 S. F. Wise, *Canadian Airmen and the First World War: The Official History of the Royal Canadian Air Force* (Toronto: Toronto University Press, 1980).

43 W. A. B. Douglas, *The Creation of a National Air Force: The Official History of the Royal Canadian Air Force* (Toronto: Toronto University Press, 1980) and Brereton Greenhous, Stephen J. Harris, William C. Johnston and William G. P. Rawling, *The Crucible of War: The Official History of the Royal Canadian Air Force* (Toronto: Toronto University Press, 1994).

44 Volume 1 is the Historical Section of the R.C.A.F., *The R.C.A.F. Overseas: The First Four Years* (Toronto: Oxford University Press, 1944). See http://www.cmp-cpm.forces.gc.ca/dhh-dhp/his/oh-ho/index-eng.asp (accessed 4 August 2014).

45 Squadron Leader J. M. S. Ross, *Royal New Zealand Air Force* (Wellington: Historical Publications Branch, 1955). See http://nzetc.victoria.ac.nz/tm/ scholarly/name-110049.html (accessed 4 August 2014).

46 Wing Commander H. L. Thompson, *New Zealanders with the Royal Air Force (Vol. I)* (Wellington: Historical Publications Branch, 1953). See http://nzetc. victoria.ac.nz/tm/scholarly/tei-WH2-1RAF.html (accessed 4 August 2014).

47 Michael Paris, *Winged Warfare: The Literature and Theory of Aerial Warfare in Britain 1859-1917* (Manchester: Manchester University Press, 1992).

48 See http://www.ref.ac.uk/panels/assessmentcriteriaandleveldefinitions/ (accessed 4 August 2014).

49 See, for example, Christina J. M. Goulter, *A Forgotten Offensive: Royal Air Force Coastal Command's Anti-Shipping Campaign, 1940-1945* (London: Cass, 1995), p. xiii where the book (and the PhD on which it was based) is dedicated to the memory of her father who flew with No. 489 (New Zealand) Squadron in Coastal Command in 1944 and 1945.

50 See, for example, Wing Commander John Stubbington, *Kept in the Dark: The Denial to Bomber Command of Vital Ultra and Other Intelligence Information during WWII*, (Barnsley: Pen and Sword, 2010), p. 15.

51 Examples are legion in this category, but include attempts to exonerate (if that was thought necessary) Leigh-Mallory; Bill Newton Dunn, *Big Wing: The Biography of Air Chief Marshal Sir Trafford Leigh-Mallory* (Shrewsbury: Airlife, 1992). Castigation includes works such as Alan Clark, *The Donkeys* (London: Pimlico, 1961).

52 For the latter, see Gary Sheffield, *The Chief: Douglas Haig and the British Army* (London: Aurum, 2011). A post-revisionist work which dispels stereotypes and attempts to take a middle ground may be J. P. Harris, *Douglas Haig and the First World War* (Cambridge: Cambridge University Press, 2008), p. 3.

53 See, for example, on aircraft, Jack Herris and Bob Pearson, *Aircraft of World War I* (Newbury: Amber, 2010) and works such as Manfred von Richtofen, *The Red Baron* (Barnsley: Pen and Sword, 2005 [1918 in German]) and William E. Burrows, *Richtofen: A True Story of the Red Baron* (London: Hart-Davis, 1970). The 'aces' theme is very popular and some works contain useful wider material. See, for example, A. D. Garrison, *Australian Fighter Aces 1914-1953* (Fairburn, ACT: RAAF Air Power Studies Centre, 1999) and Air Commodore Graham Pitchfork, *Men Behind the Medals* (Barnsley: Pen and Sword 1998).

54 Hans Ritter, *La Guerre Aérienne*, trans. Horst Gorlich (Paris: Centre d'études strategiques aérospatiales, 2012). Originally published as Hans Ritter, *Der Luftkrieg* (Berlin: Koeler, 1926) but translated and reproduced for CESA.

55 E. R. Hooton, *Phoenix Triumphant: The Rise and Rise of the Luftwaffe* (London: Arms and Armour, 1994).

56 James S. Corum, *The Luftwaffe: Creating the Operational War, 1918-1940* (Lawrence, KS: University of Kansas Press, 1997) and Williamson Murray, *Strategy for Defeat: The Luftwaffe 1933-1945* (Maxwell AFB, AL: Airpower Research Institute, 1983).

57 Including James S. Corum, *The Roots of Blitzkrieg: Hans von Seekt and German Military Reform* (Lawrence, KS: University of Kansas Press, 1994) and Robert Citino, *Path to Blitzkrieg: Doctrine & Training in the German*

Army, 1920-39 (Mechanicsburg, PA: Stackpole, 2008). See also James S. Corum, 'The Luftwaffe and the Lessons Learned in the Spanish Civil War', in *Turning Points in Air Power History from Kittyhawk to Kosovo*, ed. Sebastian Cox and Peter Gray (London: Cass, 2002), pp. 66–92.

58 Walter J. Boyne, *The Influence of Air Power on History* (New York: Pelican, 2003), p. 152.

59 Horst Boog (ed.), *The Conduct of the Air War in the Second World War: An International Comparison* (New York: Berg, 1992).

60 Jeremy Noakes (ed.), *Nazism 1919-1945: Volume 4, The German Home Front in World War II* (Exeter: University of Exeter Press, 2006 [1998]), ch. 49 on morale.

61 Jeorg Friedrich, *The Fire: The Bombing of Germany 1940-1945* (Columbia: Columbia University Press, 2006) originally published as *Der Brand* in 2004. See also Dietmar Süss, *Death from the Skies: How the British and Germans Survived Bombing during World War II* (Oxford: Oxford University Press, 2014) and Herman Knell, *To Destroy a City: Strategic Bombing and its Human Consequences in World War 2* (Cambridge, MA: Da Capo Press, 2003).

62 See Holger H. Mey, 'German Air Power: Ready to Participate in Joint and Combined Operations', in *European Air Power: Challenges and Opportunities*, ed. John Andreas Olsen (Nebraska: Potomac Press, 2014), pp. 32–63.

63 Ian Summer, *The Kings of the Air: French Aces and Airmen of the Great War* (Barnsley: Pen and Sword, 2015); see also Norman Franks and Frank W. Bailey, *Over the Front: Complete Record of the Fighter Aces and Units of the United States and French Air Services 1914-1918* (London: Grub Street, 1992).

64 Boyne, *The Influence of Air Power on History*, p. 160. Robin Higham, *Two Roads to War: The French and British air Arms from Versailles to Dunkirk* (Annapolis, MD: Naval Institute Press, 2012).

65 Air Command and Staff Course, *Air Power and its Role in the Battles of Khe San and Dien Bien Phu* (Maxwell AFB, AL: Air Command and Staff College, 2014). See also Martin Windrow, *The Last Valley: Dien Bien Phu and the French defeat in Vietnam* (London: Cassell, 2005).

66 Olivier Kaladjian, *Influence of French Air Power Strategy in the European Union's Military Operations in Africa* (Maxwell AFB, AL: School of Advanced Air Power Studies, 2011); Jean-Marc Tanguy, *Guerre Aérienne en Libye* (Paris: Histoire et Collections, 2012); and Etienne de Durand, 'French Air Power: Effectiveness through Constraints', in Olsen, *European Air Power*, p. 3.

67 Robin Higham, John T. Greenwood and Von Hardesty (eds), *Russian Aviation and Air Power in the Twentieth Century* (London: Cass, 1998).

68 James Sterret, *Soviet Air Force Theory 1918-1945* (Abingdon: Cass, 2007). See also his chapter 'Learning is Winning: Soviet Air Power Doctrine 1935-1941', in Cox and Gray (eds), *Turning Points*.

69 Phillips Payson O'Brien, *How the War was Won: Air-Sea Power and Allied Victory in World War II* (Cambridge: Cambridge University Press, 2015).

70 Sanu Kainikara, *Red Air: Politics in Russian Air Power* (Boca Raton, FL: Universal, 2007) and Soviet Russian Air Power in John Andreas Olsen (ed.), *Global Air Power* (Washington, DC: Potomac, 2011), Yefim Gordon and Dimitriy Komissarov, *Russian Air Power: Current Organisation and Aircraft of all Russian Forces* (Shrewsbury: Airlife, 2011) and Marcel de Haas, *Russian Security and Air Power 1992-2002* (Abingdon: Cass, 2004).

71 Benjamin S. Lambeth, *Russia's Air Power in Crisis: A RAND Research Study* (Washington, DC: Smithsonian, 1999).

72 Mark R. Peattie, *Sunburst: The Rise of Japanese Naval Air Power 1909-1941* (London: Chatham, 2001).

73 John Buckley, *Air Power in the Age of Total War* (London: UCL Press, 1999), pp. 170–97. See also his chapter 'Maritime Air Power and the Second World War: Britain, the USA and Japan', in Cox and Gray (eds), *Turning Points*.

74 Office of Air Force History, *The High Road to Tokyo Bay: The AAF in the Asiatic-Pacific Theater* (Washington, DC: Office of Air Force History, 2015). See also Gary Null, *Weapon of Denial: Air Power and the Battle for New Guinea* (Washington, DC: Office of Air Force History, 2013).

75 Peter Preston-Hough, *Commanding Far Eastern Skies: A Critical Analysis of the Royal Air Force Air Superiority Campaign in India, Burma and Malaya* (Solihull: Helion, 2015) and Henry Probert, *The Forgotten Air Force: The Royal Air Force and the War Against Japan 1941-1945* (London: Brassey's, 1995).

76 Bill Gillham, *The Research Interview* (London: Continuum, 2000), p. 9.

77 http://www.iwm.org.uk/collections-research/about/sound.

78 See, for example, Andrew Dorman, *The Falklands Witness Seminar Joint Services Command And Staff College June 2002* (Camberley: Strategic and Combat Studies Institute, 2003).

79 Gary Sheffield and John Bourne (eds), *Douglas Haig: War Diaries and Letters 1914-1918* (London: Weidenfeld & Nicholson, 2005).

80 Ibid., p. ix.

81 Ibid.

82 Sheffield and Bourne, *Haig's War Diaries*, pp. 2–3.

83 See also Alex Danchev and Dan Todman, *War Diaries 1939-1945: Field Marshal Lord Alanbrooke* (London: Weidenfeld & Nicholson, 2001), pp. xi–xii.

84 Ibid.

85 Sheffield and Bourne, *Haig's War Diaries*, p. 4.

86 See, for example, Robert Self, *Neville Chamberlain: A Biography* (Aldershot: Ashgate, 2006), p. 6.

87 Robert Self (ed.), *The Neville Chamberlain Diary Letters* (Aldershot: Ashgate, 4 vols, 2000–5).

88 See, for example, Ian Hunter (ed.), *Winston and Archie: The Letters of Sir Archibald Sinclair and Winston S. Churchill 1915-1960* (London: Politico, 2005). Sinclair was Secretary of State for Air under Churchill for much of the Second World War.

89   For Churchill, see Reynolds, *In Command of History*, p. xxi and Henry
     Probert, *Bomber Harris: His Life and Times* (London: Greenhill, 2001),
     p. 359 and Sir Arthur Harris, *Bomber Offensive* (London: Collins, 1947).

90   Sir Frederick Sykes, *From Many Angles: An Autobiography* (London: Harrap,
     1942), p. 105.

91   See David Jordan and Gary Sheffield, 'Douglas Haig and Airpower', in *Air
     Power Leadership: Theory and Practice*, ed. Peter W. Gray and Sebastian
     Cox (London: TSO, 2002), pp. 269 and 280 and Andrew Whitmarsh, 'British
     Army Manoeuvres and the Development of Military Aviation, 1910-1913',
     War in History 14, no. 3 (2007), p. 327.

92   See, for example, Londonderry, *Wings of Destiny*, p. 9.

93   E. H. Ware, *Wing to Wing: Bird Watching Adventures at Home and Abroad
     with the RAF* (London: Paternoster, 1946).

94   See http://www.nationalarchives.gov.uk/visit (accessed 19 January 2015).

95   AIR 8/1020, AIR 8 is the CAS Files series. Much of the correspondence is also
     copied in the Portal Papers at Christ Church Library, Oxford.

96   Air 8/1020, Minute Bufton to Portal, 5 January 1945.

97   Ibid.

98   See, for example, CAB 24/15/25, 4 June 1917 entitled War Cabinet and
     Cabinet: Memoranda (GT, CP and G War Series). 'G. T.' Series. Record Type:
     Memorandum. Former Reference: GT 925. Title: The Recent Air Raid and
     British Counter Bombing Raids. Author: Curzon and Air Board. See http://
     discovery.nationalarchives.gov.uk/SearchUI/details?Uri=D7639413 (accessed
     5 August 2104).

99   See, for example, the exchange of correspondence on medals for Bomber
     Command and other aircrew at T300/49 Minute Street to Knox dated 17
     January 1945 and in the Air Ministry at AIR 2/6762. Minute from PS to PUS
     to DGPS dated 18 January 1945. For the article from which these were taken,
     see Peter Gray, 'A Culture of Official Squeamishness? Britain's Air Ministry
     and the Strategic Air Offensive Against Germany', *Journal of Military History*
     77, no. 4 (October 2013), pp. 1349–79.

100 For examples see Simon Fowler, Peter Elliott, Roy Conyers Nesbit and
     Christina Goulter, *PRO Readers' Guide No. 8: RAF Records in the PRO*
     (London: PRO, 1994), p. 61, or online see http://www.nationalarchives.gov.
     uk/records/research-guides/raf-op.htm (accessed 8 August 2014).

101 See http://www.rafmuseum.org.uk/research/default/archive-collection/
     personal-papers.aspx (accessed 5 August 2014).

102 See http://www.rafmuseum.org.uk/research/default/archive-collection/
     company-papers.aspx (accessed 5 August 2014).

103 See http://www.baesystems.com/our-company-rzz/heritage/heritage-
     resources?_afrLoop=470902593184000&_afrWindowMode=0&_
     afrWindowId=g87x66dka_1#%40%3F_afrWindowId%3Dg87x66dka_1%26_
     afrLoop%3D470902593184000%26_afrWindowMode%3D0%26_adf.
     ctrl-state%3Dg87x66dka_69 (accessed 5 August 2014).

104 See http://www.naa.gov.au/collection/explore/defence/services.aspx (accessed 8 August 2014).
105 See, for example, No. 1 Squadron RAAF in the Second World War at http://www.awm.gov.au/units/unit_11019second_world_war.asp (accessed 8 August 2014).
106 See http://www.cmp-cpm.forces.gc.ca/dhh-dhp/his/res-rec/index-eng.asp (accessed 8 August 2014).
107 See http://www.archives.gov/research/military/air-force/ (accessed 8 August 2014).
108 See http://www.afhra.af.mil/documents/personalpapers.asp and http://www.afhra.af.mil/documents/oralhistorycatalogue.asp (both accessed 8 August 2014).
109 http://www.afhra.af.mil/studies/index.asp (accessed 8 August 2014).
110 See http://airforcehistoryindex.org/ (accessed 8 August 2014).
111 See http://www.smh-hq.org/grad/archives/afhra.html (accessed 8 August 2014). It is worth looking at their other guides at http://www.smh-hq.org/grad/researchinfo.html (accessed 8 August 2014).
112 See, for example, the Tuskegee Airmen Archive in University of California Riverside Libraries at http://library.ucr.edu/tuskegee/ (accessed 11 January 2015).
113 See http://www.nationalmuseum.af.mil/research/index.asp (accessed 11 January 2015).
114 See Gray, 'A Culture of Official Squeamishness?'.
115 See, for example, James Fyfe, 'The Great Ingratitude': Bomber Command in World War 2 (Wigtown: GCB, 1993), James Hampton, Selected for Aircrew: Bomber Command in the Second World War (Walton-on-Thames: Air Research Publications, 1993) with the subtitle of the 'Nation's Ingratitude'.
116 MRAF Sir Arthur Harris, Bomber Offensive (London: Collins, 1947), p. 268.
117 See Sir John Holmes, Military Medals Review, July 2012, https://www.gov.uk/government/publications/military-medals-review-report-by-sir-john-holmes (accessed 27 January 2015).
118 Henry Probert, Bomber Harris: His Life and Times (London: Greenhill, 2001) and Denis Richards, Portal of Hungerford: The Life of Marshal of the Royal Air Force Viscount Portal of Hungerford (London: Heinemann, 1977).
119 Gray, 'A Culture of Official Squeamishness?'.
120 See, for example, Char 20/136, Letter King George VI to Prime Minister dated 4 February 1944. See also P. Ziegler, 'Churchill and the Monarchy', in Churchill, ed. R. Blake and W. R. Louis (Oxford: Oxford University Press, 1994), pp. 187–98 and David Cannadine, 'Churchill and the British Monarchy', Transactions of the Royal Historical Society 11 (2001), p. 264.
121 The National Archive series is PRO T300.
122 T300/1, First Report of the Committee submitted to the PM, 13 April 1943.
123 T300/49, Minute Street to Knox dated 17 January 1945.

124 https://www.gov.uk/medals-campaigns-descriptions-and-eligibility#air-crew-europe-star (accessed 27 January 2015). See also AIR 2/6762, Minute from PS to PUS to DGPS dated 18 January 1945.

125 https://www.gov.uk/medals-campaigns-descriptions-and-eligibility#france-and-germany-star (accessed 27 January 2015).

126 RAFM Harris Papers, H84, Letter Harris to Sinclair dated 20 October 1944. Followed by AIR 2/9303, Letters Harris and Douglas [C-in-C Fighter Command] to Street dated 3 and 6 June 1945 when the scheme was formally announced and RAFM Harris Papers, H84 Letter Harris to Portal dated 1 June 1945 complaining of the *fait accompli*.

127 Ibid for Harris and T300/53, Minute Churchill to Sinclair dated 10 February 1944 for Churchill's comments.

128 Ibid.

129 AIR 3/9303, Minute AMP to PUS, CAS and SofS dated 31 August 1945.

Chapter 4

1 Thomas Wildenberg, *Billy Mitchell's War with the Navy: The Interwar Rivalry over Air Power* (Annapolis, MD: Naval Institute Press, 2013) and Phillip S. Meilinger, 'Billy Mitchell's War with the Navy: The Interwar Rivalry over Air Power', *Journal of Military History* 78, no. 3 (July 2014), pp. 1153–4.

2 Della Thompson (ed.), *The Concise Oxford Dictionary of Current English*, 9th edn (Oxford: Clarendon Press, 1995), p. 1446.

3 William C. Marra and Sonia K. McNeil, 'Understanding "The Loop": Regulating the Next Generation of War Machines', *Harvard Journal of Law & Public Policy* 36, no. 3 (2013), pp. 1150–51.

4 This terminology would be more correctly Remotely Piloted Air Systems except that fully autonomous systems are not remotely piloted!

5 Some authors drew on sea power precedents as in J. M. Spaight, *Air Power and the Cities* (London: Longmans, 1930).

6 Peter Paret (ed.), *The Makers of Modern Strategy from Machiavelli to the Nuclear Age* (Oxford: Clarendon Press, 1986) and the earlier version Edward Mead Earle (ed.), *The Makers of Modern Strategy from Machiavelli to Hitler* (Princeton: Princeton University Press, 1943).

7 *COED*, p. 1377.

8 Peter Paret, 'Introduction', in Paret (ed.), *The Makers of Modern Strategy*, p. 3.

9 Ibid.

10 In his preface to the second edition of *Air Power and War Rights*, Spaight, who was a senior civil servant in the Air Ministry, wrote with some pride of his book's inclusion on the reading list.

11 See Sir John Slessor, *Air Power and Armies* (Oxford: Oxford University Press, 1936). And Phillip S. Meilinger, *Airwar: Theory and Practice* (London: Cass, 2003), ch. 3 'John C. Slessor and the Genesis of Air Interdiction', p. 64. See also E. J. Kingston-McCloughry, 'Morale and Leadership', *JRUSI* 74 (1929), p. 305.

12 For the Air Corps Tactical School, see Lt. Col. Peter R. Faber, 'Interwar US
    Army Aviation and the Air Corps Tactical School: Incubators of American
    Airpower', in *The Paths of Heaven: The Evolution of Air Power Theory*,
    ed. Phillip S. Meilinger (ed. for the School of Advanced Air Power Studies)
    (Maxwell AFB, AL: Air University Press, 1997), pp. 183–238. The school was
    anything but tactical; it was the home of US strategic bombing thinking.

13 Ovid, *Metamorphoses* VIII, available at http://classics.mit.edu/Ovid/
    metam.8.eighth.html (accessed 14 August 2014).

14 H. G. Wells, *War in the Air* (London: Penguin Classics, 2005 [1908]); and
    Jules Verne, *Clipper of the Clouds* (London: Forgotten Books, 2010 [1886]).
    Jonathan Swift, *Gulliver's Travels* (London: Penguin Classics, 2012 [1726]).

15 Alfred, Lord Tennyson, *Locksley Hall* available at https://archive.org/details/
    Tennysonpoems1842vol2 (accessed 20 January 2015).

16 MRAF Sir John Slessor, *The Central Blue: Recollections and Reflections*
    (London: Cassell, 1956).

17 Richard P. Hallion, *Taking Flight: Inventing the Aerial Age from Antiquity to
    the First World War* (Oxford: Oxford University Press, 2003), p. 353.

18 David MacIsaac, 'Voices from the Central Blue: The Air Power Theorists',
    in Peter Paret (ed.), *Makers of Modern Strategy from Machiavelli to Hitler*
    (Princeton: Princeton University Press, 1943), pp. 624–47.

19 See https://archive.org/stream/warinair00well#page/n7/mode/2up (accessed 20
    January 2015).

20 Biddle, *Rhetoric and Reality in Air Warfare*, p. 150.

21 See, among others, Brett Holman, *The Next War in the Air: Britain's Fear of
    the Bomber, 1908-1941* (Farnham: Ashgate, 2014), p. 24.

22 MacIsaac, 'Voices from the Central Blue', p. 627. See also Air Vice-Marshal
    Tony Mason, *Air Power: A Centennial Appraisal* (London: Brassey's,
    1994), p. 3 where he takes the same year for his title. Fullerton was a Royal
    Engineer. Both authors use Alfred F. Hurley, *Billy Mitchell: Crusader for
    Air Power* (Bloomington, IN: Indiana University Press, 2006 [1964]). The
    full citation is Major J. D. Fullerton RE, 'Some Remarks on Aerial Warfare',
    in *Operations of the Division of Military Engineering of the International
    Congress of Engineers: Held in Chicago last August under the Auspices of the
    World's Congress Auxilliary of the Colombian Exposition* (Washington, DC:
    Government Print Office, 1894), pp. 571–4.

23 Fullerton, 'Some Remarks on Aerial Warfare', p. 574.

24 MacIsaac, 'Voices from the Central Blue', p. 627.

25 Mason, *Centennial Appraisal*, p. 3.

26 Hallion, *Taking Flight*, p. xvii.

27 See *Operations of the Division of Military Engineering of the International
    Congress of Engineers*, Contents pages and Hallion, *Taking Flight*, pp. 172–3
    for a wider commentary on the Conference.

28 Edward Warner, 'Douhet Mitchell, Seversky: Theories of Air Warfare', in Earle
    (ed.), *The Makers of Modern Strategy*, pp. 485–503.

29 Ibid., p. 485 and MacIsaac, 'Voices from the Central Blue', p. 629.

30 See, for example, Phillip S. Meilinger, 'Giulio Douhet and the Origins of Airpower Theory', in Meilinger, *Paths of Heaven*, p. 2–4 and Thomas Hippler, *Bombing the People: Giulio Douhet and the Foundations of Air-Power Strategy, 1884-1939* (Cambridge: Cambridge University Press, 2013), p. 30.

31 Hippler, *Bombing the People*, p. 30. These were signed by 'Capitano X'.

32 Ibid., p. 31 and Meilinger, 'Giulio Douhet and the Origins of Airpower Theory', p. 3.

33 Hippler, *Bombing the People*, p. 31.

34 Ibid., pp. 32–3.

35 Giulio Douhet, *The Command of the Air*, trans. Dino Ferrai (London: Faber, 1943).

36 Giulio Douhet, *Scritti critica della grande Guerra* (Rome: Berlutti, 1925) and A. Curami and G. Rochat (eds), *Scritti 1901-1915* (Rome: Stato Maggiore Aeronautica, Ufficio Storico, 1993).

37 Hippler, *Bombing the People*, p. 38.

38 Ibid., ch. 3.

39 Meilinger, 'Giulio Douhet and the Origins of Airpower Theory', p. 3.

40 Giulio Douhet, *The Command of the Air*, p. 229.

41 Meilinger, 'Giulio Douhet and the Origins of Airpower Theory', p. 13.

42 Ibid., p. 33.

43 'The Air Doctrine of General Douhet', *RAF Quarterly*, April 1933, pp. 164–7.

44 Mason, *Centennial Appraisal*, p. 45 and Alan Stephens, 'The True Believers: Air Power Between the Wars', in *The War in the Air 1914-1994*, ed. Alan Stephens (Fairbairn ACT: RAAF Air Power Studies Centre, 1994), p. 55.

45 For a wider appreciation of the debate on influence, see Robin Higham, *The Military Intellectuals in Britain: 1918-1939* (New Brunswick, NJ: Rutgers University Press, 1966), pp. 131–2 and Paris, *Winged Warfare*, pp. 114–15 and 189–90. Paris suggests early linkages with Italy through Brooke-Popham and Sykes.

46 Bernard Brodie, 'The Heritage of Douhet', in *Strategy in the Missile Age* (Princeton: Princeton University Press, 1969), ch. 3.

47 MacIsaac, 'Voices from the Central Blue', p. 632.

48 Hurley, *Billy Mitchell: Crusader for Air Power*, p. 139.

49 Mark A. Clodfelter, 'Molding Airpower Convictions: Development and Legacy of William Mitchell's Strategic Thought', in *The Paths of Heaven: The Evolution of Air Power Theory*, ed. Phillip S. Meilinger (ed. for the School of Advanced Air Power Studies) (Maxwell AFB, AL: Air University Press, 1997), pp. 79–114. See also Wildenberg, *Billy Mitchell's War with the Navy*, p. 8.

50 Clodfelter, 'Molding Airpower Convictions', p. 84.

51 Ibid., p. 91. Contrast Mitchell's approach with that of Sir David Henderson who proved to be adept at 'selling' air power; see James Pugh, 'David Henderson and Command of the Royal flying Corps', in *Stemming the Tide: Officers and Leadership in the British Expeditionary Force, 1914*, ed. Spencer Jones (Solihull: Helion, 2013), pp. 263–90.

52 See, for example, Wildenberg, *Billy Mitchell's War with the Navy*, p. 54.

53 Wildenberg, *Billy Mitchell's War with the Navy*, p. 137.

54 Clodfelter, 'Molding Airpower Convictions', p. 95.

55 Clodfelter, 'Molding Airpower Convictions', p. 107.

56 Edward Warner, 'Douhet, Mitchell, Seversky: Theories of Air Warfare', in *Makers of Modern Strategy: Military Thought from Machiavelli to Hitler*, ed. Edward Mead Earle (Princeton: Princeton University Press, 1941), pp. 485–516.

57 MacIsaac, 'Voices from the Central Blue', p. 632.

58 See generally, Phillip S. Meilinger, 'Alexander P. de Seversky and American Airpower', in *The Paths of Heaven: The Evolution of Air Power Theory*, ed. Phillip S. Meilinger (ed. for the School of Advanced Air Power Studies) (Maxwell AFB, AL: Air University Press, 1997), pp. 238–78 and James K. Libbey, *Alexander P. de Seversky and the Quest for Air Power* (Washington, DC: Potomac Books, 2013).

59 Meilinger, 'Alexander P. de Seversky', pp. 247–8.

60 Ibid., p. 258.

61 Ibid.

62 Ibid., p. 266.

63 Ibid., p. 269.

64 Libbey, *Alexander P. de Seversky*, p. 165.

65 Viscount Templewood (Sir Samuel Hoare), *Empire of the Air: The Advent of the Air Age 1922-1929* (London: Collins, 1957), p. 39.

66 Ibid., p. 41.

67 Ibid., p. 42.

68 Ibid.

69 This was laid out in Command 467, *Permanent Organization of the Royal Air Force*, 1919. Widely known as Trenchard's Memorandum of 1919.

70 Ibid., p. 4.

71 Ibid., p. 7.

72 See, for example, Jordan and Sheffield, 'Douglas Haig and Airpower', p. 272.

73 B. H. Liddell Hart, *Paris or the Future of War* (London: Kegan Paul, Trench and Trubner, 1925), pp. 46–7.

74 Higham, *The Military Intellectuals*, p. 242.

75 Webster and Frankland, *The Strategic Air Offensive Against Germany*.

76 MacIsaac, 'Voices from the Central Blue', p. 633.

77 David Omissi, *Air Power and Colonial Control: The Royal Air Force, 1919-1939* (Manchester: Manchester University Press, 1990), p. 40.

78 Omissi, *Air Power and Colonial Control*, p. 41.

79 Martin Gilbert, *Churchill, A Life* (London: Heinemann, 1991), p. 422.

80 Andrew Boyle, *Trenchard* (London: Collins, 1962), p. 370.

81 Omissi quotes 10 out of 338 in April 1921, *Air Power and Colonial Control*, p. 43.

82 Ibid., p. 21.

83 See, for example, AIR 8/6 Memorandum by the Chief of the Air Staff on Air Power Requirements of the Empire, 9 December 1918.

84 Squadron Leader J. C. Slessor, 'The Development of the Royal Air Force', *JRUSI* 76 (February and November 1931), p. 324.

85 Neville Jones, *The Beginnings of Strategic Air Power: A History of the British Bomber Force 1923-39* (London: Cass, 1987).

86 See Slessor, *The Central Blue*, p. 45.

87 Wing Commander J. C. Slessor, *Air Power and Armies* (Oxford: Oxford University Press, 1936). E. J. Kingston-McCloughry, *Winged Warfare: Air Problems of Peace and War* (London: Cape, 1937) and J. M. Spaight, *Air Power and the Cities* (London: Longmans, 1930), *Air Power in the Next War* (London: Geoffrey Bles, 1938), *The Beginnings of Organised Air Power* (London: Longmans, 1927), and *Air Power and War Rights* (London: Longmans, second edition, 1933). See also Higham, *The Military Intellectuals*.

88 Biddle, *Rhetoric and Reality*, Neville Jones, *The Origins of Strategic Bombing: A Study of the Development of British Air Strategic Thought and Practice up to 1918* (London: Kimber, 1973) and *The Beginnings of Strategic Air Power*, Harvey B. Tress, *British Strategic Bombing Policy Through 1940: Politics, Attitudes and the Formation of a Lasting Pattern* (Lewiston, NY: Mellen Press, 1988), Scott Robertson, *The Development of RAF Strategic Bombing Doctrine, 1919-1939* (Westport, CT: Praeger, 1995) and Malcolm Cooper, *The Birth of Independent Air Power* (London: Allen Unwin, 1986).

89 See Phillip S. Meilinger, 'Trenchard, Slessor and the Royal Air Force Doctrine before World War II', in Meilinger (ed.), *Paths of Heaven*, Phillip S. Meilinger, 'Trenchard and "Morale Bombing": The Evolution of Royal Air Force Doctrine Before World War II', *Journal of Military History* 60 (April 1996), pp. 243–70 and Phillip S. Meilinger, 'John C. Slessor and the Genesis of Air Interdiction', in Meilinger, *Airwar*.

90 Lawrence Freedman 'The First Two Generations of Nuclear Strategists' and Michael Carver, 'Conventional Warfare in a Nuclear Age', in Paret (ed.), *Makers of Modern Strategy*.

91 David S. Fadok, 'John Boyd and John Warden: Airpower's Quest for Strategic Paralysis', in Meilinger (ed.), *Paths of Heaven*.

92 Grant T. Hammond, *The Mind of War: John Boyd and American Security* (Washington, DC: Smithsonian, 2001).

93 Ibid., pp. 1–4.

94 Ibid., pp. 3–4.

95 Ibid., p. 2.

96 Colin S. Gray, *Modern Strategy* (Oxford: Oxford University Press, 1999), p. 91.

97 Marra and McNeil, 'Understanding "The Loop"', pp. 1150–51.

98 See John Andreas Olsen, *John Warden and the Renaissance of American Air Power* (Washington, DC: Potomac, 2007) and David R. Mets, *The Air Campaign: John Warden and the Classical Air Power Theorists* (Maxwell AFB, AL: Air University Press, 1998).

99 This thinking was challenged by the British army and under the so-called Bagnall reforms, planning at the operational level was reintroduced. This included the introduction of the Higher Command and Staff Course. See Major General J. J. G. Mackenzie and Brian Holden Reid (eds), *The British Army and the Operational Level of War* (London: Tri-service Press, 1988).

100 John A. Warden III, *The Air Campaign: Planning for Combat* (Washington, DC: NDU Press, 1988). See also Olsen, *Warden and the Renaissance of American Air Power*, p. 81.

101 Mets, *The Air Campaign*, p. 56.

102 Quotation taken from the cover of Warden's book; made by the very same Maj. Gen. Perry Smith who by then had become a major defence correspondent for CNN. See Olsen, *John Warden and the Renaissance of American Air Power*, ch. 8 for full details of the planning process and the impact of personalities and organization tussles.

103 Mets, *The Air Campaign*, p. 79.

104 See Meilinger's Foreword to Olsen, *John Warden and the Renaissance of American Air Power*.

105 See Olsen, *John Warden and the Renaissance of American Air Power*, p. 79 for a very useful critique.

106 James Neil Pugh, 'The Conceptual Origins of the Control of the Air: British Military and Naval Aviation, 1911-1918', unpublished PhD thesis, University of Birmingham, 2013.

107 AIR 8/141, 'Rules of War, Hague Rules: Air Ministry Proposals', 3 November 1932. Spaight was director of Accounts at this stage – see *The Air Force List, October 1932*. See also Higham, *The Military Intellectuals in Britain*, pp. 230–4.

108 Higham, *The Military Intellectuals in Britain*, pp. 170–76.

109 Captain Norman Macmillan, *Air Strategy* (London: Hutchinson, 1941).

110 See, for example, Peter W. Gray (ed.), *Air Power 21* (Norwich: HMSO, 2000).

111 See, for example, Sebastian Cox and Peter Gray (eds), *Turning Points in Air Power History from Kittyhawk to Kosovo* (London: Cass, 2002) and Peter Gray and Sebastian Cox (eds) *Air Power Leadership: Theory and Practice* (London: HMSO, 2002).

112 Slessor, *The Central Blue*, p. 48.

113 Ibid., pp. 48–9.

114 See, for example, Hugh Montague Trenchard, 'The Principles of Air Power in War', 1945; 'Air Power and National Security', 1946; 'The Effect of the Rise of Air Power on War', 1943. Three Papers by the Viscount Trenchard (London: Directorate of Staff Duties, May 1945). These are held at TNA AIR 20/5567 and in the RAF Museum at MFC76/1/359.

115 Higham, *The Military Intellectuals*, p. 257.
116 Ibid., p. 126.
117 Ibid. See also F. W. Lanchester, *Aircraft in Warfare: The Dawn of the Fourth Arm* (London: Constable, 1916). Henderson is widely regarded as the 'father of the RFC' and was its first senior leader.
118 Ibid.
119 Higham, *The Military Intellectuals*, p. 132.
120 Paris, *Winged Warfare*, pp. 182–3.
121 Biddle, *Rhetoric and Reality*, pp. 54–5.
122 See, for example, in Trenchard's introduction to J. M. Spaight, *The Battle of Britain – 1940* (London: Geoffrey Bles, 1941), he refers to Spaight as 'my old friend'. See also Higham, *The Military Intellectuals*, p. 230.
123 Higham, *The Military Intellectuals*, pp. 230–33.
124 'The War Object of an Air Force' produced for COS 147 (69th Chiefs of Staff Meeting). AIR 9/8 Folio 1 Air Staff 17 May 1928.
125 AIR 8/141, 'Rules of War, Hague Rules: Air Ministry Proposals', 3 November 1932.
126 AIR 8/141, and *The Air Force List, October 1932*.
127 See, for example, Emmanuelle Jouannet, *The Liberal-Welfarist Law of Nations: A History of International Law* (Cambridge: Cambridge University Press, 2012); Simon Gunn and James Vernon (eds), *The Peculiarities of Liberal Modernity in Imperial Britain* (London: Global, Area and International Archive, 2011); Douglas Mackman and Michael Mays (eds), *World War I and the Cultures of Modernity* (Jackson, MS: Mississippi University Press, 2000); Bernhard Rieger, *Technology and the Culture of Modernity in Britain and Germany 1890-1945* (Cambridge: Cambridge University Press, 2005).

Chapter 5

1 See Hallion, *Taking Flight*, p. 48.
2 Ibid., p. 32.
3 For more, see Squadron Leader Alan Riches, 'Balloons: Whatever Have They Done For Us?', *RAF Air Power Review* 3, no. 4 (Winter 2000), p. 110.
4 Hallion, *Taking Flight*, pp. 64–5.
5 The cycle of manoeuvres for the RFC has been described by Andrew Whitmarsh, 'British Army Manoeuvres and the Development of Military Aviation, 1910-1913', *War in History* 14, no. 3 (2007), p. 327.
6 See Peter Dye, 'The Genesis of Modern Warfare: The Contribution of Aviation Logistics', in *Changing War: The British Army, the Hundred Days Campaign and the Birth of the Royal Air Force, 1918*, ed. Gary Sheffield and Peter Gray (London: Bloomsbury, 2013), p. 171.

7   Sir Frederick Sykes, *From Many Angles: An Autobiography* (London: Harrap, 1942), p. 91.

8   Whitmarsh, 'British Army Manoeuvres', p. 326.

9   See, for example, Gary Sheffield, *The Chief, Douglas Haig and the British Army* (London: Aurum, 2011), pp. 61–2. David Jordan and Gary Sheffield, 'Douglas Haig and Airpower', in *Air Power Leadership: Theory and Practice*, ed. Peter W. Gray and Sebastian Cox (London: TSO, 2002), pp. 269 and 280.

10 *Field Service Regulations 1909/1912* Section 95 'The air service and air reconnaissance' pp. 118–19. https://ia600300.us.archive.org/17/items/pt1fieldservicer00greauoft/pt1fieldservicer00greauoft_bw.pdf. This stated that the air service would not 'replace other means of acquiring information' and that they would be well placed to 'co-operate with the other arms, and especially with the cavalry'.

11 David Jordan, 'The Genesis of Modern Air Power: The RAF in 1918', in Sheffield and Gray (eds), *Changing War*, p. 197.

12 See, for example, John Terraine, *The Right of the Line: The Royal Air Force in the European War 1939-1945* (London: Hodder and Stoughton, 1985), pp. 89 and 271. See also Roy M. Stanley, *To Fool a Glass Eye: Camouflage Versus Photo-Reconnaissance in World War II* (Shrewsbury: Airlife, 1998).

13 For the use of British Canberra aircraft to overfly the Soviet Union, see TNA AIR 19/1106; Project Robin and Chris Pocock, 'Operation "Robin" and the British overflight of Kapustin Yar: a historiographical note', *Intelligence and National Security* 17, no. 4 (2002), pp. 185–93.

14 See Gary Francis Powers and Curt Gentry, *Operation Overflight: A Memoir of the U-2 Incident* (Washington, DC: Brassey's, 2004 [1970]) and Michael R. Beschloss, *Mayday: Eisenhower, Kruschev and the U-2 Affair* (London: Faber and Faber, 1986).

15 William E. Burrows, *By Any Means Necessary: America's Secret Air War* (London: Arrow, 2003 [2001]), p. 133 for RAF involvement in the electronic reconnaissance.

16 See TNA AIR 20/10955 for Canberra aircraft used in this role.

17 See in particular, Phillip S. Meilinger, *Airwar: Theory and Practice* (Abingdon: Cass, 2003), p. 75. The whole chapter 'Between the Devil and the Deep Blue Sea: Britain's Fleet Air Arm Before World War II' is useful for the period in question and discusses the budgetary issues and the inter-service rivalry.

18 This therefore embraces Bomber Command's operations against capital German ships, U-boat pens and, of course, Coastal Command's work over its history. See, for example, Christina J. M. Goulter, *A Forgotten Offensive: Royal Air Force Coastal Command's Anti-Shipping Campaign, 1940-1945* (London: Cass, 1995).

19 See James Neil Pugh, 'The Conceptual Origins of the Control of the Air: British Military and Naval Aviation, 1911-1918', unpublished PhD thesis, University of Birmingham, 2013, p. 125.

20 See Hallion, *Taking Flight*, pp. 303–7 for the earliest trials and Pugh, 'Conceptual Origins of the Control of the Air', chapters 3 and 6 for the thinking.

21 See Christina J. M. Goulter, 'The Royal Naval Air Service: A Thoroughly Modern Service', in Cox and Gray (eds), *Turning Points*, p. 56.

22 See in particular, Neville Jones, *The Origins of Strategic Bombing: A Study of the Development of British Air Strategic Thought and Practice up to 1918* (London: Kimber, 1973), ch. 4 'Naval Strategic Air Operations, October 1916-1918'. A very useful alternative to Jones is George K. Williams, *Biplanes and Bombsights: British Bombing in World War I* (Maxwell AFB, AL: Air University, 1999).

23 See Peter Gray, 'The Air Ministry and the Formation of the Royal Air Force', in Sheffield and Gray (eds), *Changing War*.

24 See H. Montgomery Hyde, *British Air Policy Between the Wars 1918-1939* (London: Heinemann, 1976) in conjunction with Stephen Roskill, *Naval Policy Between the Wars* (London: Collins, 1968).

25 For the differences between Jellicoe and Beatty on the subject, see Goulter, 'The Royal Naval Air Service', p. 56.

26 See Gjert Lage Dyndal, *Land Based Air Power or Aircraft Carriers? A Case Study of the British Debate about Maritime Air Power in the 1960s* (Farnham: Ashgate, 2012).

27 See J. R. M. Butler, *Grand Strategy, Vol. II, September 1939-June 1941* (London: HMSO, 1971) through to ACM Sir Kenneth 'Bing' Cross with Vincent Orange, *Straight and Level* (London: Grub Street, 1993). Cross was commanding a Hurricane squadron aboard HMS *Glorious* when she was sunk during the evacuation from Norway. See also Winston S Churchill, *The Second World War: Volume I The Gathering Storm* (London: Cassell, 1948), pp. 516–18.

28 See, for example, A. J. Smithers, *Taranto 1940: A Glorious Episode* (Barnsley: Pen and Sword, 1995) and James Holland, *Malta: An Island Fortress under Siege* (London: Phoenix, 2003).

29 See Buckley, *Air Power in the Age of Total War*, pp. 175–86; Roberta Wohlstetter, *Pearl Harbor* (Stanford: Stanford University Press, 1966), through to Joshua Blakeney (ed.), *Japan Bites Back: Documents Contextualising Pearl Harbor* (US: Non-aligned Media, 2015) for a revisionist viewpoint.

30 Buckley, *Air Power in an Age of Total War*, p. 136. See also Corelli Barnett, *Engage the Enemy More Closely: The Royal Navy in the Second World War* (London: Hodder and Stoughton, 1991), ch. 15, p. 458, John Buckley, *The RAF and Trade Defence 1919-1945: Constant Endeavour* (Keele: Keele University Press, 1995) and Richard Overy, 'The Air War in Europe, 1939-1945', in *A History of Air Warfare*, ed. John Andreas Olsen (Washington, DC: Potomac, 2010), p. 36.

31 On the Cold War generally, it is worth looking at Sir John Hackett, *The Third World War – The Untold Story* (London: Sidgwick and Jackson, 1982); it is remarkably (or maybe not so given his distinguished military career) similar to many NATO exercise scenarios. For the more recent debates in the UK, see Peter W. Gray, 'British Air Power: Allowing the UK to Punch above its Weight', in *European Air Power: Challenges and Opportunities*, ed. John Andreas Olsen (Nebraska: Potomac Press, 2014), pp. 123–4.

32 See Hallion, *Taking Flight*, pp. 349 onwards.

33 Jordan, 'The Genesis of Modern Air Power', p. 193.

34 See T. C. G. James, *The Growth of Fighter Command 1936-1940* (London: Cass, 2002), p. 95.

35 Ibid. Note the popular view of the 'small ships' where in reality the huge majority of evacuees were taken off from the mole.

36 Works published at the time include J. M. Spaight, *The Battle of Britain – 1940* (London: Geoffrey Bles, 1941). Conventional histories include Len Deighton, *Fighter: The True Story of the Battle of Britain* (London: Collins, 1977), Richard Hough and Denis Richards, *The Battle of Britain* (London: Hodder and Stoughton, 1989), Stephen Bungay, *The Most Dangerous Enemy: A History of the Battle of Britain* (London: Aurum, 2000), Richard Overy, *The Battle of Britain* (London: Penguin, 2001), James Holland, *The Battle of Britain: Five Months that Changed History* (London: Corgi, 2010). The AHB Narratives have been published by Frank Cass in two volumes under T. C. G. James (as above) and *The Battle of Britain* (London: Cass, 2000). The experiences of the battle come out in works such as Patrick Bishop, *Fighter Boys: Saving Britain 1940* (London: Harper, 2003).

37 For the Blitz, see Juliet Gardiner, *The Blitz: The British Under Attack* (London: Harper, 2010), John Ray, *The Night Blitz 1940-1941* (London: Arms and Armour, 1996) and Paul Addison and Jeremy A. Crang (eds), *Listening to Britain: Home Intelligence Reports on Britain's Finest Hour, May to September 1940* (London: Vintage, 2011). For biographies, see those by Vincent Orange including *Park; the Biography of ACM Sir Keith Park* (London: Grub Street, 2001) and *Dowding of Fighter Command: Victor of the Battle of Britain* (London: Grub Street, 2008).

38 See Robert Wright, *Dowding and the Battle of Britain* (London: Macdonald, 1969), John Ray, *The Battle of Britain: New Perspectives, Behind the Scenes of the Great Air War* (London: Cassell, 1994) and Jack Dixon, *Dowding and Churchill: The Dark Side of the Battle of Britain* (Barnsley: Pen and Sword, 2008). It should be noted that Wright had been Dowding's personal assistant.

39 Probably the most iconic movie was that produced by Harry Salzman in 1969. TV series have given works such as Tim Clayton and Phil Craig, *Finest Hour: Book of the BBC TV Series* (London: Hodder, 1999). See also S. P. MacKenzie, *The Battle of Britain on Screen: 'The Few' in British Film and Television Drama* (Edinburgh: Edinburgh University Press, 2007).

40 Paul Addison and Jeremy A. Crang (eds), *The Burning Blue: A New History of the Battle of Britain* (London: Pimlico, 2000) and Garry Campion, *The Good Fight: Battle of Britain Propaganda and The few* (Basingstoke: Palgrave, 2009).

41 See Stephen McFarland and Wesley Phillips Newton, *To Command the Sky: The Battle for Air Superiority over Germany, 1942-1944* (Washington, DC: Smithsonian, 1991).

42 Webster and Frankland, *The Strategic Air Offensive against Germany*, AHB Narratives in AIR 41/39 onwards. See also Tooze, *The Wages of Destruction* and Biddle, *Rhetoric and Reality*.

43   See Benjamin Franklin Cooling (ed.), *Case Studies in the Achievement of Air Superiority* (Air Force History and Museums Program) available at http://www.afhso.af.mil/shared/media/document/AFD-101012-038.pdf (accessed 7 May 2015).

44   Shmuel L. Gordon, 'Air Superiority in the Israel–Arab Wars. 1967-1982', in Olsen (ed.), *A History of Air Warfare*.

45   See http://www.bbc.co.uk/news/uk-17922490 (accessed 1 May 2015) for the report on 'RAF Typhoon Jets arrive in London to test Olympic Security'. These aircrafts were backed up by RAF Regiment snipers in helicopters.

46   Sebastion Cox, 'The Air/Land Relationship – an historical perspective', *RAF Air Power Review* 11, no. 2 (Summer 2008), p. 1.

47   On the latter, see Mary Hudson, 'A History of military Aeromedical Evacuation', *Royal Air Force Air Power Review* 11, no. 2 (Summer 2008), pp. 74–101.

48   See, for example, Roger Annett, *Lifeline in Helmand: RAF Front-Line Air Supply in Afghanistan: 1310 Flight in Action* (Barnsley: Pen and Sword, 2012).

49   See, for example, Georges Bernage, *Red Devils: The 6th Airborne Division in Normandy* (Bayeux: Heindal, 2002), or Sebastian Ritchie, *Arnhem: Myth and Reality: Airborne Warfare, Air Power and the Failure of Operation Market Garden* (London: Hale, 2011).

50   See Jonathan Boff, 'Air/Land Integration in the 100 Days: The Case of Third Army', *Royal Air Force Air Power Review* 12, no. 3 (Winter 2009), pp. 78–88 and David Jordan, 'The Royal Air Force and Air/Land Integration in the 100 Days, August-November 1918', *Royal Air Force Air Power Review* 11, no. 2 (Summer 2008), pp. 12–29 for the Fourth Army.

51   Cox, 'The Air/Land Relationship', p. 2. See also J. C. Slessor, *Air Power and Armies* (Oxford: Oxford University Press, 1936), p. 170 in which the author laments the lack of 'information, expert advice and reconnaissance' in the planning process prior to the Battle of Amiens.

52   See David Omissi, *Air Power and Colonial Control: The Royal Air Force, 1919-1939* (Manchester: Manchester University Press, 1990), Philip Towle, *Pilots and Rebels: The Use of Aircraft in Unconventional warfare 1918-1988* (London: Brassey's, 1989) and Peter Gray, 'The Myths of Air Control and the Realities of Imperial Policing', *Royal Air Force Air Power Review* 4, no. 2 (Summer 2001), pp.37–52. More broadly, see Richard P. Hallion, *Strike from the Sky: The History of Battlefield Air Attack, 1911-1945* (Washington, DC: Smithsonian, 1989). See also Sebastian Ritchie, *The RAF, Small Wars and Insurgencies in the Middle East 1919-1939* (Shrivenham: Centre for Air Power Studies, 2011).

53   TNA AIR 41/56, AHB Narrative, *The RAF in the Bombing Offensive Against Germany, Vol. VI, The Final Phase March 1944-May 1945*, p. 7.

54   Ibid., p. 230.

55   See Haywood S. Hansell Jr., *The Air Plan that Defeated Hitler* (Atlanta, GA: Higgins, 1972), p. 40.

56 See W. Hays Parks, '"Precision" and "Area" Bombing: Who Did Which and When?', in *Airpower: Theory and Practice*, ed. John Gooch (London: Cass, 1995), pp. 145–74.

57 See, for example, Tami Davis Biddle, 'British and American Approaches to Strategic bombing: Their Origins and Implementation in the World War II Combined Bomber Offensive', in Gooch (ed.), *Airpower*.

58 See Gray, *Leadership and Direction*, p. 208 for the Casablanca Conference.

59 Buckley, *Air Power in an Age of Total War*, p. 127.

60 See David Ian Hall, *Strategy for Victory: The Development of British Tactical Air Power 1919-1943* (London: Praeger, 2008), p. 37.

61 See ibid., and Brad William Gladman, *Intelligence and Anglo American Air Support in World War II: The Western Desert and Tunisia 1940-1943* (Basingstoke: Palgrave, 2008).

62 See Jones, *The Origins of Strategic Bombing*, p. 13.

63 See Gian P. Gentile, *How Effective is Strategic Bombing: Lessons Learned from World War II to Kosovo* (New York: New York University Press, 2001) which deals in particular with the US Bombing Survey. For the British equivalent, see Air Ministry, *The Strategic Air War Against Germany 1939-1945: Official Report of the British Bombing Survey Unit* (London: Cass, 1998); also available without forewords as TNA AIR 10/3866.

64 Gentile, *How Effective is Strategic Bombing*, p. 147. For the growth of the Russian equivalent, see David R. Jones, 'The Emperor and the Despot: Statesmen, Patronage and the strategic Bomber in Imperial and Soviet Russia, 1909-1959', in *The Influence of Airpower upon History: Statesmanship, Diplomacy and Foreign Policy since 1903*, ed. Robin Higham and Mark Parillo (Lexington, KY: University of Kentucky Press, 2013), p. 137.

65 'Putin honours submarine rescue team', *Guardian* 5 October 2005, http://www.theguardian.com/uk/2005/oct/05/russia.world (accessed 2 May 2015).

66 Ian Gooderson, *Air Power at the Battlefront: Allied Close Air Support in Europe 1943-1945* (London: Cass, 1998) draws on the Operational Research Team's reporting.

67 Tooze, *Wages of Destruction*, p. 602.

68 This is most pronounced in the chapter on China by Andrew S. Erickson, 'Chinese Statesmen and the Use of Airpower', in Higham and Parillo (eds), *The Influence of Airpower*, p. 237.

Chapter 6

1 James MacGregor Burns, *Leadership* (New York: Harper, 1979), p. 2.

2 Ibid.

3 These issues are discussed at length in Gray, *Leadership, Direction and Legitimacy of the RAF Bomber Offensive*. They are also influenced by many discussions with senior military and civilian colleagues in the course of the

author's directorship of the Defence Leadership and Management Centre in the Defence Academy.

4 These remain Crown Copyright and are used with permission. They have been published in, for example, Gray, *Leadership, Direction and Legitimacy of the RAF Bomber Offensive* and Peter W. Gray and Jonathan Harvey in 'Strategic Leadership Education', in *In Pursuit of Excellence: International Perspectives of Military Leadership*, ed. Colonel Bernd Horn and Lieutenant-Colonel Allister MacIntyre (Kingston, ON: Canadian Defence Academy Press, 2006).

5 Brian Howieson and Howard Kahn, 'Leadership, Management and Command: The Officers' Trinity', in Gray and Cox (eds), *Air Power Leadership*, p. 16.

6 James G. Hunt, *Leadership: A New Synthesis* (London: Sage, 1991), p. 4. See also Kimberley B. Boal and Robert Hooijberg, 'Strategic Leadership research: Moving On', *Leadership Quarterly* 11 (2001), pp. 515–49. For the extension of Hunt's work into the military context see Leonard Wong, Paul Bliese and Dennis McGurk, 'Military leadership: A context specific review', *Leadership Quarterly* 14 (2003), pp. 657–92.

7 Andrew Kakabadse and Nada Kakabadse, *Essence of Leadership* (London: Thomson, 1999), pp. 298–9.

8 See, for example, John Keegan, *The Mask of Command: A Study of Generalship* (London: Pimlico, 1999 [1987]), pp. 40–4.

9 David V. Day and Robert G. Lord, 'Executive Leadership and Organizational Performance: Suggestions for a New Theory and Methodology', *Journal of Management* 14, no. 3 (1988), pp. 459–61.

10 See Hunt, *Leadership: A New* Synthesis, p. 71 for the stratified systems theory approach. For a more conventional view, see John Adair, *Effective Strategic Leadership* (London: Pan, 2003), p. 95.

11 This was particularly true of the discussion in Chiefs of Staff meetings in the mid-1930s. See, for example, Bond, *British Military Policy Between the Two World Wars*. Bond is far more eloquent on the subject than his air counterpart Montgomery Hyde, *British Air Policy Between the Wars 1918-1939*.

12 Field Marshal Lord Alanbrooke, *War Diaries 1939-1945*, ed. Alex Danchev and Daniel Todman (London: Wiedenfeld & Nicholson, 2001), and Gray, *Leadership, Direction and Legitimacy of the RAF Bomber Offensive*, p. 178.

13 This is broadly constant in the literature, but for a brief guide, see Adair, *Effective Strategic Leadership*, p. 95.

14 See H. Rittell and M. Webber, 'Dilemmas in a General Theory of Planning', *Policy Sciences* 4 (1973), pp. 155–69. For the application of this typology to the military environment, see Keith Grint, *Leadership, Management and Command; Rethinking D-Day* (Basingstoke: Palgrave Macmillan, 2008), pp. 11–18.

15 This applies equally to other services. See Lawrence M. Hanser, Louis W. Miller, Herbert J. Shukiar and Bruce Newsome, *Developing Senior Navy Leaders: Requirements for Flag Officer Expertise Today and in the Future* (Santa Monica, CA: RAND, 2008), p. 8. In addition, the British army places a huge emphasis on performance in command, or field, appointments in their promotion system.

16 See, for example, Peter Gray, 'The Balkan Air Wars: Air Power as a Weapon of First Political Choice', in *A Century of Military Aviation 1914–2014*, ed. Wing Commander Keith Brent (Canberra, CT: Air Power Development Centre, 2014), pp. 171–86.

17 Annual Chief of Defence Staff Lecture, 3 December 2009, available at https:// www.rusi.org/events/past/ref:E4B184DB05C4E3/ (accessed 26 August 2014).

18 AIR 10/1910, Air Publication 1300, *Royal Air Force War Manual; Part I Operations*. ch. III.

19 Ibid., p. 8.

20 Ibid., p. 14.

21 London, LHCMA, KCL, Brooke-Popham Papers 1/5/3 and 1/5/4 for the opening address and 1/6/1 for *Some Notes on Morale*.

22 Squadron Leader C. F. A. Portal DSO, MC, 'An Essay on Morale', Air Publication 956, *A Selection of Essays From the Work of Officers Attending the First Course at the Royal Air Force Staff College 1922-1923*. Ch. VIII. See also Gray, *Leadership, Direction and Legitimacy of the RAF Bomber Offensive*, pp. 39–45.

23 Examples include *A Guide to Reading on Professionalism and Leadership* (Canadian Forces Leadership Institute); Allan English (ed.), *The Operational Art: Canadian Perspectives, Leadership and Command* (Kingston, ON: Canadian Defence Academy Press, 2006) and Gray and Cox (ed.), *Air Power Leadership*.

24 AP 3000, 3rd edn. p. 1.3.1 and AP 3000, 4th edn. p. 61.

25 Ibid., and Lord Tedder, *Air Power in War: The Lees Knowles Lectures by Marshal of the Royal Air Force The Lord Tedder* (London: Hodder and Stoughton, 1947), p. 91.

26 For short biographies of all the chiefs, see Henry Probert, *High Commanders of the Royal Air Force* (London: HMSO, 1991).

27 Tedder, *Air Power in War*, p. 89.

28 Ibid., p. 91.

29 Ibid., p. 92.

30 Ibid., pp. 92–3.

31 See Gray, *Leadership, Direction and Legitimacy of the RAF Bomber Offensive*, on the Casablanca Conference, pp. 208–12.

32 This was evident during the First World War with Henderson, Sykes and Trenchard maintaining direct reporting links to Haig's headquarters.

33 *Concise Oxford Dictionary*, p. 327.

34 Clausewitz, *On War*, ch. 5, p. 639.

35 Richard E. Simkin, *Race to the Swift: Thoughts on Twenty-First Century Warfare* (London: Brasseys, 1985), pp. 227–55.

36 Simkin, *Race to the Swift*, p. 230.

37 JWP 0-01, *British Defence Doctrine*, 2nd edn. pp. 3–7, and JDP 0-01, 4th edn. pp. 5–5.

38 Ibid.

39 JDP 0-01, *British Defence Doctrine*, 4th edn. p. 5–5. This phrase does not appear in the 2nd edn.

40 See, for example, AP 3000, 4th edn. p. 61. But see also Section 3, 'Air command and control' in JDP 0-30.

41 JP 3-30 *Command and Control of Joint Air Operations* (US Joint Staff, 10 February 2014) available at http://www.dtic.mil/doctrine/new_pubs/jp3_30.pdf (accessed 1 September 2014).

42 This tension is discussed, and circumnavigated in AP 3000, 4th edn. pp. 62–3. See also JP 3-30, pp. 1-3–1-4.

43 See Air Commodore Stuart Peach, 'The Airman's dilemma: To Command or To Control', in Peter W. Gray (ed.), *Air Power 21: Challenges for the New Century* (Norwich: HMSO, 2000), p. 126.

44 Although the language used is along the lines of showing 'some flaws', see Florence Gaub, *The North Atlantic Treaty Organization and Libya: Reviewing Operation Unified Protector* (Carlisle, PA: Strategic Studies Institute, June 2013), p. viii. See http://www.strategicstudiesinstitute.army.mil/pdffiles/PUB1161.pdf (accessed 1 September 2014).

45 Clausewitz, *On War*, Book VIII, ch. 6B, p. 731.

46 Ibid.

47 For a wider treatment, see Beatrice Heuser, *Reading Clausewitz* (London: Pimlico, 2002), ch. 3. See also the supporting essays in the Howard and Paret translation.

48 In conducting research, and taking evidence, for the University of Birmingham Policy Commission Report. *Implications for Policy Makers*, this was frequently referred to colloquially as 'Predator Porn'.

49 Mark Clodfelter, *The Limits of Air Power; The American Bombing of North Vietnam* (New York: Free Press, 1989), p. 37.

50 See https://www.gov.uk/government/organisations/national-security/groups/national-security-council (accessed 3 September 2014).

51 Sir Lawrence Freedman, *The Official History of the Falklands Campaign: Volume II, War and Diplomacy* (London: Routledge, 2005), pp. 22–3.

52 It is not worth explaining this in detail; it is very much the province of staff colleges. It is also bound to be subject to amendment, fluctuation and so forth. See JDP 5-00, *Campaign Planning* (2nd edn, change 2, July 2013).

53 Freedman, *The Official History of the Falklands Campaign: Volume II*, p. 21. Quotation taken from Peter Hennessy, *The Prime Minister: The Office and its Holders Since 1946* (London: Allen, 2000), ch. 16.

54 Gray, *Leadership, Direction and Legitimacy of the RAF Bomber Offensive*, p. 276.

55 For the importance, see Tooze, *The Wages of Destruction*, p. 648.

56 Probert, *Bomber Harris*, p. 303.

57 Webster and Frankland, *Strategic air Offensive against Germany*, Vol. III, p. 45 onwards.

58 Harris, *Bomber Offensive*, p. 215.

59   Webster and Frankland, *Strategic Air Offensive against Germany*, Vol. IV,
     App.8 (xl), Directive by Air Marshal Norman Bottomley, deputy chief of the
     Air Staff and General Carl Spaatz.

60   Ibid.

61   Webster and Frankland, *Strategic Air Offensive against Germany*, Vol. IV, App.
     25, Note, Tedder to Portal on 'Air Policy to be adopted with a View to Rapid
     Defeat of Germany' dated 25 October 1944.

62   AIR 41/56, pp.152–3.

63   AIR 37/1013, Letter Harris to Portal dated 1 November 1944.

64   Ibid.

65   Webster and Frankland, *Strategic Air Offensive against Germany*, Vol. III, p. 83.

66   Portal Papers, Folder 10, E32A, Letter Portal to Harris dated 5 November
     1944.

67   Ibid.

68   See Goulter, 'British Official Histories of the Air War', p. 141 and Frankland,
     History at War, p. 88.

69   Ibid.

70   Portal Papers, Folder 10, E32b, Letter Harris to Portal dated 6 November 1944.

71   Ibid.

72   Portal Papers, Folder 10, E32c, Letter Portal to Harris dated 12 November 1944.

73   Portal Papers, Folder 10 (1945), E1, Letter Harris to Portal dated 12 December
     1944.

74   Ibid.

75   Richards, *Portal*, p. 320.

76   File copy on AIR 8/1020.

77   Portal Papers, Folder 10 (1945), E2, Letter Portal to Harris dated 22 December
     1944.

78   Ibid.

79   Portal Papers, Folder 10 (1945), E3, Letter Harris to Portal dated 28 December
     1944.

80   Webster and Frankland, *Strategic Air Offensive against Germany*, Vol. III, p. 87.

81   Ibid.

82   Portal Papers, Folder 10 (1945), E3, Letter Harris to Portal dated 28 December
     1944.

83   AIR 8/1020, Minute Bufton to Portal dated 3 January 1945.

84   Cox, Introduction to Harris, *Despatch*, pp. xxii–xxiv. See also Cox, 'Sir Arthur
     Harris and the Air Ministry', in *Air Power Leadership: Theory and Practice*,
     ed. Peter Gray and Sebastian Cox (London: HMSO, 2002), p. 224.

85   AIR 8/1020, Minute Bufton to Portal dated 3 January 1945.

86   Portal Papers, Folder 10 (1945), E3, Letter Harris to Portal dated 28
     December 1944. For life on the receiving end, see Martin Middlebrook (ed.),

*The Everlasting Arms: The War Memoirs of Air Commodore John Searby
DSO, DFC* (London: William Kimber, 1988), ch. X.

87 Portal Papers, Folder 10, E3a, Letter Portal to Harris dated 8 January 1945.

88 Webster and Frankland, *Strategic Air Offensive against Germany*, Vol. III, p. 90.

89 The official historians make a perfectly valid case on the war of attrition that was being fought between Bomber Command and the German fighter force, alone at first and then with the huge numbers the USSTAF was able to throw at the conflict; see Webster and Frankland, *Strategic Air Offensive against Germany*, Vol. III, pp. 90–93.

90 Portal Papers, Folder 10, E3b, Letter Harris to Portal dated 18 January 1945.

91 Ibid.

92 Portal Papers, Folder 10, E3c, Letter Portal to Harris dated 20 January 1945.

93 Probably the best analysis of the validity of the criticisms of Harris is by Cox in his introduction to Harris, *Despatch*, pp. xxii–xxiv.

94 Harris's disagreement over Pathfinders has been quoted above; for disagreement even on the post mortem, see Portal Papers, Folder 10, E15, Letter Portal to Harris dated 12 April 1944 and subsequent reply. For incendiaries, see Portal Papers' Folder 9, E3c, Letter Harris to Portal, dated 28 February 1942, in response to Cherwell's advocacy of the plan.

95 This was the nickname used to describe Churchill's late night discussions.

96 Portal Papers, Folder 6, E7, Minute Churchill to CAS dated 28 January 1945.

97 Ibid.

98 Portal Papers, Folder 6, E7, Minute Portal to Churchill dated 28 January 1945.

Chapter 7

1 University of Birmingham Policy Commission VI, *The Security Impact of Drones: Challenges and Opportunities for the UK* (University of Birmingham, October 2014), http://www.birmingham.ac.uk/Documents/research/policycommission/remote-warfare/final-report-october-2014.pdf (accessed 3 January 2015). See p. 56 onwards for the ethical debate.

2 Adam Roberts, 'Land Warfare: From Hague to Nuremberg', in *The Laws of War: Constraints on Warfare in the Western World*, ed. Michael Howard, George J. Andreopoulos and Mark R. Shulman (New Haven: Yale University Press, 1994), pp. 119–20.

3 Ibid.

4 Clausewitz, *On War*, p. 83.

5 Michael Howard, '*Temperamenta Belli*: Can War be Controlled?', in *Restraints on War: Studies in the Limitation of Armed Conflict*, ed. Michael Howard (Oxford: Oxford University Press, 1979), p. 3.

6 Ibid.

7 Ibid., p. 4.

8 Widely attributed to the descriptions of the proposed air campaign in the build up to the second Gulf War in 2003.

9 Rosalyn Higgins, *Problems and Processes: International Law and How We Use It* (Oxford: Oxford University Press, 1994), chapters. 1 and 2 generally and p. 13 in particular.

10 W. Hays Parks, 'Air War and the Law of War', *Air Force Law Review* 32, no. 2 (1990), pp. 1–225, fn. 5. The use of this quotation by an eminent military lawyer is interesting in itself. The original, which is not cited by Parks, was from H. Lauterpacht, 'The Problem of the Revision of the Law of War', *British Yearbook of International Law* (1952), p. 382.

11 See, for example: Andrew Clapham (ed.), *The Oxford Handbook of International Law in Armed Conflict (Oxford Handbooks in Law)* (Oxford: Oxford University Press, 2014), Adam Roberts and Richard Guelff (eds), *Documents on the Laws of War* (Oxford: Oxford University Press, 2000), A. P. Rogers, *Law on the Battlefield* (Manchester: Juris Publishing, 2004), Christine Gray, *International Law and the use of Force* (Oxford: Oxford University Press, 2008). The list of general books is both extensive and expensive!

12 See, for example, Gary D. Solis, *The Law of Armed Conflict: International Humanitarian Law in War* (Cambridge: Cambridge University Press, 2010), Elisabeth Wilmshurst, *International Law and the Classification of Conflicts* (Oxford: Oxford University Press, 2012) and Travers Macleod, *Rule of Law in War: International Law and United States Counterinsurgency in Iraq and Afghanistan* (Oxford: Oxford University Press, 2015).

13 William H. Boothby, *The Law of Targeting* (Oxford: Oxford University Press, 2012), Noam Lubell, *Extraterritorial Use of Force Against Non-State Actors* (Oxford: Oxford University Press, 2010), Claire Finkelstein, Jens David Ohlin and Andrew Altman (eds), *Targeted Killings: Law and Morality in an Asymmetrical World* (Oxford: Oxford University Press, 2012) and Nils Melzer, *Targeted Killing in International Law* (Oxford: Oxford University Press, 2008).

14 See the translated French text, Olivier Corten, *The Law Against War: The Prohibition on the Use of Force in Contemporary International Law* (Oxford: Hart, 2010).

15 Charter of the United Nations 1945, Ch. 1 Art. 2, para. 4, available at http://www.un.org/en/documents/charter/chapter1.shtml (accessed 5 January 2015).

16 UN Charter, Ch. 7, Art 39. See, for example, UNSCR 678 which authorized member states 'to use all necessary means' in the war against Iraq after its illegal occupation of Kuwait.

17 UN Charter, Ch. 7, Art 51. See also North Atlantic Treaty, Art. 5.

18 Higgins, *Problems and Processes*, p. 230.

19 See JSP 383, *Manual of the Law of armed Conflict*, para. 1.6, available at https://www.gov.uk/government/uploads/system/uploads/attachment_data/file/27874/JSP3832004Edition.pdf (accessed 5 January 2015).

20 Ian Brownlie, *Principles of Public International Law*, 4th edn (Oxford: Clarendon, 1990 [1966]), pp. 4–11.

21 Roberts and Guelff, *Documents on the Laws of War*, pp. 12–13.

22 Ibid., p.13.

23 Roberts and Guelff, *Documents on the Laws of War*, pp. 35 and 59. For detailed commentary see Parks, 'Air War and the Law of War', pp. 9–12.

24 Roberts and Guelff, *Documents on the Laws of War*, p. 67.

25 Ibid., p. 78.

26 Ibid.

27 See M. W. Royse, *Aerial Bombardment and the International Regulation of Warfare* (New York: Harold Vinal, 1928), pp. 215–16.

28 Roberts and Guelff, *Documents on the Laws of War*, p. 140. The full text is at App. 3.

29 Ibid., p. 140.

30 Tami Davis Biddle, 'Air Power', in Howard, Andreopoulos and Shulman (eds), *The Laws of War*, p. 148.

31 See Gray, *Leadership, Direction and Legitimacy of the RAF Bomber Offensive*, pp. 54–7.

32 Ibid.

33 HC Deb, 21 June 1938, Vol. 337, cc919-1045.

34 Ibid.

35 See Gray, 'The Gloves Will Have to Come Off' for the debates within the Air Ministry.

36 Roberts and Guelff, *Documents on the Laws of War*, pp. 20 and 175–8 and JSP 383, para. 1.29.

37 Roberts and Guelff, *Documents on the Laws of War*, chapters 17–20.

38 Ibid., p. 442.

39 Ibid.

40 Ibid., p. 10.

41 JSP 383, para. 2.2.3.

42 See JSP 383, para. 2.4 and Roberts and Guelff, *Documents on the Laws of War*, pp. 8–10.

43 See JSP 383, para. 2.5 and Roberts and Guelff, *Documents on the Laws of War*, pp. 447–52.

44 AP I, Article 50 of; Roberts and Guelff, *Documents on the Laws of War*, p. 448.

45 JSP 383, para. 2.5.3.

46 Roberts and Guelff, *Documents on the Laws of War*, pp. 9–10.

47 AP I, Article 51(5)(b), Roberts and Guelff, *Documents on the Laws of War*, p. 449.

48 See, for example, Yoram Dinstein, *Non-International Armed Conflicts in International Law* (Cambridge: Cambridge University Press, 2014).

49 Ibid., p. 3.

50 Roberts and Guelff, *Documents on the Laws of War*, p. 481.

51 Ibid., pp. 483–512.

52 JSP 383, para. 15.3.1.

53 Dinstein, *Non-International Armed Conflict*, p. 3. See also UoB Policy Commission VI, *The Security Impact of Drones*, p. 45.

54 UoB Policy Commission VI, *The Security Impact of Drones*, p. 45 citing the International Court of Justice, Armed Activities on the Territory of the Congo (Democratic Republic of the Congo v. Uganda), Judgment, I.C.J. Reports 2005, p. 243, http://www.icj-cij.org/docket/files/116/10455.pdf (accessed 5 January 2015).

55 *Concise Oxford Dictionary*, p. 463.

56 For the latter, see UoB Policy Commission VI, *The Security Impact of Drones*, ch. 4.

57 Carlo D'Este, *Warlord: A Life of Churchill at War 1874–1945* (London: Allen Lane, 2008), p. 732.

58 See, for example, A. C. Grayling, *Among the Dead Cities: Was the Allied Bombing of Civilians in WW2 a Necessity or a Crime?* (London: Bloomsbury, 2006). Note also the chapter by Donald Bloxham, 'Dresden as a War Crime', in *Firestorm: The Bombing of Dresden in 1945*, ed. Paul Addison and Jeremy A. Crang (London: Pimlico, 2006), pp. 180–208. For the economist's view, see Tooze, *The Wages of Destruction*.

59 General Viscount Wolseley, *The Life of John Churchill, Duke of Marlborough to the Accession of Queen Anne* (London: Richard Bentley and Son, 1894), Vol. 2, p. 84.

60 Wolseley was Commander-in-Chief of the British army from 1895 to 1901; see Hew Strachan, *Politics of the British Army* (Oxford: Clarendon Press. 1997), pp. 65–6.

61 See Bernard Williams, 'Ethics', in *Philosophy 1: A Guide to the Subject*, ed. A. C. Grayling (Oxford: Oxford University Press, 1995), p. 551. See also 'Who was Jeremy Bentham?' at http://www.ucl.ac.uk/Bentham-Project/who (accessed 7 January 2015).

62 Jeremy Bentham and John Stuart Mill, *Utilitarianism and other Essays* (London: Penguin 1987). There is obviously a considerably wider literature, but this provides the basics.

63 Ibid., p. 65.

64 Williams, 'Ethics', p. 554.

65 See Paul R. Viotti and Mark V. Kauppi, *International Relations Theory: Realism, Pluralism, Globalism* (New York: Macmillan, 1987), p. 37.

66 W. V. Herbert Esq., (late Captain, Turkish Army), 'The Ethics of Warfare', *JRUSI* 42, no. 2 (1898 July/December), p. 1022.

67 Ibid., p. 1024.

68 Ibid., p. 1025.

69 Ibid., p. 1028.

70 Ibid., p. 1029.

71 Ibid., p. 1032.

72 Gary Wills, *Saint Augustine* (London: Phoenix, 2000 [1999]), p. 121.

73 Charles Guthrie and Michael Quinlan, *Just War: The Just War Tradition, Ethics in Modern Warfare* (London: Bloomsbury, 2007), p. 7. See also Fritz Allhof, Nicholas G. Evans and Adam Henschke (eds), *Routledge Handbook of Ethics and War: Just war Theory in the Twenty-first Century* (Abingdon: Routledge, 2013), p. 1.

74 Ibid.

75 Michael Walzer, *Just and Unjust Wars: A Moral Argument with Historical Illustrations* (New York: Basic Books, 1977). The fourth edition (2006) includes Walzer's comments on the invasion of Iraq. The Vietnam link is at the very opening of the Preface to the original edition which features, with differing page numbers, in all editions.

76 See also Michael Walzer, *Arguing about War* (New Haven, CT: Yale University Press, 2004) and Jean Bethke Elshtain (ed.), *Just War Theory* (Oxford: Blackwell, 1992).

77 Walzer, *Just and Unjust Wars*, 4th edn, p. 251.

78 Ibid., pp. 251–5.

79 Ibid., pp. 256–7.

80 On the latter, see Dr Peter Lee, 'Rights, Wrongs and Drones: Remote Warfare, Ethics and the Challenge of Just War Reasoning', *RAF Air Power Review* 16, no. 3 (Autumn/Winter 2013), pp. 30–49.

81 See, for example, John Quigley, 'The United States' Withdrawal from International Court of justice Jurisdiction in Consular Cases: Reasons and Consequences', *Duke Journal of Comparative and International Law* 19, no. 263 (2009), available at http://scholarship.law.duke.edu/cgi/viewcontent.cgi?article=1057&context=djcil (accessed 6 January 2015).

82 See, for example, *Report of the International Court of Justice, 1 August 2013-31 July 2014*, General Assembly A/69/4 available at http://www.icj-cij.org/court/en/reports/report_2013-2014.pdf (accessed 6 January 2015).

83 UoB Policy Commission VI, *The Security Impact of Drones*, ch. 4.

84 Guthrie and Quinlan, *Just War*, pp. 47–9.

85 HC Deb, 21 June 1938, Vol.m 337, cc919-1045. Mr Noel-Baker, c920.

86 The Prime Minister, ibid., c936.

87 Ibid.

88 Ibid. These were based on the Draft Hague Rules.

89 AIR 20/22, Minute J. B. Abraham to C-in-C Bomber Command dated 15 September 1938. See also AIR 41/5, Section D, 'Air Ministry Instructions of 15 September 1938'.

90 Ibid.

91 Ibid.

92 AIR 41/5, Section D, 'Admiralty Proposals 1939'.

93 Ibid. Group Captain J. C. Slessor forwarded a copy of *Bomber Command Operation Instruction No.2* to Malkin to inform the meeting. ADM 116/4155, Minute dated 9 August 1939. The Committee was under the chairmanship of Sir William Malkin, legal advisor to the Foreign Office. AIR 41/5, Section D, 'The Malkin Proposals Dropped'. Parks, 'Air War and the Law of War', p. 43. Full report at ADM 116/4155, *Sub-Committee on the Humanisation of Aerial Warfare: Report*, dated 15 July 1938.

94 AIR 41/5, Section D, 'Interdepartmental Committee. August 1939'.

95 AIR 41/5, Section D, 'Proposed Permissible Objectives'.

96 AIR 41/5, Section D, 'Air Council Instructions of 22 August 1939'.

97 Ibid.

98 Ibid.

99 Ibid.

100 Ibid.

101 Parks, 'Air War and the Law of War', p. 50.

102 Ibid.

103 Beyond the works of Spaight, see Philip Landon, 'Aerial Bombardment & International Law', *JRUSI* 77 (1932), p. 44.

104 Parks, 'Air War and the Law of War', p. 49.

105 Webster and Frankland, *Strategic Air Offensive against Germany*, Vol. I, p. 129. They quote this for the first two years of the war.

106 AIR 41/5, Section D, 'Our Long-term Policy'.

107 AIR 14/194, Paper by D of Plans dated 7 September 1939, 'Note on the Question of Relaxing the Bombardment Instructions and Initiating Extended Air Attack'.

108 Webster and Frankland, *Strategic Air Offensive against Germany*, Vol. I, p. 135.

109 Ibid.

110 AIR 2/4474, Telegram CAS to Barratt dated 16 October 1939, encl 14A. Dean, who was in the civil directorate S6 at the time agreed that bombing in the west was not carried out because it suited Britain, France and Germany; Maurice Dean, The *Royal Air Force and Two World Wars* (London: Cassell, 1979), p. 264.

111 Directive (DCAS – Douglas) to Portal dated 4 June 1940; Webster and Frankland, *Strategic Air Offensive against Germany*, Vol. IV, App. 8 (xi). AIR 14/77 in which 'in no circumstances should night bombing degenerate into mere indiscriminate action, which is contrary to the policy of His Majesty's Government'.

112 Self, *Chamberlain*, p. 393. See also Robert Self (ed.), *The Neville Chamberlain Diary Letters, Vol IV; The Downing Street Years, 1934–1940* (Aldershot: Ashgate, 2005): Letter to Ida dated 10 September 1939.

113 Self, *Chamberlain*, p. 237.

114 Self, *The Diary Letters*, Letter to Ida dated 10 September 1939.

115 AIR 41/5, Section D, 'Bombing Instructions of 4 June 1940'.

116 Parks, 'Air War and the Law of War', p. 47.

117 AIR 41/5, Section D, 'Berlin'.

118 Ibid.

119 AIR 14/194, Minute SASO to Groups dated 14 June 1940.

120 AIR 41/5, Section D, 'Directive of 30th October 1940'. See also Webster and Frankland, *Strategic Air Offensive against Germany*, Vol. IV, p. 128, para. 3.

121 Ibid., p. 129, para. 3(b).

122 Ibid., p. 129, para. 4 (ii).

123 Ibid.

124 Webster and Frankland, *Strategic Air Offensive against Germany*, Vol. IV, p. 133 for the former directive dated 9 March 1941, and p. 135 for the latter dated 9 July 1941. See also Vol. II, p. 167ff for the discussion on the move to area bombing.

125 AIR 41/5, Section D, 'Help for Russia'.

126 Webster and Frankland, *Strategic Air Offensive against Germany*, Vol. IV, p. 138, Directive dated 9 July, App. A, para. 3.

127 Ibid.

128 COS Memo 31 July 1941 in Webster and Frankland, *Strategic Air Offensive against Germany*, Vol. II, pp. 180–1.

129 Ibid., p. 182.

130 Ibid., pp. 183–5.

131 Ibid., pp. 185–7.

132 Webster and Frankland, *Strategic Air Offensive against Germany*, Vol. IV, p. 142, Directive dated 13 November 1941.

133 Ibid., p. 143, Directive dated 14 February 1942, para. 1.

134 Ibid., p. 144, para. 4(ii).

135 Ibid., p. 144, para. 5.

136 Churchill, op. cit.

137 W. V. Herbert, 'The Ethics of Warfare', p. 1029.

138 The world of experimental psychology emphasizes this with the work of Stanley Milgram in particular. In his now infamous experiment (now considered highly unethical) Milgram demonstrated that under the guidance and authority of a scientist, the subject would eventually apply lethal electric shocks to the victim (a stooge) but the incremental nature made the whole possible. The same is said to apply to the persecution of the Jews in Nazi Germany. See Stanley Milgram, *Obedience to Authority: An Experimental View* (London: Tavistock, 1974).

Chapter 8

1 Joint Doctrine Publication 0-01 (JDP 0-01), *UK Defence Doctrine*, 5th edn, November 2014, p. 19.

2 As occurred, for example, just before the start of Operation *Desert Fox* in December 1998; personal interview with author.

3   See, for example, Lord Tedder, *With Prejudice: The War Memoirs of MRAF Lord Tedder* (London: Cassell, 1966), pp. 412–13 where the prime minister is complaining of a lack of information over air operations.

4   Webster and Frankland, *The Strategic Air Offensive against Germany*, Vol. II, p. 158.

5   JDP 0-01, second and fifth editions.

6   COS (42) 466 (O). Final. Dated 31 December 1942. 'American-British strategy in 1943'. Reproduced in full at Michael Howard, *Grand Strategy*, Vol. IV (London: HMSO, 1970), App. III (A).

7   See Gray, *The Leadership, Direction and Legitimacy of the RAF Bomber Offensive*, pp. 208–12.

8   See Freedman, *The Official History of the Falklands Campaign*, Vol. II, p. 155 which covers the extent of military support.

9   General Sir John Reith evidence to the Iraq Inquiry, 18 January 2010, available at http://www.iraqinquiry.org.uk/media/42508/100115am-reith.pdf (accessed 6 January 2014). The Goldwater-Nichols legislation was introduced in an attempt to eliminate inter-service rivalry in the United States. The senior joint force commander was entitled to go directly to the civilian political leadership.

10   JDP 0-01, *UK Defence Doctrine*, p. 7.

11   See RAND Corporation, *After Saddam: Prewar Planning and the Occupation of Iraq* (Santa Monica, CA: RAND, 2008). As with many RAND reports, this was commissioned by one of the services, in this case the US Army.

12   Part of this is because desk officers move on and their replacements are looking for something new to say. The same is true at senior levels. Occasionally, a more intellectually appropriate concept comes along.

13   AP 3000, third edition, 2.6.

14   Ibid.

15   See Peter Gray, 'The Balkan Air War(s): Air Power as a Weapon of First Choice', in *A Century of Military Aviation 1914-2014: Proceedings of the 2014 RAAF Air Power Conference*, ed. Keith Brent (Canberra, ACT: Air Power Development Centre, 2014), pp. 161–2. See also Benjamin S. Lambeth, *NATO's Air War for Kosovo: A Strategic and Operational Assessment* (Santa Monica, CA: RAND, 2001), Stephen T. Hosmer, *The Conflict over Kosovo: Why Milosevic Decided to settle When He Did* (Santa Monica, CA: RAND, 2001).

16   Discussion with the author during US JFACC courses on which the author taught at Hurlbert AFB. Lambeth, *NATO's Air War*, p. 190.

17   Lambeth, *NATO's Air War*, pp. 190–91. Short used to regale audiences on the JFACC course with stories of this.

18   Peter Gray, 'Air Power: Strategic Lessons from an Idiosyncratic Campaign', in *The Falklands Conflict Twenty Years On: Lessons for the Future*, ed. Stephen Badsey, Mark Grove and Rob Havers (London: Cass, 2005), p. 253.

19   See, for example, A. D. Redmond, 'Operation Irma acted as a catalyst', *British Medical Journal* 307 (1993), p. 1425, available at http://www.ncbi.

nlm.nih.gov/pmc/articles/PMC1679624/pdf/bmj00049-0065a.pdf (accessed 7 January 2015).

20   See, for example, Helena P. Schrader, *The Blockade Breakers: The Berlin Airlift* (Stroud: The History Press, 2008) or Roger G. Miller, *To save a City: The Berlin Airlift 1948-1949* (Bolling, DC: Air Force History and Museums Program, 2013).

21   JDP 0-01, *UK Defence Doctrine*, p. 7.

22   Holden Reid, *Studies in British Military Thought*, p. 17.

23   John Kiszely, 'Thinking about the Operational Level', *JRUSI* (December 2005), p. 38.

24   David T. Zabecki, *The German 1918 Offensives: A Case Study in the Operational Level of War* (Abingdon: Routledge, 2006), pp. 11–12. Zabecki took his analogy from the US Army Command and Staff College and warned that, while useful, it should not be pushed too far.

25   Vallance (ed.), *Air Power*, p. xviii.

26   Edward N. Luttwak, 'The Operational Level of War', *International Security 5*, no. 3 (Winter 1980/81), p. 61.

27   Mackenzie and Holden Reid (eds), *The British Army and the Operational Level of War*, p. 10.

28   The author is a graduate of the HCSC and was assistant director for the 2001 course. He subsequently provided strategic leadership education for the students.

29   Shimon Naveh, *In Pursuit of Military Excellence: The Evolution of Operational Theory*, (Abingdon: Cass, 1997), p. 9.

30   Ibid., pp. 10–11 for Russian thinking and 11–13 for US developments.

31   Stephen J. Zaccaro, *The Nature of Executive Leadership: A Conceptual and Empirical Analysis of Success* (Washington, DC: American Psychological Association, 2001), pp. 7 and 12.

32   See Gray, *The Leadership, Direction and Legitimacy of the RAF Bomber Offensive*, pp. 246–7.

33   Portal Papers, Folder 9, E63, Letter Portal to Harris dated 10 October 1942.

34   Tedder, *With Prejudice*, p. 460.

35   Colonel Phillip S. Meilinger, 'Ten Propositions: Emerging Air Power', *Airpower Journal* (Spring 1996), p. 2. Available at http://www.au.af.mil/au/awc/awcgate/au/meil.pdf (accessed 7 January 2015). The Propositions were also published as a small pamphlet and widely distributed through the USAF and more widely.

36   R. V. Jones, 'Intelligence and command', in *Leaders and Intelligence*, ed. Michael I. Handel (London: Cass, 1989), p. 288.

37   See, for example, Douglas Barrie, 'Show but Don't Tell', *Aerospace* 42, no. 1 (January 2015), p. 38 covers a visit to the Chinese Zhuhai Air Show in November 2014. See also http://aerosociety.com/News/Insight-Blog/2697/Rising-eagle-preWW2-German-air-power (accessed 7 January 2015) for an article on open-source material on the Luftwaffe in the interwar years.

38 See Sebastian Cox, 'Sources and Organisation of RAF Intelligence', in *The Conduct of the Air War in the Second World War: An International Comparison*, ed. Horst Boog (Oxford: Berg, 1992), p. 553.

39 See AIR 20/8143 for the absence of reporting. Webster and Frankland, *Strategic Air Offensive against Germany*, Vol. II, p. 255. See PREM 3/193/6A, JIC (43) 367 Final dated 9 September 1943 'Probabilities of a German Collapse'.

40 For the so-called 'dodgy dossier' see http://news.bbc.co.uk/nol/shared/spl/hi/ middle_east/02/uk_dossier_on_iraq/pdf/iraqdossier.pdf (accessed 7 January 2015).

41 See, for example, Paul K. Davies, *Effects-Based Operations: A Grand Challenge for the Analytical Community* (Santa Monica, CA: RAND, 2001) and Brigadier General David A. Deptula, *Effects-Based Operations: Change in the Nature of Warfare* (Arlington, VA: Aerospace Education Foundation, 2001).

42 See Webster and Frankland, *Strategic Air Offensive against Germany*, Vol. IV, App. 8 (xl), Directive by Air Marshal Norman Bottomley, deputy chief of the Air Staff to C-in-C Bomber Command dated 25 September 1944.

43 AIR 3/9303, Minute AMP to PUS, CAS and SofS dated 31 August 1945.

44 See Peter Gray, 'A Culture of Official Squeamishness?' p. 1375.

45 See James Gow, *Triumph of the Lack of Will: International Diplomacy and the Yugoslav War* (New York: Columbia University Press, 1997), p. 17.

46 Rugova was a quietly spoken academic who shunned all question of militant action against the Serbs. He would expound at great length how a softly-softly approach was the only way to challenge the Serbs.

47 For a detailed discussion on the international legal aspects of these talks, see Marc Weller, 'The Rambouillet Conference on Kosovo', *International Affairs* 75, no. 2 (1999), pp. 211–51. Weller has acted as counsel to the Bosnian Muslims and the Kosovo Albanians.

48 See *Interim Agreement for Peace and Self-Government In Kosovo*, 23 February 1999. Available at http://jurist.law.pitt.edu/ramb.htm (accessed 5 February 2104). See in particular Chapter 7. See also.

49 See also Hosmer, *Why Milosevic Decided to Settle*, pp. 12–16.

50 See Richard Holbrooke, *To End a War* (New York: Modern Library, 1999 [1998]) for a comprehensive discussion on this and Milosevic's attitudes. Albright was the US permanent representative to the UN in the first Clinton administration. For the air warfare dimension, see Colonel Robert C. Owen, *Deliberate Force: A Case Study in Effective Air Campaigning* (Maxwell AFB, AL: Air University Press, 2000).

51 Lawrence Freedman, 'The Spilt-screen War: Kosovo and Changing Concepts of the use of Force', in *Kosovo and the Challenge of Humanitarian Intervention: Selective Indignation, Collective Action and International Citizenship*, ed. Albrecht Schnabel and Ramesh Thakur (New York: United Nations Press, 2000), pp. 423–4.

52 Ibid.

53 Lambeth, *NATO's Air War*, p. 190 and General Wesley K. Clark, *Waging Modern War: Bosnia, Kosovo and the Future of Combat* (New York: Public Affairs, 2001), pp. 243–4.

54 Discussion with the author during US JFACC courses on which the author taught at Hurlbert AFB. Lambeth, *NATO's Air War*, p. 190.

55 Lambeth, *NATO's Air War*, pp. 190–91. Short used to regale audiences on the JFACC course with stories of this.

56 Hosmer, *Why Milosevic Decided to Settle*, p. 40.

57 For a full breakdown in the Soviet supplied SAM and radar systems, see *The Military Balance 1998/1999* (London: IISS, 1998), p. 100.

58 http://www.afhso.af.mil/topics/factsheets/factsheet.asp?id=18652 (accessed 5 February 2014).

59 Ibid. But notwithstanding the extensive use of drones over North Vietnam and of AQM 34 Firebees 'near' North Korea from 1970 to 1973. http://www.nationalmuseum.af.mil/factsheets/factsheet.asp?id=4044 (accessed 5 February 2014).

60 Milosevic's ground forces systematically confiscated passports and other documents to prevent Albanians from returning.

61 See Nicholas Wheeler, 'The Kosovo Bombing Campaign', in *The Politics of International Law*, ed. Christian Reus-Smit (Cambridge: Cambridge University Press, 2004), p. 189 et seq. See also Nicholas J. Wheeler, 'Reflections on the Legality and Legitimacy of NATO's intervention in Kosovo', *International Journal of Human Rights* 4, no. 3–4 (2000).

62 Ibid.

63 Hosmer, *Why Milosevic Decided to Settle*, p. 43.

64 Ibid., pp. 46–7.

65 Ibid., p. 51.

66 TNA INF 1/292, Part 2 'Home Morale and Public Opinion', dated 22 September 1941 produced by Stephen Taylor MD MRCP.

67 Hosmer, *Why Milosevic Decided to Settle*, pp. 54–5.

68 Ibid., p. 58.

69 Ibid., p. 67. See also Anthony P. Cordesman, *The Lessons and Non-Lessons of the Air and Missile Campaign in Kosovo*, available at http://csis.org/files/media/csis/pubs/kosovolessons-full.pdf (accessed 5 February 2014), pp. 151–74.

70 Hosmer, *Why Milosevic Decided to Settle*, p. 67.

71 Conversation between the author and General Short.

72 Lambeth, *NATO's Air War*, p. 234.

73 Reported in Greg Seigle, 'USA claims France hindered raids', *Jane's Defence Weekly* 27 (October 1999), p. 3.

74 Lambeth, *NATO's Air War*, p. 234.

75 Wheeler, 'The Kosovo bombing campaign'.

76 Writing in the *Daily Telegraph*, Keegan had long been an advocate of 'boots on the ground' decrying air power. Following the successful termination of *Allied Force* his headline ran 'So the bomber got through to Milosevic after all'. *Daily Telegraph*, 4 June 1999, p. 28. See also John Keegan, 'Yes, we won this war; let's be proud of it.' *Daily Telegraph*, 24 June 1999, p. 26. Contrast this with General Sir Michael Rose, 'Peacekeepers fight a better war than bombers', *Sunday Times*, 20 June 1999, p. 26.

BIBLIOGRAPHY

Official publications – UK

Field Service Regulations 1909/1912 Section 95 'The air service and air reconnaissance'.
Command 467, *Permanent Organization of the Royal Air Force*, 1919.
Air Publication 956, *A Selection of Essays From the Work of Officers Attending the First Course at the Royal Air Force Staff College 1922-1923*.
Air Publication 1300, *Royal Air Force War Manual; Part I Operations*.
The Air Force List, October 1932.
Joint Warfare Publication 0-01, *British Defence Doctrine*, 2nd edn, October 2001.
Joint Doctrine Publication 0-01, *British Defence Doctrine*, 4th edn, November 2011.
Joint Doctrine Publication 0-01, *UK Defence Doctrine*, 5th edn, November 2014.
Joint Doctrine Publication 0-30, *UK Air and Space Doctrine*, July 2013.
Joint Doctrine Publication 5-00, *Campaign Planning*, 2nd edn, change 2, July 2013.
JSP 383, *Manual of the Law of armed Conflict*
MOD DCDC: *Global Strategic Trends – Out to 2045*, 5th Edition, July 2014
Air Publication 3000, *British Air Power Doctrine*, 3rd edn, 1999.
Air Publication 3000, *British Air and Space Power Doctrine*, 4th edn, Undated.
Joint Concept Note 3/12, *Future Air and Space Concept*, September 2012.
Sir John Holmes, *Military Medal Review*, July 2012.

Official publications – NATO

North Atlantic Treaty Organization, NATO Standardization Agency, AAP-6 (2009) *NATO Glossary of Terms and Definitions* (Brussels: NATO Standardization Agency, 2009).

Official publications – Australia

Australian Air Publication 1000, *The Air Power Manual*, 6th edn, September 2013.

Official publications – United States

Air Force Doctrine Document 1, *Air Force Basic Doctrine, Organization and Command*, 14 October 2011.
MCDP 1-0, *Marine Corps Operations*, 9 August 2011.
RAND Corporation, *After Saddam: Prewar Planning and the Occupation of Iraq* (Santa Monica, CA: RAND, 2008).

Official publications – Canada

B-GA-400-000/FP-000, *Canadian Forces Aerospace Doctrine*, edition 2.
A Guide to Reading on Professionalism and Leadership (Canadian Forces Leadership Institute).

Official publications – United Nations

Charter of the United Nations 1945
Report of the International Court of Justice, 1 August 2013-31 July 2014, General Assembly A/69/4

Official histories – UK

Sir Lawrence Freedman, *The Official History of the Falklands Campaign: Volume II, War and Diplomacy* (London: Routledge, 2005).
Michael Howard, *Grand Strategy*, Vol. IV (London: HMSO, 1970).
Walter Raleigh and H. H. Jones, *The War in the Air: Being the Story of the part played in the Great War by the Royal Air Force* (Oxford: Clarendon Press, six volumes, 1922–37).
Sir Charles Webster and Noble Frankland, *The Strategic Air Offensive against Germany, 1939-1945* (London: Her Majesty's Stationary Office, 1960).

Official histories – US

Wesley Frank Craven and James Lea Cate (eds), *The Army Air Forces in World War II* (Chicago: University of Chicago Press, 1948–58; Reprinted Washington, DC: Office of Air Force History, 1983).
Maurer Maurer (ed.), *The U.S. Air Service in WWI: Vol. I, The Final Report and a Tactical History* (Washington, DC: Office of Air Force History, 1978).
Lt. Col. Ralph A. Rowley, *Tactics and Techniques of Close Air Support Operations 1961-1973* (Washington, DC: Office of Air Force History, 1976).
USAF Historical Division Liaison Office, *USAF Airborne Operations in WWII and Korea* (1962).

Official histories – Australia

F. M. Cutlack, *Official History of Australia in the War of 1914-1918: Volume VIII, The Australian Flying Corps in the Western and Eastern Theatres of War, 1914-1918*, 11th edn (Sydney: Angus and Robertson, 1941).

Douglas Gillison, *Australia in the War of 1939-1945. Series 3 – Air Vol. 1: The Royal Australian Air Force 1939-1942* (Canberra: Australian War Memorial, 1962).

John Herington, *Australia in the War of 1939-1945. Series 3 – Air Vol. II: Air War against Germany and Italy 1939-1945* (Canberra: Australian War Memorial, 1954).

John Herington, *Air Power over Europe 1944-1945* (Canberra: Australian War Memorial, 1963).

George Odgers, *Australia in the War of 1939-1945. Series 3 – Air Vol. II: Air War against Japan, 1943-1945* (Canberra: Australian War Memorial, 1957).

Official histories – Canada

W. A. B. Douglas, *The Creation of a National Air Force: The Official History of the Royal Canadian Air Force* (Toronto: Toronto University Press, 1980).

Brereton Greenhous, Stephen J. Harris, William C. Johnston and William G. P. Rawling, *The Crucible of War: The Official History of the Royal Canadian Air Force* (Toronto: Toronto University Press, 1994).

Historical Section of the R.C.A.F., *The R.C.A.F. Overseas: The First Four Years* (Toronto: Oxford University Press, 1944).

Historical Section of the R.C.A.F., *The R.C.A.F. Overseas: The Fifth Year* (Toronto: Oxford University Press, 1945).

Historical Section of the R.C.A.F., *The R.C.A.F. Overseas: The Sixth Year* (Toronto: Oxford University Press, 1949).

S. F. Wise, *Canadian Airmen and the First World War: The Official History of the Royal Canadian Air Force* (Toronto: Toronto University Press, 1980).

Official histories – New Zealand

Squadron Leader J. M. S. Ross, *Royal New Zealand Air Force* (Wellington: Historical Publications Branch 1955).

Wing Commander H. L. Thompson, *New Zealanders with the Royal Air Force (Vol. I)* (Wellington: Historical Publications Branch, 1953).

Wing Commander H. L. Thompson, *New Zealanders with the Royal Air Force (Vol. II)* (Wellington: Historical Publications Branch, 1956).

Wing Commander H. L. Thompson, *New Zealanders with the Royal Air Force (Vol. III)* (Wellington: Historical Publications Branch, 1959).

Archival materials

Air historical branch narratives

AIR 41/5, *International Law of the Air, 1939-1945. Confidential supplement to Air Power and War Rights.*
AIR 41/14, *The Growth of Fighter Command, 1936-1940.*
AIR 41/39, *The RAF in the Bomber Offensive against Germany.*

AIR series

AIR 8, Files of the Chief of the Air Staff
AIR 9, Air Plans
AIR 10, Air Publications
AIR 14, Bomber Command
AIR 15, Coastal Command
AIR 16, Fighter Command

Reference works

Della Thompson (ed.), *The Concise Oxford Dictionary of Current English*, 9th edn (Oxford: Clarendon Press, 1995).

Books

ACM Sir Kenneth 'Bing' Cross with Vincent Orange, *Straight and Level* (London: Grub Street, 1993).
John Adair, *Effective Strategic Leadership* (London: Pan, 2003).
Air Ministry, *The Strategic Air War Against Germany 19390194S: Official Report of the British Bombing Survey Unit* (London: Cass, 1998).
Roger Annett, *Lifeline in Helmand: RAF Front-Line Air Supply in Afghanistan: 1310 Flight in Action* (Barnsley: Pen and Sword, 2012).
Paul Addison and Jeremy A. Crang (eds), *The Burning Blue: A New History of the Battle of Britain* (London: Pimlico, 2000).
Paul Addison and Jeremy A. Crang (eds), *Firestorm: The Bombing of Dresden in 1945* (London: Pimlico, 2006).
Paul Addison and Jeremy A. Crang (eds), *Listening to Britain: Home Intelligence Reports on Britain's Finest Hour – May to September 1940* (London: Vintage, 2011).
Group Captain A. K. Agarwal, *The Third Dimension: Air Power in Combating the Maoist Insurgency* (New Delhi: Vij Books, 2013).
Air Command and Staff Course, *Air Power and its Role in the Battles of Khe San and Dien Bien Phu* (Maxwell, AL: Air Command and Staff College, 2014).
Fritz Allhof, Nicholas G. Evans and Adam Henschke (eds), *Routledge Handbook of Ethics and War: Just War Theory in the Twenty-first Century* (Abingdon: Routledge, 2013).

Stephen E. Ambrose, *D-Day: The Daring British Airborne Raid* (London: Simon & Schuster, 1985).

Stephen Badsey, Mark Grove and Rob Havers (eds), *The Falklands Conflict Twenty Years On: Lessons for the Future* (London: Cass, 2005).

Claudia Baldoli, Andrew Knapp and Richard Overy (eds), *Bombing States and Peoples in Western Europe 1940-1945* (London: Continuum, 2011).

Corelli Barnett, *Engage the Enemy More Closely: The Royal Navy in the Second World War* (London: Hodder and Stoughton, 1991).

David L. Bashow, *No Prouder Place: Canadians and the Bomber Command Experience, 1939-1945* (St Catherines, ON: Vanwell, 2005).

Jeremy Bentham and John Stuart Mill, *Utilitarianism and other Essays* (London: Penguin 1987).

Michael R. Beschloss, *Mayday: Eisenhower, Kruschev and the U-2 Affair* (London: Faber and Faber, 1986).

Georges Bernage, *Red Devils: The 6th Airborne Division in Normandy* (Bayeux: Heindal, 2002).

Uri Bialer, *The Shadow of the Bomber: The Fear of Air Attack and British Politics, 1932-1939* (London: RHS, 1980).

Tami Davis Biddle, *Rhetoric and Reality in Air Warfare: The Evolution of British and American Ideas about Strategic Bombing, 1914–1945* (Princeton: Princeton University Press, 2002).

Patrick Bishop, *Fighter Boys Saving Britain 1940* (London: Harper, 2003).

Patrick Bishop, *Bomber Boys: Fighting Back 1940-1945* (London: Harper, 2008).

Jeremy Black and Donald M. MacRaild, *Studying History* (Basingstoke: Palgrave, 2000).

Jeremy Black, *Rethinking Military History* (London: Routledge, 2004).

Nicholas Black, *The British Naval Staff in the First World War* (Woodbridge: Boydell, 2009).

Robert Blake and William R. Louis (eds), *Churchill* (Oxford: Oxford University Press, 1994).

Joshua Blakeney (ed.), *Japan Bites Back: Documents Contextualising Pearl Harbor* (US: Non-aligned Media, 2015).

Marc Bloch, *The Historian's Craft*, trans. Peter Putman (Manchester: Manchester University Press, 1992).

Brian Bond, *British Military Policy Between the Two World Wars* (Oxford: Clarendon, 1980).

Horst Boog (ed.), *The Conduct of the Air War in the Second World War: An International Comparison* (Oxford: Berg, 1992).

William H. Boothby, *The Law of Targeting* (Oxford: Oxford University Press, 2012).

Timothy Bowman and Mark Connelly, *The Edwardian Army: Recruiting, Training and Deploying the British Army, 1902-1914* (Oxford: Oxford University Press, 2012).

Andrew Boyle, *Trenchard* (London: Collins, 1962).

Walter J. Boyne, *The Influence of Air Power on History* (New York: Pelican, 2003).

Bernard Brodie, *Strategy in the Missile Age* (Princeton: Princeton University Press, 1969).

Ian Brownlie, *Principles of Public International Law*, 4th edn (Oxford: Clarendon, 1990 [1966]).

James MacGregor Burns, *Leadership* (New York: Harper, 1979).

John Buckley, *The RAF and Trade Defence 1919-1945: Constant Endeavour* (Keele: Keele University Press, 1995).

John Buckley, *Air Power in the Age of Total War* (London: UCL Press, 1999).

Stephen Bungay, *The Most Dangerous Enemy: A History of the Battle of Britain* (London: Aurum, 2000).

William E. Burrows, *Richtofen: A True Story of the Red Baron* (London: Hart-Davis, 1970).

James Ramsay M. Butler, *Grand Strategy, Vol. II, September 1939-June 1941* (London: HMSO, 1971).

Garry Campion, *The Good fight: Battle of Britain Propaganda and the Few* (Basingstoke: Palgrave, 2009).

Edward H. Carr, *What is History?* (London: Penguin, 1990 [1961]).

Winston S. Churchill, *The Second World War: The Gathering Storm*, vol. 1 (London: Cassell, 1948).

Winston S. Churchill, *The Second World War* (London: Cassell, six volumes, 1949).

Robert Citino, *Path to Blitzkrieg: Doctrine & Training in the German Army, 1920-39* (Mechanicsburg, PA: Stackpole, 2008).

Alan Clark, *The Donkeys* (London: Pimlico, 1961).

General Wesley K. Clark, *Waging Modern War: Bosnia, Kosovo and the Future of Combat* (New York: Public Affairs, 2001).

Carl von Clausewitz, *On War*, ed. Michael Howard and Peter Paret (London: Everyman, 1993).

Tim Clayton and Phil Craig, *Finest Hour: Book of the BBC TV Series* (London: Hodder, 1999).

Mark Clodfelter, *The Limits of Air Power; The American Bombing of North Vietnam* (New York: Free Press, 1989).

Benjamin Franklin Cooling (ed.), *Case Studies in the Achievement of Air Superiority* (Air Force History and Museums Program), available at http://www.afhso.af.mil/shared/media/document/AFD-101012-038.pdf.

Malcolm Cooper, *The Birth of Independent Air Power* (London: Allen Unwin, 1986).

Julian S. Corbett, *Principles of Maritime Strategy* (London: Longmans, 1911).

James S. Corum, *The Roots of Blitzkrieg: Hans von Seekt and German Military Reform* (Lawrence, KS: University of Kansas Press, 1994).

James S. Corum, *The Luftwaffe: Creating the Operational War, 1918-1940* (Lawrence, KS: University of Kansas Press, 1997).

Olivier Corten, *The Law Against War: The Prohibition on the Use of Force in Contemporary International Law* (Oxford: Hart, 2010).

Sebastian Cox and Peter Gray (eds), *Turning Points in Air Power History from Kittyhawk to Kosovo* (London: Cass, 2002).

Paul K. Davies, *Effects-Based Operations: A Grand Challenge for the Analytical Community* (Santa Monica, CA: RAND, 2001).

Maurice Dean, The *Royal Air Force and Two World Wars* (London: Cassell, 1979).

Len Deighton, *Fighter: The True Story of the Battle of Britain* (London: Collins, 1977).

Brigadier General David A. Deptula, *Effects-Based Operations: Change in the Nature of Warfare* (Arlington, VA: Aerospace Education Foundation, 2001).

Carlo D'Este, *Warlord: A Life of Churchill at War 1874 1945* (London: Allen Lane, 2008).

Yoram Dinstein, *Non-International Armed Conflict in International Law* (Cambridge: Cambridge University Press, 2014).

Jack Dixon, *Dowding and Churchill: The Dark Side of the Battle of Britain* (Barnsley: Pen and Sword, 2008).

Andrew Dorman, *The Falklands Witness Seminar Joint Services Command And Staff College June 2002* (Camberley: Strategic and Combat Studies Institute, 2003).

Giulio Douhet, *The Command of the Air*, trans. Dino Ferrai (London: Faber, 1943).

Giulio Douhet, *SScriit critica della grande* Guerra (Rome: Berlutti, 1925).

Giulio Douhet, A. Curami and G. Rochat (eds), *Scritti 1901-1915* (Rome: Stato Maggiore Aeronautica, Ufficio Storico, 1993).

Bill Newton Dunn, *Big Wing: The Biography of Air Chief Marshal Sir Trafford Leigh-Mallory* (Shrewsbury: Airlife, 1992).

Gjert Lage Dyndal, *Land Based Air Power or Aircraft Carriers? A Case Study of the British Debate about Maritime Air Power in the 1960s* (Farnham: Ashgate, 2012).

Edward Mead Earle (ed.), *Makers of Modern Strategy: Military Thought from Machiavelli to Hitler* (Princeton: Princeton University Press, 1941).

Edward Mead Earle (ed.), *The Makers of Modern Strategy from Machiavelli toHitler* (Princeton: Princeton University Press, 1943).

David Edgerton, *England and the Aeroplane: Militarism, Modernity and Machines* (London: Penguin, 2013).

Jean Bethke Elshtain (ed.), *Just War Theory* (Oxford: Blackwell, 1992).

Allan D. English, *The Cream of the Crop: Canadian Aircrew 1939-1945* (Montreal: McGill-Queen's University Press, 1996).

Allan English (ed.), *The Operational Art: Canadian Perspectives, Leadership and Command* (Kingston, ON: Canadian Defence Academy Press, 2006).

Byron Farwell, *For Queen and Country: A Social History of the Edwardian and Victorian Army* (London: Penguin, 1991).

Claire Finkelstein, Jens David Ohlin and Andrew Altman (eds), *Targeted Killings: Law and Morality in an Asymmetrical World* (Oxford: Oxford University Press, 2012).

Simon Fowler, Peter Elliott, Roy Conyers Nesbit and Christina Goulter, *PRO Readers' Guide No. 8: RAF Records in the PRO* (London: PRO, 1994).

Martin Francis, *The Flyer: British Culture and the Royal Air Force 1939-1945* (Oxford: Oxford University Press, 2008).

Noble Frankland, *History at War: The Campaigns of an Historian* (London: de la Mare, 1998).

Norman Franks and Frank W. Bailey, *Over the Front: Complete Record of the Fighter Aces and Units of the United States and French Air Services 1914-1918* (London: Grub Street, 1992).

David French, *Military Identities: The Regimental System, the British Army & the British People c1870-2000* (Oxford: Oxford University Press, 2005).

David French, *The British Way in Counter-Insurgency 1945-1967* (Oxford: Oxford University Press, 2011).

Jeorg Friedrich, *The Fire: The Bombing of Germany 1940-1945* (Columbia: Columbia University Press, 2006).

Robert Frank Futtrell (ed.), *Ideas, Concepts, Doctrine: Basic Thinking in the United States Air Force, Vol.1, 1907-1960* (Birmingham, AL: Air University Press, 1999).

Robert Frank Futtrell (ed.), *Ideas, Concepts, Doctrine: Basic Thinking in the United States Air Force, Vol. 2. 1961-1984* (Birmingham, AL: Air University Press, 1999).

James Fyfe, *'The Great Ingratitude': Bomber Command in World War 2* (Wigtown: GCB, 1993).

Juliet Gardiner, *The Blitz: The British Under Attack* (London: Harper, 2010).

Stephen A. Garrett, *Ethics and Airpower in World War II: The British Bombing of German Cities* (New York: St. Martins, 1993).

A. D. Garrison, *Australian Fighter Aces 1914-1953* (Fairburn ACT: RAAF Air Power Studies Centre, 1999).

Florence Gaub, *The North Atlantic Treaty Organization and Libya: Reviewing Operation Unified Protector* (Carlisle, PA: Strategic Studies Institute, June 2013).

Gian P. Gentile, *How Effective is Strategic Bombing: Lessons Learned from World War II to Kosovo* (New York: New York University Press, 2001).

Martin Gilbert, *Churchill, A Life* (London: Heinemann, 1991).

Bill Gillham, *The Research Interview* (London: Continuum, 2000).

Brad William Gladman, *Intelligence and Anglo American Air Support in World War II: The Western Desert and Tunisia 1940-1943* (Basingstoke: Palgrave, 2008).

Alfred Gollin, *The Impact of Air Power on the British People and their Government, 1909-14* (London: Macmillan, 1989).

John Gooch (ed.) *Airpower: Theory and Practice* (London: Cass, 1995).

Ian Gooderson, *Air Power at the Battlefront: Allied Close Air Support in Europe 1943-1945* (London: Cass, 1998).

Andrew Gordon, *The Rules of the Game: Jutland and British Naval Command* (London: John Murray, 1996).

Yefim Gordon and Dimitriy Komissarov, *Russian Air Power: Current Organisation and Aircraft of all Russian Forces* (Shrewsbury: Airlife, 2011).

Christina J. M. Goulter, *A Forgotten Offensive: Royal Air Force Coastal Command's Anti-Shipping Campaign, 1940-1945* (London: Cass, 1995).

James Gow, *Triumph of the Lack of Will: International Diplomacy and the Yugoslav War* (New York: Columbia University Press, 1997).

Matthew Grant, *British Way in Cold Warfare: Intelligence, Diplomacy and the Bomb, 1945-1975* (London: Continuum, 2009).

Colin S. Gray, *Modern Strategy* (Oxford: Oxford University Press, 1999).

Peter W. Gray (ed.), *Air Power 21: Challenges for the New Century* (Norwich: HMSO, 2000).

Peter Gray and Sebastian Cox (eds), *Air Power Leadership: Theory and Practice* (London: HMSO, 2002).

Peter Gray, *The Leadership, Direction and Legitimacy of the RAF Bomber Offensive from Inception to 1945* (London: Continuum, 2012).

Anthony C. Grayling, *Philosophy 1: A Guide to the Subject* (Oxford: Oxford University Press, 1995).

Anthony C. Grayling, *Among the Dead Cities: Was the Allied Bombing of Civilians in WWII a Necessity or a Crime?* (London: Bloomsbury, 2006).

Keith Grint, *Leadership, Management and Command; Rethinking D-Day* (Basingstoke: Palgrave Macmillan, 2008).

Jeffrey Grey (ed.), *The Last Word? Essays on Official History in the United States and British Commonwealth* (Westport, CT: Praeger, 2003).

Simon Gunn and James Vernon (eds), *The Peculiarities of Liberal Modernity in Imperial Britain* (London: Global, Area and International Archive, 2011).

Charles Guthrie and Michael Quinlan, *Just War: The Just War Tradition, Ethics in Modern Warfare* (London: Bloomsbury, 2007).

Marcel de Haas, *Russian Security and Air Power 1992-2002* (Abingdon: Cass, 2004).

David Ian Hall, *Strategy for Victory: The Development of British Tactical Air Power 1919-1943* (London: Praeger, 2008).

Richard P. Hallion, *Strike from the Sky: The History of Battlefield Air Attack, 1911-1945* (Washington, DC: Smithsonian, 1989).

Richard P. Hallion, *Taking Flight: Inventing the Aerial Age from Antiquity to the First World War* (Oxford: Oxford University Press, 2003).

James Hampton, *Selected for Aircrew: Bomber Command in the Second World War* (Walton-on-Thames: Air Research Publications, 1993)

Michael I. Handel (ed.), *Leaders and Intelligence* (London: Cass, 1989).

Haywood S. Hansell Jr., *The Air Plan that Defeated Hitler* (Atlanta, GA: Higgins, 1972).

Lawrence M. Hanser, Louis W. Miller, Herbert J. Shukiar and Bruce Newsome, *Developing Senior Navy Leaders: Requirements for Flag Officer Expertise Today and in the Future* (Santa Monica, CA: RAND, 2008).

Sir Arthur Harris, *Bomber Offensive* (London: Collins, 1947).

J. P. Harris, *Douglas Haig and the First World War* (Cambridge: Cambridge University Press, 2008).

Max Hastings, *Bomber Command* (London: Pan Macmillan, 1993).

Seamus Heaney (trans.), *Beowulf* (London: Faber, 2000).

Peter Hennessy, *The Prime Minister: The Office and its Holders Since 1946* (London: Allen, 2000).

Jack Herris and Bob Pearson, *Aircraft of World War I* (Newbury: Amber, 2010).

Beatrice Heuser, *Reading Clausewitz* (London: Pimlico, 2002).

Rosalyn Higgins, *Problems and Processes: International Law and How We Use It* (Oxford: Oxford University Press, 1994).

Robin Higham, *The Military Intellectuals in Britain: 1918-1939* (New Brunswick, NJ: Rutgers University Press, 1966).

Robin Higham, *The French and British Air Arms from Versailles to Dunkirk* (Annapolis, MD: Naval Institute Press, 2012).

Robin Higham and Mark Parillo (eds), *The Influence of Airpower upon History: Statesmanship, Diplomacy and Foreign Policy since 1903* (Lexington, KY: University of Kentucky Press, 2013).

Thomas Hippler, *Bombing the People: Giulio Douhet and the Foundations of Air-Power Strategy, 1884-1939* (Cambridge: Cambridge University Press, 2013).

Richard Holbrooke, *To End a War* (New York: Modern Library, 1999 [1998]).

Brian Holden-Reid, *Studies in British Military Thought: Debates with Fuller and Liddell Hart* (Nebraska, NE: Nebraska University Press, 1998).

James Holland, *Malta: An Island Fortress under Siege* (London: Phoenix, 2003).

James Holland, *The Battle of Britain: Five Months that Changed History* (London: Corgi, 2010).

Brett Holman, *The Next War in the Air: Britain's Fear of the Bomber, 1908-1941* (Farnham: Ashgate, 2014).

Edward R. Hooton, *Phoenix Triumphant: The Rise and Rise of the Luftwaffe* (London: Arms and Armour, 1994).

Colonel Bernd Horn and Lieutenant-Colonel Allister MacIntyre (eds), *In Pursuit of Excellence: International Perspectives of Military Leadership* (Kingston, ON: Canadian Defence Academy Press, 2006).

Stephen T. Hosmer, *The Conflict over Kosovo: Why Milosevic Decided to Settle When He Did* (Santa Monica, CA: RAND, 2001).

Richard Hough and Denis Richards, *The Battle of Britain* (London: Hodder and Stoughton, 1989).

Michael Howard (ed.), *Restraints on War: Studies in the Limitation of Armed Conflict* (Oxford: Oxford University Press, 1979).

Michael Howard, *The Causes of War and Other Essays* (Hounslow: Temple Smith, 1983).

Michael Howard, *The Lessons of History* (Oxford: Oxford University Press, 1991).

Michael Howard, George J. Andreopoulos and Mark R. Shulman (eds), *The Laws of War: Constraints on Warfare in the Western World* (New Haven, CT: Yale University Press, 1994).

Matthew Hughes and William J. Philpott (eds), *Modern Military History* (Basingstoke: MacMillan, 2006).

Matthew Hughes (ed.), *British Ways of Counter-insurgency: A Historical Perspective* (London: Routledge, 2013).

Alfred F. Hurley, *Billy Mitchell: Crusader for Air Power* (Bloomington, IN: Indiana University Press, 2005[1964]).

H. Montgomery Hyde, *British Air Policy Between the Wars 1918-1939* (London: Heinemann, 1976).

IISS, *The Military Balance 1998/1999* (London: IISS, 1998).

John James, *The Paladins: The Story of the RAF up to the Outbreak of World War II* (London: Futura, 1991).

T. C. G. James, *Air Defence of Great Britain, Volume I: The Growth of Fighter Command 1936-1940* (London: Whitehall History Publishing with Cass, 2002).

T. C. G. James, *The Battle of Britain* (London: Cass, 2000).

Edgar Jones and Simon Wessely, *Shell Shock to PTSD* (Hove: Psychology Press, 2005).

Neville Jones, *The Beginnings of Strategic Air Power: A History of the British Bomber Force 1923-39* (London: Cass, 1987).

Neville Jones, *The Origins of Strategic Bombing: A Study of the Development of British Air Strategic Thought and Practice up to 1918* (London: Kimber, 1973).

Spencer Jones (ed.), *Stemming the Tide: Officers and Leadership in the British Expeditionary Force, 1914* (Solihull: Helion, 2013).

Emmanuelle Jouannet, *The Liberal-Welfarist Law of Nations: A History of International Law* (Cambridge: Cambridge University Press, 2012).

Sanu Kainikara, *Red Air: Politics in Russian Air Power* (Boca Raton, FL: Universal, 2007).

Andrew Kakabadse and Nada Kakabadse, *Essence of Leadership* (London: Thomson, 1999).

John Keegan, *The Mask of Command: A Study of Generalship* (London: Pimlico, 1999 [1987]).

Paul Kennedy, *Rise and Fall of the Great Powers: Economic Change and Military Conflict from 1500-2000* (London: Fontana, 1989).

Edgar J. Kingston-McCloughry, *Winged Warfare: Air Problems of Peace and War* (London: Cape, 1937).

Herman Knell, *To Destroy a City: Strategic Bombing and its Human Consequences in World War 2* (Cambridge, MA: Da Capo Press, 2003).

Lt Col (USAF) Karen U. Kwiatowski, *Expeditionary Air Operations in Africa: Challenges and Solutions* (Birmingham, AL: Fairchild Papers/Air University Press, 2012).

Benjamin S. Lambeth, *Russia's Air Power in Crisis: A RAND Research Study* (Washington, DC: Smithsonian, 1999).

Benjamin S. Lambeth, *NATO's Air War for Kosovo: A Strategic and Operational Assessment* (Santa Monica, CA: RAND, 2001).

Frederick W. Lanchester, *Aircraft in Warfare: The Dawn of the Fourth Arm* (London: Constable, 1916).

H. Lauterpacht, 'The Problem of the Revision of the Law of War', *British Yearbook of International Law* (1952). Published under the auspices of the Royal Institute of International Affairs (London: Oxford University Press, 1953).

J. Lee Thompson, *Northcliffe: Press Baron in Politics 1865-1922* (London: Murray, 2000).

James K. Libbey, *Alexander P. de Seversky and the Quest for Air Power* (Washington, DC: Potomac Books, 2013).

Basil H. Liddell Hart, *Paris or the Future of War* (London: Kegan Paul, Trench and Trubner, 1925).

Lord Londonderry, *Wings of Destiny* (London: MacMillan, 1943).

Noam Lubell, *Extraterritorial Use of Force Against Non-State Actors* (Oxford: Oxford University Press, 2010).

Niccolo Machiavelli, *The Art of War*, trans. Neal Wood (Cambridge, MA: Perseus, 1965).

Major General J. J. G. Mackenzie and Brian Holden Reid (eds), *The British Army and the Operational Level of War* (London: Tri-service Press, 1988).

S. P. MacKenzie, *The Battle of Britain on Screen: 'The Few' in British Film and Television Drama* (Edinburgh: Edinburgh University Press, 2007).

Douglas Mackman and Michael Mays (eds), *World War I and the Cultures of Modernity* (Jackson, MS: Mississippi University Press, 2000).

Travers Macleod, *Rule of Law in War: International Law and United States Counterinsurgency in Iraq and Afghanistan* (Oxford: Oxford University Press, 2015).

Captain Norman Macmillan, *Air Strategy* (London: Hutchinson, 1941).

Markus Mäder, *In Pursuit of Conceptual Excellence: The Evolution of British Military-Strategic Doctrine in the Post-Cold War Era, 1989–2002* (Bern: Peter Lang, 2004).

Air Vice-Marshal Tony Mason, *Air Power: A Centennial Appraisal* (London: Brassey's, 1994).

Stephen McFarland and Wesley Phillips Newton, *To Command the Sky: The Battle for Air Superiority over Germany, 1942-1944* (Washington, DC: Smithsonian, 1991).

Nils Melzer, *Targeted Killing in International Law* (Oxford: Oxford University Press, 2008).

Phillip S. Meilinger (Ed. for the School of Advanced Air Power Studies), *The Paths of Heaven: The Evolution of Air Power Theory* (Maxwell AFB, AL: Air University Press, 1997).

Phillip S. Meilinger, *Airwar: Theory and Practice* (London: Cass, 2003).

David R. Mets, *The Air Campaign: John Warden and the Classical Air Power Theorists* (Maxwell AFB, AL: Air University Press, 1998).

Keith Middlemass and John Barnes, *Baldwin: A Biography* (London: Weidenfeld and Nicholson, 1969).

Stanley Milgram, *Obedience to Authority: An Experimental View* (London: Tavistock, 1974).

Roger G. Miller, *To Save a City: The Berlin Airlift 1948-1949* (Bolling, DC: Air Force History and Museums Program, 2013).

Stephen Morillo (with Michael F. Pavkovic), *What is Military History?* (Cambridge: Polity, 2006).

Williamson Murray, *Strategy for Defeat: The Luftwaffe 1933-1945* (Maxwell, AL: Airpower Research Institute, 1983).

Williamson Murray and Richard Hart Sinnreich (eds), *The Past as Prologue: The Importance of History to the Military Profession* (Cambridge: Cambridge University Press, 2006).

Shimon Naveh, *In Pursuit of Military Excellence: The Evolution of Operational Theory* (Abingdon: Cass, 1997).

Jeremy Noakes (ed.), *Nazism 1919-1945: Volume 4, The German Home Front in World War II* (Exeter: University of Exeter Press, 2006 [1998]).

Gary Null, *Weapon of Denial: Air Power and the Battle for New Guinea* (Washington, DC: Office of Air Force History, 2013).

Phillips Payson O'Brien, *How the War was Won: Air-Sea Power and Allied Victory in World War II* (Cambridge: Cambridge University Press, 2015).

Office of Air Force History, *The High Road to Tokyo Bay: The AAF in the Asiatic-Pacific Theater* (Washington, DC: Office of Air Force History, 2015).

John Andreas Olsen, *John Warden and the Renaissance of American Air Power* (Washington, DC: Potomac, 2007).

John Andreas Olsen (ed.), *A History of Air Warfare* (Washington, DC: Potomac, 2010).

John Andreas Olsen (ed.), *Global Air Power* (Washington, DC: Potomac, 2011).

John Andreas Olsen (ed.), *European Air Power: Challenges and Opportunities* (Nebraska: Potomac Press, 2014).

David Omissi, *Air Power and Colonial Control: The Royal Air Force, 1919-1939* (Manchester: Manchester University Press, 1990).

Vincent Orange, *Park; the Biography of ACM Sir Keith Park* (London: Grub Street, 2001).

Vincent Orange, *Dowding of Fighter Command: Victor of the Battle of Britain* (London: Grub Street 2008).

Richard J. Overy, *The Air War 1939-1945* (New York: Stein and Day, 1980).

Richard J. Overy, *The Battle of Britain* (London: Penguin, 2001).

Richard J. Overy, *The Bombing War: Europe 1939-1945* (London: Penguin, 2014).

Ovid, *Metamorphoses* VIII.

Colonel Robert C. Owen, *Deliberate Force: A Case Study in Effective Air Campaigning* (Birmingham, AL: Air University Press, 2000).

Peter Paret (ed.), *The Makers of Modern Strategy from Machiavelli to the Nuclear Age* (Oxford: Clarendon Press, 1986).

Michael Paris, *Winged Warfare: The Literature and Theory of Aerial Warfare in Britain 1859-1917* (Manchester: Manchester University Press, 1992).

Mark R. Peattie, *Sunburst: The Rise of Japanese Naval Air Power 1909-1941* (London: Chatham, 2001).

Graham Pitchfork, *Men Behind the Medals* (Barnsley: Pen and Sword, 1998).

Graham Pitchfork, *The Sowreys* (London: Grub Street, 2012).

Gary Francis Powers and Curt Gentry, *Operation Overflight: A Memoir of the U-2 Incident* (Washington, DC: Brassey's, 2004 [1970]).

Henry Probert, *High Commanders of the Royal Air Force* (London: HMSO, 1991).

Henry Probert, *The Forgotten Air Force: The Royal Air Force and the War Against Japan 1941-1945* (London: Brassey's, 1995).

Peter Preston-Hough, *Commanding Far Eastern Skies: A Critical Analysis of the Royal Air Force Air Superiority Campaign in India, Burma and Malaya* (Solihull: Helion, 2015).

Henry Probert, *Bomber Harris: His Life and Times* (London: Greenhill, 2001).

Stanley J. Rachman, *Fear and Courage* (New York: Freeman and Company, 1990).

John Ray, *The Battle of Britain: New Perspectives, Behind the Scenes of the Great Air War* (London: Cassell, 1994).

John Ray, *The Night Blitz 1940-1941* (London: Arms and Armour, 1996).

Christian Reus-Smit (ed.), *The Politics of International Law* (Cambridge: Cambridge University Press, 2004).

David Reynolds, *In Command of History: Churchill Fighting and Writing the Second World War* (London: Allen Lane, 2004).

Denis Richards, *Portal of Hungerford: The Life of Marshal of the Royal Air Force Viscount Portal of Hungerford* (London: Heinemann, 1977).

Manfred von Richtofen, *The Red Baron* (Barnsley: Pen and Sword, 2005 [1918 in German]).

Bernhard Rieger, *Technology and the Culture of Modernity in Britain and Germany 1890-1945* (Cambridge: Cambridge University Press, 2005).

Sebastian Ritchie, *Industry and Air Power: The Expansion of British Aircraft Production 1935-1941* (Abingdon: Routledge, 1997).

Sebastian Ritchie, *The RAF, Small Wars and Insurgencies in the Middle East 1919-1939* (Shrivenham: Centre for Air Power Studies 2011).

Sebastian Ritchie, *Arnhem: Myth and Reality: Airborne Warfare, Air Power and the Failure of Operation Market Garden* (London: Hale, 2011).

Hans Ritter, *La guerre aérienne*, trans. Horst Gorlich (Paris: CESA, 2012). Originally published as Hans Ritter, *Der Luftkrieg* (Berlin: Koeler, 1926).

Scott Robertson, *The Development of RAF Strategic Bombing Doctrine, 1919-1939* (Westport, CT: Praeger, 1995).

Stephen Roskill, *Naval Policy Between the Wars* (London: Collins, 1968).

Morton W. Royse, *Aerial Bombardment and the International Regulation of Warfare* (New York: Harold Vinal, 1928).

Helena P. Schrader, *The Blockade Breakers: The Berlin Airlift* (Stroud: The History Press, 2008).

Robert Self (ed.), *The Neville Chamberlain Diary Letters* (Aldershot: Ashgate, 4 vols. 2000–5).

Robert Self, *Neville Chamberlain: A Biography* (Aldershot: Ashgate, 2006).

Desmond Seward, *Wings Over the Desert: In Action with an RFC pilot in Palestine 1916-18* (Yeovil: Haynes, 2009)

Gary Sheffield and John Bourne (eds), *Douglas Haig: War Diaries and Letters 1914-1918* (London: Weidenfeld and Nicholson, 2005).

Gary Sheffield (ed.), *War Studies Reader: From the Seventeenth Century to the Present Day and Beyond* (London: Continuum, 2010).

Gary Sheffield, *The Chief: Douglas Haig and the British Army* (London: Aurum, 2011).

Gary Sheffield and Peter Gray (eds), *Changing War: The British Army, the Hundred Days Campaign and the Birth of the Royal Air Force, 1918* (London: Bloomsbury, 2013).

Richard E. Simkin, *Race to the Swift: Thoughts on Twenty-First Century Warfare* (London: Brasseys, 1985).

Fred Singleton, *A Short History of the Yugoslav Peoples* (Cambridge: Cambridge, 1985).

Colin Sinnott, *The Royal Air Force and Aircraft Design 1923-1939: Air Staff Operational Requirements* (London: Cass, 2001).

Sir John Slessor, *Air Power and Armies* (Oxford: Oxford University Press, 1936).

MRAF Sir John Slessor, *The Central Blue: Recollections and Reflections* (London: Cassell, 1956).

A. J. Smithers, *Taranto 1940: A Glorious Episode* (Barnsley: Pen and Sword, 1995).

Gary D. Solis, *The Law of Armed Conflict: International Humanitarian Law in War* (Cambridge: Cambridge University Press, 2010).

James Maloney Spaight, *The Beginnings of Organised Air Power* (London: Longmans, 1927).

James Maloney Spaight, *Air Power and the Cities* (London: Longmans, 1930).

James Maloney Spaight, *Air Power and War Rights* (London: Longmans, second edition, 1933).

James Maloney Spaight, *Air Power in the Next War* (London: Geoffrey Bles, 1938).

James Maloney Spaight, *The Battle of Britain – 1940* (London: Geoffrey Bles, 1941).

Roy M. Stanley, *To Fool a Glass Eye: Camouflage Versus Photo-Reconnaissance in World War II* (Shrewsbury: Airlife, 1998).

Alan Stephens (ed.), *The War in the Air 1914-1994* (Canberra: Air Power Studies Centre, 1994).

James Sterret, *Soviet Air Force Theory 1918-1945* (Abingdon: Cass, 2007).

Hew Strachan, *Politics of the British Army* (Oxford: Clarendon Press, 1997).

Robert D. Strassler (ed.), *The Landmark Thucydides: A Comprehensive Guide to the Peloponnesian War* (New York, NY: Touchstone, 1996).

Robert B. Strassler (ed.), *The Landmark Herodotus: The Histories* (London: Quercus, 2007).

Alan Stephens (ed.), *The War in the Air 1914-1994* (Fairbairn, ACT: RAAF Air power Studies Centre, 1994).

Wing Commander John Stubbington, *Kept in the Dark: The Denial to Bomber Command of Vital Ultra and Other Intelligence Information during WWII* (Barnsley: Pen and Sword, 2010).

Ian Summer, *The Kings of the Air: French Aces and Airmen of the Great War* (Barnsley: Pen and Sword, 2015).

Dietmar Süss, *Death from the Skies: How the British and Germans Survived Bombing During World War II* (Oxford: Oxford University Press, 2014).

Jonathan Swift, *Gulliver's Travels* (London: Penguin Classics, 2012 [1726]).

Sir Frederick Sykes, *From Many Angles: An Autobiography* (London: Harrap, 1942).

Jean-Marc Tanguy, *Guerre Aérienne en Libye* (Paris: Histoire et Collections, 2012).

Lord Tedder, *Air Power in War: The Lees Knowles Lectures by Marshal of the Royal Air Force The Lord Tedder* (London: Hodder and Stoughton, 1947).

Lord Tedder, *With Prejudice: The War Memoirs of MRAF Lord Tedder* (London: Cassell, 1966).

Major General A. C. Temperley, *The Whispering Gallery of Europe* (London: Collins, 1938).

Viscount Templewood (Sir Samuel Hoare), *Empire of the Air: The Advent of the Air Age 1922-1929* (London: Collins, 1957).

John Terraine, *The Right of the Line: The Royal Air Force in the European War 1939-1945* (London: Hodder and Stoughton, 1985).

Adam Tooze, *The Wages of Destruction: The Making & Breaking of the Nazi Economy* (London: Penguin, 2007).

John Tosh (ed.), *Historians on History* (Harlow: Longman, 2000).

Harvey B. Tress, *British Strategic Bombing Policy Through 1940: Politics, Attitudes and the Formation of a Lasting Pattern* (Lewiston, NY: Mellen Press, 1988).

Philip Towle, *Pilots and Rebels: The Use of Aircraft in Unconventional warfare 1918-1988* (London: Brassey's, 1989).

Sun Tzu, *The Art of War*, foreword by James Clavell (London: Hodder and Stoughton, 1981).

Group Captain Andrew Vallance (ed.), *Air Power: Collected Essays on Doctrine* (Bracknell: D Def S (RAF), 1990).

Jules Verne, *Clipper of the Clouds* (London: Forgotten Books, 2010 [1886]).

Anthony Verrier, *The Bomber Offensive* (London: Batsford, 1968).

Paul R. Viotti and Mark V. Kauppi, *International Relations Theory: Realism, Pluralism, Globalism* (New York: Macmillan, 1987).

Michael Walzer, *Just and Unjust Wars: A Moral Argument with Historical Illustrations* (New York: Basic Books, 1977).

Michael Walzer, *Arguing about War* (New Haven, CT: Yale University Press, 2004).

John A. Warden III, *The Air Campaign: Planning for Combat* (Washington, DC: NDU Press, 1988).

E. H. Ware, *Wing to Wing: Bird Watching Adventures at Home and Abroad with the RAF* (London: Paternoster, 1946).

Herbert G. Wells, *War in the Air* (London: Penguin Classics, 2005 [1908]).

Mark K. Wells, *Courage and Air Warfare: The Allied Aircrew Experience in the Second World War* (London: Frank Cass, 1995).

Thomas Wildenberg, *Billy Mitchell's War with the Navy: The Interwar Rivalry over Air Power* (Annapolis, MD: Naval Institute Press, 2013).

George K. Williams, *Biplanes and Bombsights: British Bombing in World War I* (Maxwell AFB, AL: Air University Press, 1999).

Gary Wills, *Saint Augustine* (London: Phoenix, 2000 [1999]).

Elisabeth Wilmshurst, *International Law and the Classification of Conflicts* (Oxford: Oxford University Press, 2012).

Martin Windrow, *The Last Valley: Dien Bien Phu and the French defeat in Vietnam* (London: Cassell, 2005).

Jay Winter and Antoine Prost, *The Great War in History: Debates and Controversies, 1914 to the Present* (Cambridge: Cambridge University Press, 2005).

Robert Wright, *Dowding and the Battle of Britain* (London: Macdonald, 1969).

Roberta Wohlstetter, *Pearl Harbor* (Stanford: Stanford University Press, 1966).

General Viscount Wolseley, *The Life of John Churchill, Duke of Marlborough to the Accession of Queen Anne* (London: Richard Bentley and Son, 1894).

David T. Zabecki, *The German 1918 Offensives: A Case Study in the Operational Level of War* (Abingdon: Routledge, 2006).

Stephen J. Zaccaro, *The Nature of Executive Leadership: A Conceptual and Empirical Analysis of Success* (Washington, DC: American Psychological Association, 2001).

Book chapters

Tami Davis Biddle, 'British and American Approaches to Strategic bombing: Their Origins and Implementation in the World War II Combined Bomber Offensive', in John Gooch (ed.), *Airpower: Theory and Practice* (London: Cass, 1995), pp. 99–144.

Donald Bloxham, 'Dresden as a War Crime', in Paul Addison and Jeremy A. Crang (eds), *Firestorm: The Bombing of Dresden in 1945* (London: Pimlico, 2006), pp. 180–208.

Sydney Brandon, 'LMF in Bomber Command 1939-1945: Diagnosis or denouncement', in Hugh Freeman and German E. Berrios (eds), *150 Years of British Psychiatry Volume II: The Aftermath* (London: Athlone Press, 1996), pp. 119–29.

Joanna Bourke, 'New Military History', in Matthew Hughes and William J. Philpott (eds), *Modern Military History* (Basingstoke: MacMillan, 2006), pp. 258–80.

John Buckley, 'Maritime Air Power and the Second World War: Britain, the USA and Japan', in Sebastian Cox and Peter Gray (eds), *Turning Points in Air Power History from Kittyhawk to Kosovo* (London: Cass, 2002), pp. 125–41.

Michael Carver, 'Conventional Warfare in a Nuclear Age', in Peter Paret (ed.), *Makers of Modern Strategy from Machiavelli to Hitler* (Princeton: Princeton University Press, 1943), pp. 779–814.

Mark A. Clodfelter, 'Molding Airpower Convictions: Development and Legacy of William Mitchell's Strategic Thought', in Phillip S. Meilinger (Ed. for the School of Advanced Air Power Studies), *The Paths of Heaven: The Evolution of Air Power Theory* (Maxwell AFB, AL: Air University Press, 1997), pp. 79–114.

James S. Corum, 'The Luftwaffe and the Lessons Learned in the Spanish Civil War', in Sebastian Cox and Peter Gray (eds), *Turning Points in Air Power History from Kittyhawk to Kosovo* (London: Cass, 2002), pp. 66–92.

Sebastian Cox, 'Sources and Organisation of RAF Intelligence', in Horst Boog (ed.), *The Conduct of the Air War in the Second World War: An International Comparison* (Oxford: Berg, 1992), pp. 553–79.

Sebastian Cox, 'Sir Arthur Harris and the Air Ministry', in Peter Gray and Sebastian Cox (eds), *Air Power Leadership: Theory and Practice* (London: HMSO, 2002), pp. 210–26.

Sebastian Cox, 'Setting the Historical Agenda: Webster and Frankland and the debate over the Strategic Bombing Offensive against Germany, 1939-1945', in Jeffrey Grey (ed.), *The Last Word? Essays on Official History in the United States and British Commonwealth* (Westport, CT: Praeger, 2003), pp. 147–74.

Peter Dye, 'The Genesis of Modern Warfare: The Contribution of Aviation Logistics', in Gary Sheffield and Peter Gray (eds), *Changing War: The British Army, the Hundred Days Campaign and the Birth of the Royal Air Force, 1918* (London: Bloomsbury, 2013), pp. 171–90.

Etienne de Durand, 'French Air Power: Effectiveness through Constraints', in John Andreas Olsen (ed.), *European Air Power: Challenges and Opportunities* (Nebraska: Potomac Press, 2014), pp. 3–31.

Andrew S. Erickson, 'Chinese Statesmen and the Use of Airpower', in Robin Higham and Mark Parillo (eds), *The Influence of Airpower upon History: Statesmanship, Diplomacy and Foreign Policy since 1903* (Lexington, KY: University of Kentucky Press, 2013), pp. 237–72.

Lt. Col. Peter R. Faber, 'Interwar US Army Aviation and the Air Corps Tactical School: Incubators of American Airpower', in Phillip S. Meilinger (Ed. for the School of Advanced Air Power Studies), *The Paths of Heaven: The Evolution of Air Power Theory* (Maxwell AFB, AL: Air University Press, 1997), pp. 183–238.

David S. Fadok, 'John Boyd and John Warden: Airpower's Quest for Strategic Paralysis', in Phillip S. Meilinger (ed.), *Paths of Heaven: The Evolution of Air Power Theory* (Maxwell AFB, AL: Air University Press, 1997), pp. 357–98.

Lawrence Freedman, 'The First Two Generations of Nuclear Strategists', in Peter Paret (ed.), *Makers of Modern Strategy from Machiavelli to Hitler* (Princeton: Princeton University Press, 1943), pp. 735–78.

Shmuel L. Gordon, 'Air Superiority in the Israel-Arab Wars. 1967-1982', in John Andreas Olsen (ed.), *A History of Air Warfare* (Washington, DC: Potomac, 2010), pp. 127–56.

Christina J. M. Goulter, 'The Royal Naval Air Service: A Thoroughly Modern Service', in Sebastian Cox and Peter Gray (eds), *Turning Points in Air Power History from Kittyhawk to Kosovo* (London: Cass, 2002), pp. 51–65.

Christina J. M. Goulter, 'British Official Histories of the Air War', in Jeffrey Grey (ed.), *The Last Word? Essays on Official History in the United States and British Commonwealth* (Westport, CT: Praeger, 2003), pp. 133–46.

Peter W. Gray, 'Air Power: Strategic Lessons from an Idiosyncratic Campaign', in Stephen Badsey, Mark Grove and Rob Havers (eds), *The Falklands Conflict Twenty Years On: Lessons for the Future* (London: Cass, 2005), pp. 253–64.

Peter W. Gray, 'Why Study Military History', in Gary Sheffield (ed.), *War Studies Reader: From the Seventeenth Century to the Present Day and Beyond* (London: Continuum, 2010), pp. 17–34.

Peter W. Gray, 'The Air Ministry and the Formation of the Royal Air Force', in Gary Sheffield and Peter Gray (eds), *Changing War: The British Army, The Hundred Days Campaign and the Birth of the Royal Air Force, 1918* (London: Bloomsbury, 2013), pp. 135–48.

Peter W. Gray, 'The Balkan Air War(s): Air Power as a Weapon of First Choice', in Keith Brent (ed.), *A Century of Military Aviation 1914-2014: Proceedings of the 2014 RAAF Air Power Conference* (Canberra, ACT: Air Power Development Centre, 2014), pp. 171–86.

Peter W. Gray, 'British Air Power: Allowing the UK to Punch above its Weight', in John Andreas Olsen (ed.), *European Air Power: Challenges and Opportunities* (Nebraska: Potomac Press, 2014), pp. 106–38.

Peter W. Gray and Jonathan Harvey, 'Strategic Leadership Education', in Colonel Bernd Horn and Lieutenant-Colonel Allister MacIntyre (eds), *In Pursuit of Excellence: International Perspectives of Military Leadership* (Kingston, ON: Canadian Defence Academy Press, 2006), pp. 81–96.

Jeffrey Grey, 'Introduction', in Jeffrey Grey (ed.), *The Last Word? Essays on Official History in the United States and British Commonwealth* (Westport, CT: Praeger, 2003), pp. ix–xiii.

Michael Howard, '*Temperamenta Belli*: Can War be Controlled?', in Michael Howard (ed.), *Restraints on War: Studies in the Limitation of Armed Conflict* (Oxford: Oxford University Press, 1979), pp. 1–16.

Michael Howard, 'Military History and the History of War', in Williamson Murray and Richard Hart Sinnreich (eds), *The Past as Prologue: The Importance of History to the Military Profession* (Cambridge: Cambridge University Press, 2006), pp. 12–22.

Brian Howieson and Howard Kahn, 'Leadership, Management and Command: The Officers' Trinity', in Peter Gray and Sebastian Cox (eds), *Air Power Leadership: Theory and Practice* (London: HMSO, 2002), pp. 15–40.

James G. Hunt, *Leadership: A New Synthesis* (London: Sage, 1991).

Reginald V. Jones, 'Intelligence and Command', in Michael I. Handel (ed.), *Leaders and Intelligence* (London: Cass, 1989), pp. 288–98.

David R. Jones, 'The Emperor and the Despot: Statesmen, Patronage and the strategic Bomber in Imperial and Soviet Russia, 1909-1959', in Robin Higham and Mark Parillo (eds), *The Influence of Airpower upon History: Statesmanship, Diplomacy and Foreign Policy since 1903* (Lexington, KY: University of Kentucky Press, 2013), pp. 115–44.

David Jordan and Gary Sheffield, 'Douglas Haig and Airpower', in Peter W. Gray and Sebastian Cox (eds), *Air Power Leadership: Theory and Practice* (London: TSO, 2002), pp. 264–82.

Sanu Kainikara, 'Soviet Russian Air Power', in John Andreas Olsen (ed.), *Global Air Power* (Washington, DC: Potomac, 2011).

David MacIsaac, 'Voices from the Central Blue: The Air Power Theorists', in Peter Paret (ed.), *The Makers of Modern Strategy from Machiavelli to the Nuclear Age* (Oxford: Clarendon Press, 1986), pp. 624–47.

Iain McNicholl, 'Campaigning: An Air Force Perspective', in Jonathan Bailey, Richard Iron and Hew Strachan (eds), *British Generals in Blair's Wars* (Farnham: Ashgate, 2013), pp. 265–72.

Phillip S. Meilinger, 'Giulio Douhet and the Origins of Airpower Theory', in Phillip S. Meilinger (ed.), *Paths of Heaven: The Evolution of Air Power Theory* (Maxwell AFB, AL: Air University Press, 1997), pp. 1–40.

Phillip S. Meilinger, 'Alexander P. de Seversky and American Airpower', in Phillip S. Meilinger (Ed. for the School of Advanced Air Power Studies), *The Paths of Heaven: The Evolution of Air Power Theory* (Maxwell AFB, AL: Air University Press, 1997), pp. 239–78.

Phillip S. Meilinger, 'Trenchard, Slessor and the Royal Air Force Doctrine before World War II', in Phillip S. Meilinger (ed.), *Paths of Heaven: The Evolution of Air Power Theory* (Maxwell AFB, AL: Air University Press, 1997), pp. 41–78.

Phillip S. Meilinger, 'John C. Slessor and the Genesis of Air Interdiction', in Phillip S. Meilinger (ed.), *Airwar: Theory and Practice* (Abingdon: Cass, 2003), pp. 64–74.

Holger H. Mey, 'German Air Power: Ready to Participate in Joint and Combined Operations', in John Andreas Olsen (ed.), *European Air Power: Challenges and Opportunities* (Nebraska: Potomac Press, 2014), pp. 32–63.

Richard Overy, 'The Air War in Europe, 1939-1945', in John Andreas Olsen (ed.), *A History of Air Warfare* (Washington, DC: Potomac, 2010), pp. 27–52.

W. Hays Parks, '"Precision" and "Area" Bombing: Who Did Which and When?', in John Gooch (ed.), *Airpower: Theory and Practice* (London: Cass, 1995), pp. 145–74.

Air Commodore Stuart Peach, 'The Airman's dilemma: To Command or To Control', in Peter W. Gray (ed.) *Air Power 21: Challenges for the New Century* (Norwich: HMSO, 2000), pp. 123–52.

James Pugh, 'David Henderson and Command of the Royal flying Corps', in Spencer Jones (ed.), *Stemming the Tide: Officers and Leadership in the British Expeditionary Force, 1914* (Solihull: Helion, 2013), pp. 263–90.

Adam Roberts, 'Land Warfare: From Hague to Nuremberg', in Michael Howard, George J. Andreopoulos and Mark R. Shulman (eds), *The Laws of War: Constraints on Warfare in the Western World* (New Haven, CT: Yale University Press, 1994), pp. 116–39.

Alan Stephens, 'The True Believers: Air Power Between the Wars', in Alan Stephens (ed.), *The War in the Air 1914-1994* (Fairbairn ACT: RAAF Air power Studies Centre, 1994), pp. 47–80.

James Sterrett, 'Learning is Winning: Soviet Air Power Doctrine, 1935-1941', in Sebastian Cox and Peter Gray (eds), *Turning Points in Air Power History from Kittyhawk to Kosovo* (London: Cass, 2002), pp. 173–87.

Edward Warner, 'Douhet, Mitchell, Seversky: Theories of Air Warfare', in Edward Mead Earle (ed.), *Makers of Modern Strategy: Military Thought from Machiavelli to Hitler* (Princeton: Princeton University Press, 1941), pp. 485–516.

Nicholas Wheeler, 'The Kosovo Bombing Campaign', in Christian Reus-Smit (ed.), *The Politics of International Law* (Cambridge: Cambridge University Press, 2004), pp. 189–216.

Bernard Williams, 'Ethics', in Anthony C. Grayling (ed.), *Philosophy 1: A Guide to the Subject* (Oxford: Oxford University Press, 1995), pp. 545–82.

P. Ziegler, 'Churchill and the Monarchy', in Robert Blake and William R. Louis (eds), *Churchill* (Oxford: Oxford University Press, 1994), pp. 187–98.

Journal articles

Anon. 'The Principles of War and the R.A.F. – Security', *The Royal Air Force Quarterly* VII, no. 3 (July 1936), p. 300.

Douglas Barrie, 'Show but Don't Tell', *Aerospace* 42, no. 1 (January 2015), pp. 38–40.

Kimberley B. Boal and Robert Hooijberg, 'Strategic Leadership research: Moving On', *Leadership Quarterly* 11 (2001), pp. 515–49.

Jonathan Boff, 'Air/Land Integration in the 100 Days: The Case of Third Army', *Royal Air Force Air Power Review* 12, no. 3 (Winter 2009), pp. 77–88.

David Cannadine, 'Churchill and the British Monarchy', *Transactions of the Royal Historical Society* 11 (2001), pp. 249–72.

Sebastion Cox, 'The Air/Land Relationship – an Historical Perspective', *Royal Air Force Air Power Review* 11, no. 2 (Summer 2008), pp. 1–11.

David V. Day and Robert G. Lord, 'Executive Leadership and Organizational Performance: Suggestions for a New Theory and Methodology', *Journal of Management* 14, no. 3 (1988), pp. 453–64.

A. D. English, 'A Predisposition to Cowardice? Aviation Psychology and the Genesis of "Lack of Moral Fibre"', *War & Society* 13, no. 1 (May 1995), pp. 15–34.

N. S. Gilchrist, 'An Analysis of Causes of Breakdown in Flying', *British Medical Journal* 12 (October 1918), pp. 401–3.

Peter Gray, 'The Myths of Air Control and the Realities of Imperial Policing', *Royal Air Force Air Power Review* 4, no. 2 (Summer 2001), pp. 37–52.

Peter Gray, 'The Gloves Will Have to Come Off: A Reappraisal of the Legitimacy of the RAF Bomber Offensive Against Germany', *Royal Air Force Air Power Review* 13, no. 3 (Autumn/Winter 2010), pp. 9–40.

Peter Gray, 'A Culture of Official Squeamishness? Britain's Air Ministry and the Strategic Air Offensive Against Germany', *Journal of Military History* 77, no. 4 (October 2013), pp. 1349–78.

W. Hays Parks, 'Air War and the Law of War', *Air Force Law Review* 32, no. 2 (1990), pp. 1–125.

W. V. Herbert Esq. (late Captain, Turkish Army), 'The Ethics of Warfare', *JRUSI* 42, no. 2 (July/December 1898).

Mary Hudson, 'A History of military Aeromedical Evacuation', *Royal Air Force Air Power Review* 11, no. 2 (Summer 2008), pp. 74–101.

David Jordan, 'The Royal Air Force and Air/Land Integration in the 100 Days, August-November 1918', *Royal Air Force Air Power Review* 11, no. 2 (Summer 2008), pp. 12–29.

Edgar J. Kingston-McCloughry, 'Morale and Leadership', *JRUSI* 74 (1929), pp. 305–10.

John Kiszely, 'Thinking about the Operational Level', *JRUSI* (December 2005), pp. 23–38.

Philip Landon, 'Aerial Bombardment & International Law', *JRUSI* 77 (1932), pp. 40–5.

Peter Lee, 'Rights, Wrongs and Drones: Remote Warfare, Ethics and the Challenge of Just War Reasoning', *Royal Air Force Air Power Review* 16, no. 3 (Autumn/Winter 2013), pp. 30–49.

Ignacio Brescó de Luna, 'Memory, History and Narrative: Shifts of Meaning when (Re)constructing the Past', *Europe's Journal of Psychology* 8, no. 2 (2012), pp. 300–10.

William C. Marra and Sonia K. McNeil, 'Understanding "The Loop": Regulating the Next Generation of War Machines', *Harvard Journal of Law & Public Policy* 36, no. 3 (2013), pp. 1139–86.

Phillip S. Meilinger, 'Ten Propositions: Emerging Air Power', *Airpower Journal* (Spring 1996), pp. 1–18.

Phillip S. Meilinger, 'Billy Mitchell's War with the Navy: The Interwar Rivalry over Air Power', *Journal of Military History* 78, no. 3 (July 2014), p. 1153.

Phillip S. Meilinger, 'Trenchard and "Morale Bombing": the Evolution of Royal Air Force Doctrine Before World War II', *Journal of Military History* 60 (April 1996), pp. 243–70.

Mark Moyar, 'The Current State of Military History', *The Historical Journal* 50, no. 1 (2007), pp. 225–240.

Richard Overy, 'Doctrine Not Dogma: Lessons from the Past', *Royal Air Force Air Power Review* 3, no. 1 (2000), pp. 32–47.

Peter Paret, 'The Annales School and the History of War, *The Journal of Military History* 73 (October 2009), pp. 1289–94.

Chris Pocock, 'Operation "Robin" and the British overflight of Kapustin Yar: A Historiographical Note", *Intelligence and National Security* 17, no. 4 (2002), pp. 185–93.

John Quigley, 'The United States' Withdrawal from International Court of justice Jurisdiction in Consular Cases: Reasons and Consequences', *Duke Journal of Comparative and International Law* 19, no. 263 (2009), pp. 263–306.

D. Redmond, 'Operation Irma Acted as a Catalyst', *British Medical Journal* 307, no. 6916 (27 November 1993), pp. 1424–5.

Squadron Leader Alan Riches, 'Balloons: Whatever Have They Done For Us?', *RAF Air Power Review* 3, no. 4 (Winter 2000), pp. 109–23.

Horst W. J. Rittell and Melvin M. Webber, 'Dilemmas in a General Theory of Planning', *Policy Sciences* 4 (1973), pp. 155–69.

Elli P. Schachter, 'Narrative Identity Construction as a Goal-orientated Endeavour: Reframing the Issue of "big vs. Small" Story Research', *Theory and Psychology* 21, no. 1 (2011), pp. 107–13.

Greg Seigle, 'USA Claims France Hindered Raids', *Jane's Defence Weekly* (27 October 1999).

Squadron Leader J. C. Slessor, 'The Development of the Royal Air Force', *Royal United Service Institute Journal* 76 (May 1931), p. 328.

Marc Weller, 'The Rambouillet Conference on Kosovo', *International Affairs* 75, no. 2 (1999), pp. 211–51.

Nicholas J. Wheeler, 'Refelections on the Legality and Legitimacy of NATO's intervention in Kosovo', *International Journal of Human Rights* 4, no. 3–4 (2000). Special Issue: The Kosovo Tragedy The Human Rights Dimension.

Hayden White, 'The Question of Narrative in Contemporary Historical Theory', *History and Theory* 23, no. 1 (February 1984), pp. 1–33.

Andrew Whitmarsh, 'British Army Manoeuvres and the Development of Military Aviation, 1910-1913', *War in History* 14, no. 3 (2007), pp. 325–46.

Leonard Wong, Paul Bliese and Dennis McGurk, 'Military Leadership: A Context Specific Review', *Leadership Quarterly* 14 (2003), pp. 657–92.

Periodicals

Herbert G. Wells, 'The war in the air: And particularly how Mr Bert Smallways fared while it lasted', *Pall Mall Magazine* (1908).

Reports and papers

University of Birmingham Policy Commission VI, *The Security Impact of Drones: Challenges and Opportunities for the UK* (University of Birmingham, October 2014).

Tami Davis Biddle and Robert M. Citino, 'The role of Military History in the Contemporary Academy', Society of Military History White Paper, available at http://www.smh-hq.org/docs/SMHWhitePaper.pdf.

Conference proceedings

Michael Duffy, Theo Farrell and Geoffrey Sloan (eds), *Doctrine and Military Effectiveness: Prceedings of the Conference held at The Britannia Royal Naval College, January 1997* (Exeter: Strategic Policy Studies Group, 1997).

Jorg Echternkamp, 'North Africa: A forgotten theatre of War? Identity, Legitimization and the Shifts in German Memory Culture since 1945', conference paper, presented at The Desert War: International Workshop, Madrid 17–18 October 2014.

Major J. D. Fullerton RE, 'Some Remarks on Aerial Warfare', *Operations of the Division of Military Engineering of the International Congress of Engineers: Held in Chicago last August under the Auspices of the World's Congress Auxilliary of the Colombian Exposition* (Washington, DC: Government Print Office, 1894), pp. 571–4.

Peter Gray, 'The Balkan Air Wars: Air Power as a Weapon of First Political Choice', in Wing Commander Keith Brent (ed.), *A Century of Military Aviation 1914-2014* (Canberra, CT: Air Power Development Centre, 2014).

Theses and dissertations

Olivier Kaladjian, *Influence of French Air Power Strategy in the European Union's Military Operations in Africa* (Maxwell, AL: School of Advanced Air Power Studies, 2011).

James Neil Pugh, 'The Conceptual Origins of the Control of the Air: British Military and Naval Aviation, 1911-1918', unpublished PhD thesis, University of Birmingham, 2013.

INDEX

Printed in Poland
by Amazon Fulfillment
Poland Sp. z o.o., Wrocław

61600284R00114